Once again, the authors have identified the industry trends we all need to understand. From Millennial patterns to the rise of online reviews, the factors explored in Game Changers *will go a long way in determining who's successful five, 10 or 15 years from now. And who isn't.*

– Margaret Kelly, CEO, RE/MAX LLC

Steve Murray proves once again why he is one of the great minds in real estate. He and his team have conducted exhaustive research. They've asked the right questions of the right people and presented key insights to help all real estate professionals make sense of the market and the opportunities and challenges ahead. Steve, Lon and Lorne have provided a great service by seeing this ambitious project to completion.

– Mark Willis, CEO
Keller Williams Realty International

Game Changers *provides an insightful and thought-provoking look at some of the factors that will affect the residential brokerage business in the coming years. Even better, the authors suggest strategies that astute leaders may wish to consider to not only remain relevant but to capitalize on the opportunities that will arise as a result of these circumstances.*

– Pam O'Connor, President/CEO
Leading Real Estate Companies of the World

The title of the book says it all - it's a Game Changer*! Steve Murray, Lon Welsh and Lorne Wallace have produced a deeply researched, clearly presented analysis of the fears and challenges that are driving change in the real estate business. Every agent, broker and owner will benefit from reading it today!.*

– Mary Tennant, President
Keller Williams Realty International

The authors have done an excellent job of raising some serious issues for the industry that need to be considered and discussed. Game Changers *is a must-read for anyone in a leadership position in real estate.*

– Bob Hale, President & CEO
Houston Association of Realtors

Game Changers

The Unfounded Fears and Future Prosperity of the Residential Real Estate Industry

April 2014

ISBN: 978-0-615-99430-7

Art Direction and Design:
Paul Salley, REAL *Trends*, Inc.,
Chief Creative Image, LLC
Elizabeth, CO - Phone 303-683-4815,
Jeremy Conti, Your Castle Real Estate
and Tiffany Chin, Your Castle Real Estate

Edited by:
Special thanks to Ellie Sheldon, co-owner,
XMedia Communication

Published by REAL *Trends*, Inc. and Your Castle Real Estate

7501 Village Square Drive, Ste. 200	9085 E. Mineral Circle, Ste. 360
Castle Rock, CO 80108	Centennial, CO 80112
Phone 303-741-1000	Phone 303-9-CASTLE

Order online: www.gamechangersrealestate.com

Foreward

Every business leader fears something about the future. Whether this concern focuses on their own company or on their industry, leaders are riveted on change and how it will affect their business. Former Intel CEO Andrew Grove wrote a book entitled *Only the Paranoid Survive.* That sums it up nicely. Concern about change is a constant.

Leaders in residential realty services are no different. Of course there are inevitable cyclical and seasonal changes. These are fairly routine and, while not easy to swallow, today's leaders have learned to manage them. But what most concerns leaders are structural changes—the kinds that underpin the entire business. These are typically far more serious. And while these changes appear somewhere out on the horizon, they tend to capture the attention of anyone with a significant stake in this business.

Among these hovering-in-the-distance structural changes are:

- The possibility that the homeownership rate will continue to fall and head towards 50 percent, moving from its current 64 percent

- The potential for housing consumers to start looking for their agents online and use ratings, which could move the referred rate (percentage of housing consumers who find and select their agent due to a personal relationship or referral) from its current level of nearly 70 percent to somewhere in the neighborhood of 50 percent or less

- A change in IRS rules, disqualifying real estate agents as independent contractors and forcing them to take on employee status

- That consumers will actually begin to want to control more of the process of selling and purchasing their homes, and the assisted rate (percentage of consumers using real estate agents to buy or sell) falls from today's nearly 82 percent to less than 65 percent

Any one of these changes to the underlying structure of our industry has the potential to cause a huge transformation in how realty businesses are operated—and even have a significant impact on how many brokerages and agents the industry can sustain. The future could produce a scenario where several fundamentals of residential realty services all shift to some extent—concurrently.

The challenge of technology

In a general sense, it is technology that is changing everything. This encompasses consumers' interactions with technology, how these interactions have changed their views towards how they do business—and whom they do business with. This also includes the notion that access to technology and "big data" are changing consumers' approaches to buying and selling housing. And further, that although we cannot see how all of this will play out in the future, the manner in which it does will probably not favor the incumbents' way of doing business.

Whether it is the use of "big data," the move towards an era of "data visualization," or the ability of technology to burrow ever deeper into the process of buying and selling homes, technology evokes concern. But it is not so much the evolution of technology that concerns industry leaders the most. Rather, it is whether consumers, particularly Millennials, will make use of it in a wholesale fashion. Here there *should* be concern. For while older established professionals take pride in the accuracy of the MLS dataset, today's housing consumers seem to brush aside such concerns. How else to explain their use of leading portals where the data is not nearly as "pure"?

The challenge of the regulatory environment

For as long as government has existed there have been rules and regulations governing the conduct of the citizenry. And for as long as government has existed, the rules and regulations governing business conduct have expanded—and will continue to expand. The Dodd Frank Act is but the most recent example of a government intervention that will directly impact housing sales.

Of great concern is not only how this new group of regulations will affect housing, but what is coming next. An example of a regulatory change that few in realty services have had to deal with—yet—is "disparate impact." This new set of fair housing rules that determine whether a firm or person has acted in a discriminatory manner is based not on actual discrimination, but whether one's business rules or policies end up discriminating—even if unintentionally.

And few have yet to sound the alarm about the formation of a new task force/ working group focused on the "health" of housing. Nearly a dozen federal agencies are discussing the (apparently) unhealthy homes that most of us live in. While they are commencing as an "advisory" group, one can almost see the future when unless and until a house is deemed "healthy" one cannot sell it to another. The green movement is a part of this effort; one can also imagine the government (either state or national) creating rules and regulations that require a home to be brought up to some standard for energy efficiency before title can pass. This has already been attempted in several states.

Lastly, how federal and state authorities deal with the tax-favored status of housing could have significant implications for housing. It is not just the mortgage and property tax deductions that should be of concern. It is the move to tax the real estate transaction and/or the taxation of business services that could have an even-broader impact on our industry. Further, as proposed in January 2014, the new Camp tax proposals would do away with deductions for state and federal property taxes and cap the mortgage interest deduction—among other items. Any of these changes could have a profound impact on the health of housing sales.

So whether it is technology, changing consumers, or changes in government regulation, the realty industry may have many future surprises in store.

Game Changers will examine several of these potential outcomes going out to the year 2025. We'll address their implications for industry participants, and address the probability that any of these will happen and the impact they may have. We'll also present ideas on how various participants can prosper in a future environment that looks substantially different from how our business appears today.

In a previous book, *Game Plan,* released in 2011, the point was made that many of the most important changes to the structure of residential realty services had occurred from forces within the industry. New forms of sales agent compensation drove most change that occurred between 1985 and 2005. While outside influences such as liberalized rules for one-stop shopping also had an impact, it was chiefly intensified competition for real estate agents that drove the restructuring of the industry. This form of competition continues today.

What hasn't changed significantly thus far is consumer behavior as it relates to real estate agents. Consumers still find and select agents as they always have through personal knowledge or a referral from a trusted source. In terms of executing a purchase or sale of residential property, consumers still use agents at about the same percentage levels as they have for the past 40 years—even after the shocks of the last 10 years. Even the impacts of the web and mobility have not changed the business as expected. While consumers flock to real estate websites, their habits and practices in their interactions with the realty industry have simply not budged significantly—yet.

Steve Murray, Lorne Wallace, and Lon Welsh
April 2014

Dedications

Steve:

I dedicate this book to Doniece Welch whose positive spirit and can do attitude has been instrumental in the 27 year success of REAL *Trends* and all that we have accomplished working together. Doniece thanks for all that you do.

Lorne:

I'd would like to dedicate this book to the memory of my real estate agent grandfather, Robert Lawrence, who sent a little 5 year old child up the street with a stack of "Just Sold" postcards and started my life-long involvement with real estate. And to my real estate mother, Patricia Wallace, who supported a family through lots of missed dinners and open house weekends. And to my real estate broker wife, Kelli Todd, who took a chance on what was then a little company from Canada. There have been a lot of interesting chapters with more to write…

Lon:

I'd like to dedicate this book to the amazing team at Your Castle Real Estate. I've learned so much from you, and this book would not have been possible without your support.

Special Thanks

We wish to acknowledge MRIS and its CEO, David Charron for their assistance in the research we conducted with the consumer portion of this study. Also our thanks to David for his wise input into various chapters and themes of the book.

Table of Contents

Introduction

The housing marketplace in the United States and Canada is a marvelous engine of commerce. Real estate professionals have designed a system that provides abundant market information, along with a set of rules that enable home buyers, home sellers, and real estate professionals to efficiently transfer homeownership from one party to another. No other system in the world accomplishes this so well.

This system has survived numerous challenges since it was first conceived nearly a half century ago. The Multiple Listing Services (MLSs), where real estate professionals share their inventory with one another, and the system of "cooperation and compensation," which helps make the system consistent and easy to understand, together form the foundation of the system. The rule-making bodies, both Realtor associations and the MLSs, create a marketplace where participants know how to navigate a transaction and do so in a manner convenient to all parties engaged in the sale and purchase of housing.

Brokerage firms and sales agents have been able to build predictable businesses on this foundation. It has enabled the industry to flourish. While numerous changes have occurred in the past 30 years in the structure of brokerage, that foundation continues to serve the interests of all parties in a remarkable way.

Historically, change in our industry has been evolutionary—not revolutionary. There have been few, if any, radical divergences from the norm. While different forms of brokerage have appeared, along with shifts in the delivery of service to housing consumers, the basics of real estate brokerage have remained mostly unchanged.

Evolutionary change is often the most dangerous. The analogy that's frequently applied is the "boiling of the frog": Slow change can often leave those who are being impacted unaware of just how much change is occurring. This kind of change can be so slight and so elongated that few react when there is still time to do so effectively.

We believe that such is the case today.

Game Changers looks at many major changes underway in the market for residential real estate services. The changes we discuss are those we believe will have the most impact on how real estate services are delivered, how brokerage firms are structured, and whether MLSs and Associations of Realtors as currently configured will survive in a recognizable way. Each by itself could have a significant impact on the industry as we know it today.

In the following pages, we'll present our views on the factors that could cause changes to occur and the probability that they will. We'll discuss what forces counter these changes and the implications, for industry participants, of all of this potential upheaval. We'll also present some possible solutions. *Game Changers* is meant more as a primer for leaders to begin the process of thinking about the "what ifs." We are confident that many others will have their own ideas concerning which potential changes are more important—and whether any material changes will occur.

The authors wish to express our sincere thanks to the many industry leaders who shared their time and thoughts with us in the creation of *Game Changers.* Without this invaluable input this book would not have been possible.

We trust that *Game Changers* will, in some way, contribute to the ongoing conversation about what the future holds for all of us engaged in this great industry, and how we can continue to engage in ways that ensure it remains the best the world has to offer.

Methodology

The research that underlies *Game Changers* included interviews with nearly 50 industry leaders. These included CEOs of leading brokerage firms, both regional and national, as well as leaders of multiple listing services and associations of Realtors as well as nearly 20 leading agents and teams. These interviews were conducted between December 2013 and January 2014.

A national survey of more than 1,350 of the largest regional and local realty firms from all brands, regions of the country, and business models was conducted by REAL *Trends*. In addition, nearly 6,000 of the highest-producing sales agents took part in a survey. Both realty firm leaders and sales agents were questioned about their views of the future.

To gain insights into recent buyer and seller attitudes about their selection and use of real estate agents, we utilized the unquestioned leader in consumer surveying and polling, Harris Interactive, to conduct a national consumer survey.

Chapter One

Counselors and Facilitators – The Segmentation of Sales Agents

Probability: High
Impact: Moderate

Cream rises to the top. So it is with real estate sales professionals. The best sales agents are capturing more market share. They accomplish this via the thoughtful use of technology, more advanced customer relationship management tools, hard work, and intense focus. The trend to concentrate market share among the highest producers is accelerating.

What does this mean for an industry built on the egalitarian basis of "cooperation"? "Facilitators" perform a lower-value role as processors of transactions for housing consumers. "Counselors" have the ability to create additional value through knowledge, experience, and superior market insight. Historically, they have been paid the same commissions—will that be the case in the future? The increasing segregation of Facilitators and Counselors will have profound impacts on the industry in the years ahead. This creates opportunities for agents, brokerages, and related companies like title and mortgage who can position themselves appropriately for the trend.

Historically, sales agent productivity has been distributed in typical bell-curve proportions. Most agents sat in the middle of the curve with some seven to ten deals, while a few low-producing sales agents (less than three deals per year) and high-producing sales agents (more than 25 deals) made up the tail distributions.

In 2013, the average productivity was 8.5 transactions per sales agent per year—not a departure from historical numbers. But in recent years, the bell curve has flattened—and in fact, is not a bell curve at all. Now, for example, there is a huge uptick in the no-production end of the "curve." Exhibit 1-1 shows the distribution for the Denver metropolitan area. Other data suggest that this distribution is common in other metropolitan areas across the country.

Since the housing downturn, more agents have achieved limited or no volume. In addition, the number of high-volume agents and teams has increased. There are fewer agents in the middle achieving a moderate amount of volume. Note that the Denver statistics in Exhibit 1-1 vary from the NAR (National Association of Realtors) statistics. That is because about half of the licensees in Denver are not Realtors. Most of these non-Realtor agents have very low or no volume. Thus, to just look at the NAR stats ignores the almost 50% of the licensees across the U.S. who are not Realtors.

Exhibit 1-1: Distribution of 2013 agent production. 44% of licensees had no production in 2013.

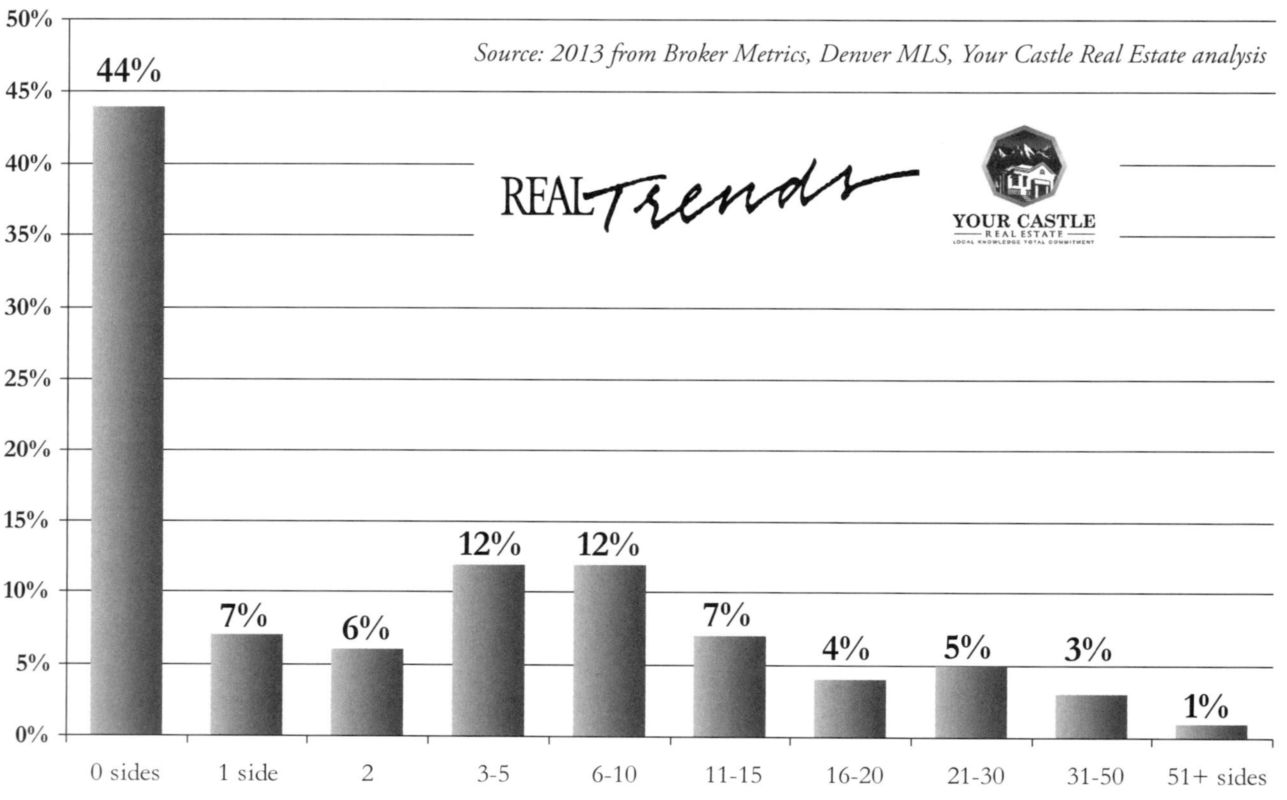

Counselors

Due to their experience in the market and level of productivity, we view high-volume agents as true **"Counselors"** to their clients. These agents have common attributes:

- An intense focus on activities that produce more business
- Quick to adopt technology that will enable better business processes

- Expertise and knowledge in housing markets
- Mastery of the complexities of the buying and selling transaction

Since they bring a lot of value to the transaction, these Counselors are better able to justify—and receive —high commissions.

Facilitators

Agents who do far less business than their Counselor counterparts also have common traits. We refer to this group as **"Facilitators"**: They can process a sale or purchase fairly well, but often are not in a position to add more value—consulting, for example. Here is how we define Facilitators:

- They have access to technologies that enable easier deal navigation for their clients, but they have not adopted them as extensively as high-volume agents have.
- They lack transaction experience. These agents are not as skilled in the details of either the market or the transaction.
- Generally, they have far less experience overall. Facilitators are not in a position to offer as much in the way of true guidance to their clients and customers.

Since they offer less value, when the customer asks for a reduced listing commission or a rebate on the buyer commission, these agents have less success in maintaining their fees.

Top-volume agents want to form relationships with other high producers. This is a challenge to the industry (though not to top-volume agents!). Numerous cities have "off-market" listing exchanges, and in some cities, these have grown to take up significant portions of the available inventory.

The rise of listing portals has made possible new methods of reaching home buyers and sellers, making the MLS less valuable than it was in the past. This trend also challenges the very notion of "cooperation and compensation." These days, high-volume agents appear to be experiencing growing frustration when working with low producers. To these top producers, sharing a commission is not as equitable when they are having to perform more of the work to close a transaction.

Change in consumer perceptions

We engaged Harris Interactive to interview over a thousand consumers that recently completed a real estate transaction. We asked these consumers a number of questions, summarized in Exhibit 1-2. We segmented the results by generation (age) of the consumer. Generally, consumers of different ages tended to answer the questions in about the same way. The most material difference was in the last question, "Are real estate agent services less valuable now that so much information is available on the Internet?"

Millennials, under 33 years old, agreed 49% of the time. Traditional consumers, those over 61 years old, only agreed with this statement 30% of the time. The real estate transaction is complex enough that we doubt that many of these consumers will adopt FSBO (for sale by owner). But they may feel comfortable shouldering more of the workload, and assign less responsibility to real estate agents.

Exhibit 1-2: Consumers by Generations: How much do you agree with…
Younger consumers see less value in real estate agents than older consumers.

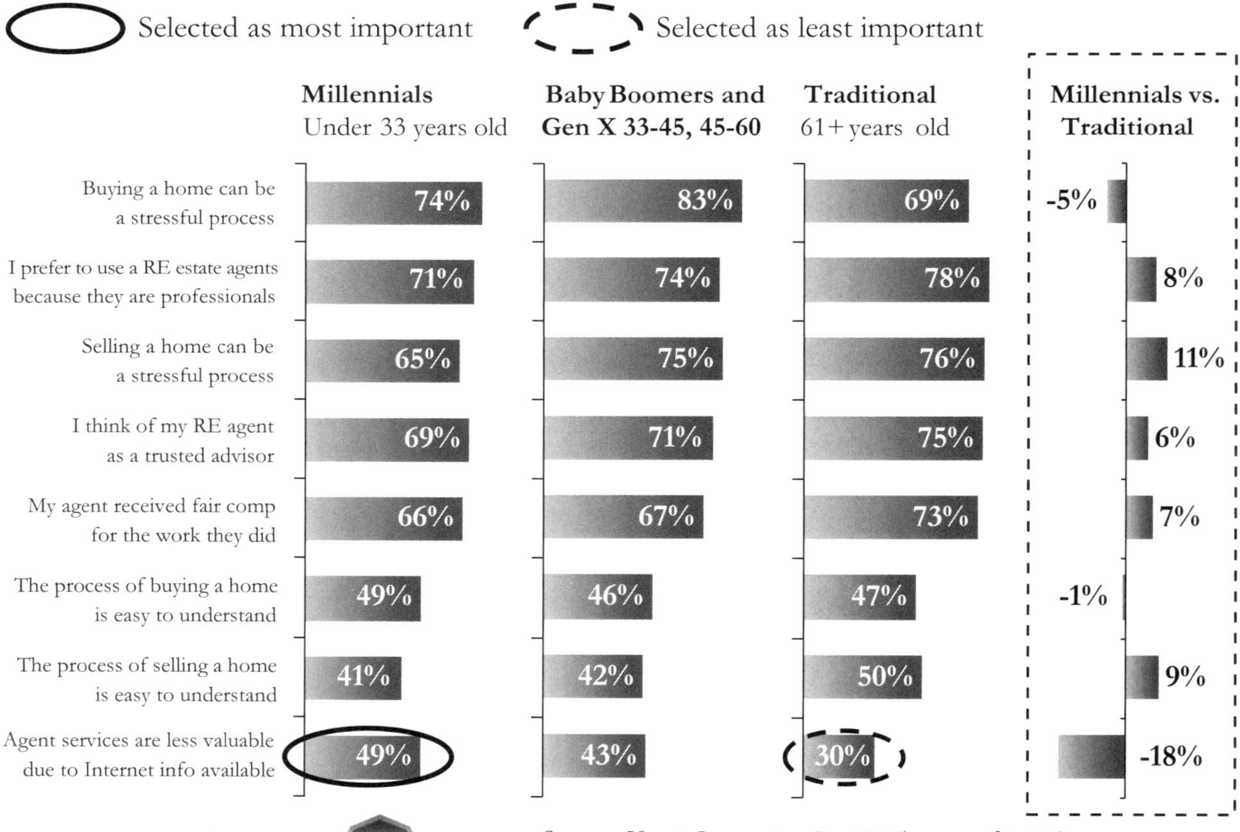

Source: Harris Interactive: Jan 2014 survey of 1,004 consumers. Does not include 178 (18%) that didn't use an agent.

Forces moving in favor of sales agent segmentation

Four major forces are currently driving the business done by high-volume agents.

- Technology is making it more efficient to close higher volumes of deals.
- These agents are capitalizing on their ability to grow incremental business from online sources
- The team model has evolved as an acceptable way to conduct business.
- A segment of consumers, empowered with market knowledge from the internet, will choose a middle path between hiring a "counselor" agent and FSBO (for sale by owner). They may pick a lower cost, lower value "Facilitator" instead.

Below, we will discuss the ripple effect these forces are having on sales agent segmentation.

1. As production has consolidated among fewer sales agents, they gather a higher share of the commission revenue. This has led to further investment in their marketing and business-building capabilities.
2. High-volume agents typically now have the scale to be able to afford to advertise online. In taking advantage of this tool, they are taking increasing share from low-volume agents.
3. Agents that are more productive can build teams. Teams generate leads in greater quantities. They can afford the people and the systems to better incubate prospects, service customers, and respond to growth opportunities.
4. The complexities of the real estate transaction and growing a real estate business make being an agent far more challenging than it was in the past. The dollar cost may not be much higher to enter the business of real estate. However, to build a business that produces even average earnings is far more time consuming and expensive than it has been historically.
5. In Chapter Three, *Ratings and reviews move the bar for agents*, we discuss several changes in consumer behavior. Both of these consumer trends will drive business to high-volume agents:
    - Consumers are interested in using ratings websites to research their next agent.
    - A sizable number of younger consumers would prefer to use an agent with specific expertise vs. one referred to them.

6. As we discuss in our chapter on homeownership rates, the investor share of the market is likely to grow modestly. This will occur at the expense of the owner-occupant share. Investors are typically more experienced in real estate nuances than owner-occupant clients are. The investor segment tends to favor the more experienced high-volume agents who have the skills they desire.
7. As we present in other chapters of this book, there are parties with a clear stake in preventing change in our industry. For example:
   - In Chapter Four, *The not-so-safe safe harbor* (employees vs. independent contractors), many industry players are poised to fight legislative change.
   - In Chapter Three, *Ratings*, we discuss how poorly rated agents will lose market share: They will oppose ratings sites.

   In this case, there is not one overarching entity (e.g., the government that can be lobbied, NAR rolling out "Agent Match") to oppose. The market-share gains of the Counselors will be fought at a grass-roots level. This will be difficult to measure and even more difficult to fight.
8. A segment of consumers always chooses the cheapest option. This continues to be true in real estate, even as the Facilitator/Counselor segmentation evolves. The Facilitators will remain very busy, but they will be under increasing commission pressure.

Countering these segmentation forces

1. The median age of a Realtor is 55+. A large proportion of the high-volume agents are those in their last decade of working before retirement (often their most productive years). Anecdotal evidence indicates that younger agents want more work/life balance. Many may not have the desire or drive to go for the higher levels of volume reached by their Traditional and Boomer generation counterparts. The move towards the "80/20" rule of sales may not hold as older-generation Realtors retire.
2. The economics of real estate firms will drive higher levels of training for new agents. This offsets the loss of income from high-producing and high cost agents. A new trend: training that is more intensive with accountability systems to assist new agents in growing their volume faster than in the past.
3. Consumers of all age cohorts continue to favor relationships as the preferred method to locate and select their sales agent. Our consumer study shows that Millennials believe that a referral from a trusted source is the most important factor

in the choice of an agent. This reliance on personal relationships will offset the trend of choosing an agent solely due to their experience and sales volume. New and lower-volume agents will continue to have business opportunities as a result.

Overall, it is likely that residential real estate will continue this split between Facilitators and Counselors. What opportunities and challenges would that present for you? We conducted 50 detailed interviews with industry leaders in December 2013 and January 2014.

Here is what they shared with us on this topic:

Perspectives from Industry Leaders

Owner of a large independent firm with $4 billion+ volume:

The opportunities and challenges are the same. Maybe 60% of real estate sales people are Facilitators; they do not have the skill set, because they have not done enough transactions. They have not moved their game up to a high-enough level to be a Counselor in the future. They just present offers and show properties. Ten years ago—that was all you needed. Now the clients have all the information and you need to be an interpreter, not a provider. All that shifts to the counseling side of things. The concern: How much will the industry shift to facilitating needs for the clients versus counseling needs for clients?

In the future, we will have two groups:

1. *High-level advisory and counseling because of experience, knowledge and skills. You're able to really add value to your client's decision making on buying a home or investment property.*
2. *Somebody who says, "You want to go to those four homes, I will take you there. I will help you fill out that documentation, do the paperwork and get the deal closed."*

Facilitators and Counselors get the same commission today, but not in the future.

– Dan Elsea, President, Real Estate One, Detroit, MI

President of a large franchised brokerage, $5 billion+ volume:

Buyers are becoming more efficient and sophisticated. With the current technology that is available, their first showing is typically on the web. Although this may eventually affect a broker's pricing model, there is presently no sign of this.

Another issue is that some clients may be more technologically savvy than their agent. Clients may spend much more time searching the Internet in a particular price range or neighborhood, which causes them to become more knowledgeable than their agent. This gap could potentially affect the way buyers view agents.

– Joan Docktor, President, Berkshire Hathaway HomeServices Fox & Roach, Realtors/The Trident Group, Philadelphia (4,000 agents)

President of a large independent brokerage, $28 billion volume:

What is the role of the Realtor in today's real estate world? In the not too distant past, the role of a Realtor was to "show product" and "negotiate the price." Today, the role is far more than that. Today, the Realtor's role is to be a project manager. Not only do they need to oversee and manage all aspects and moving parts of bringing a purchase or sale of a property to fruition, it's important that they are local real estate experts who know their markets and appropriate values. They need to manage home inspectors, appraisers, mortgage financiers, insurance providers, settlement companies, etc. They need to coordinate all the components and pieces required to meet the simple needs of a customer trying to buy or sell a property.

It takes a "village" to bring today's real estate transaction to fruition and the Realtor is the team coordinator and relationship manager.

– Jeff Detwiler, President/COO, The Long & Foster Companies, Inc., Mid-Atlantic Region

---

CEO of a large MLS:

The vast majority of Realtors are part timers. Not to say you can't do this part time, but if you are part time because you have three other "jobs" then you are not focused

on the transaction and cannot possibly do a good job. I believe the number of part timers is about 70% of the pool. That would be 700,000 out of a million Realtors.

– Russ Bergeron, CEO, Midwest Real Estate Data LLC (MRED Chicago MLS)

President of a large franchise brokerage, $3 billion+ volume:

Globalization will continue even while the business becomes more hyper-localized. Big data will influence where and how real estate brands, companies, and Realtors market homes. The current demographic information available to Realtors is just the beginning. In the very near future, there will be so much detailed data easily accessible that a Realtor will know the odds of someone selling their home in the next six months; information on recent purchasing habits; which country the next four buyers in a neighborhood may come from; extraordinary detailed information on each and every home, etc.

The successful Realtors are already shifting from being salespeople to consultants, advisors, Counselors, data analysts, and data interpreters. While technology will make some portions of the transaction easier, faster, and more seamless, with a focus on the customer's "experience," the transaction will be more challenging with additional regulation, liability, and risk. Realtors will remain relevant and important as buying and selling homes becomes more complex. The consumer will look to full-time, highly skilled trusted advisors to help them, which could help alleviate commission compression. Training from brands and brokers will need to be more sophisticated and specialized, which will help alleviate pressure on the company dollar.

—Chad Ochsner, Broker/Owner, RE/MAX Alliance, Arvada (Denver), CO

Senior franchise executive:

What are significant strengths of our business? I'll look at it from a macro level. When I say our business, it is everyone's business in real estate.

- *It's the fact that Realtors are able to navigate an extremely dysfunctional environment in order to meet or exceed the customer's expectations.*
- *It's the fact that a home is an asset that cannot be commoditized since it's unique and emotional.*

- *It's the fact that the human element in this business will always prevail over technology. Despite often comparable access to capital, programs and tools, there are always significant disparities in performance between brokerages and agents. It all boils down to the level of commitment, execution, ability to build trust with the consumer, deliver the service, and make it happen. It is still a very person-to-person business in that regard.*

When I look at what often differentiates our brand and brokers, it's the respect garnered within the brokerage community for our overall level of professionalism, our focus on the consumer, our commitment to quality control, resolution of any issue that affects others, and our core values. When companies reach a point where they have stepped away from those obligations in the pursuit of short-term economics the business ultimately suffers. It's the beginning of the end. The reputation of the firm is really no more than the reputation of all the agents that work there, and you can't afford to compromise.

When considering the weaknesses of the industry, perhaps the greatest is the inability to deliver a consistent consumer experience. I've always said that the value of any brand, regardless of industry, and whether at an agent, firm or franchise level, is ultimately based on its ability to deliver a consistent consumer experience, and all within our industry have significant room for progress due to the unique nature of each transaction and the point of service provider.

– Budge Huskey, President & CEO, Coldwell Banker Real Estate LLC, Madison, NJ

Regional Owner, Keller Williams Realty

It is appropriate for the best agents to do most of the business. The lead agents are building teams today and taking advantage of the skills they apply to the market place and taking advantage of their ability to generate leads and serve more consumers effectively. If you want to do more business then get better at the business. It creates a great opportunity for talented individuals that wish to apply themselves to their craft. Real estate is a field with limitless opportunities, the only thing holding anyone back from maximizing those opportunities are their willingness to learn and their willingness to take action.

– David Osborn, Keller Williams Realty

CEO of a large franchise brokerage:

> *How the transaction gets done is important to us. Consumers are going to be buying experience. Not data. Not slogans. Not marketing. We are the trusted advisor; help you negotiate; get a deal done as pleasantly as possible. Consumers won't buy data. Realtors won't buy data from brokerages either, but they will work for a brokerage that packages all of it for them.*
>
> *This will need new business rules and leadership models different than most brokerages used in the past. Not easy. We must bring accountability to the consumer's "experience." How you deliver the experience changes as technology evolves. But the key elements for the home buy and sell process are timeless. If the agent doesn't do this, then the consumer might as well use the cheapest options.*
>
> – Mark Woodroof, CEO, Better Homes and Gardens Gary Greene Real Estate

---

Leader of a large real estate team, $134 million in 2013:

> *Are you gaining share by specializing? Yes, absolutely, 100%. This is Business 101. Best people get better, and as they improve, they gain market share. A lot of agents are lazy, lack focus, and are not motivated. There is something to be said for working smart. But specialists that know their content and work hard will always have more business.*
>
> – Lisa Burridge, Lisa Burridge & Associates, Casper, WY

High-production individual Realtor, 310 deals in 2012:

> *Consumers want a good deal, but it is a people business. Not everyone wants the best "deal" from agents. Most people want to get the best service, from someone knowledgeable. Achieve the client's goal (sell fast, get a good price, make it less of a hassle). A segment of consumers does not want to bother with technology. They want to hear it from the Realtor; want the relationship with someone they trust.*
>
> – Trish Nash, individual professional, EXIT Realty Gallery of Homes, Henderson, NV

High-production individual Realtor, $100+ million in 2012:

Focus on a high ethical standard. Our industry is too focused on closing of a sale and taking short cuts. Make a judgment call—before starting your real estate career—you have to be an educator to your client, first. You don't get paid to educate, but that gives better results for clients. And in the long run, you will be much better off for it. And no one else might agree—ethics, training, education.

Get in touch with your own strengths. Find what makes you unique in your market. What is your mission? What makes you tick? If you want to be a digital agent, you can position yourself accordingly. And you will be more attractive to clients. It is OK to be passionate for a sub-segment of a community (e.g., tri-athletes). There are too many generalists.

– Marie Chung, individual professional, Modern Realty Co., Cerritos, CA

High-production individual Realtor, 600+ sides in 2012:

Technology is attempting to devalue the role of the Realtor. The average buyer or seller has gone online and done their homework on pricing. It is critical to develop the relationship with the clients by providing value-added services such as expertise in the local market and transaction management. Prepare buyers and sellers with the mechanics of the transaction and highlight the pain points. This includes the hurdles of the mortgage process. These items are much more valuable than taking the clients in a car and driving them around, although that is a good opportunity to develop the relationship.

– Ayoub Rabah, Founder, Great Street Properties, Chicago, IL

High-production team, $100+ million in 2012:

Biggest threats / what keeps you up at night?

- *To compete, you have to differentiate from discount brokerages or /and Zillow.*
- *Discount brokerages dilute the value of the Realtor. NAR and the local boards need to step up. We don't explain the value we add to consumers.*
- *Associations don't add enough value themselves. In Atlanta, there are more non-Realtors than Realtors. Denver too. Agents that are not a member of a board and still doing well. NAR needs to show value.*

Biggest opportunities for the next decade?

- *Very business-minded Realtors will thrive due to their mindset. Get a competitive advantage. We're mass marketers that happen to be in the RE biz. You see more of the 80/20 rule going to 90/10 .... The market will concentrate.*
- *Technology and websites like Redfin and Zillow make successful Realtors work harder. We are competitive people at heart. We want to grow market share. We can compete with the portals; specifically if we focus on our local market. In the process, we will take market share from small Realtors.*

Most-valuable services you provide today and why? In the future?

- *My value is local knowledge. Always has been, always will be local knowledge. You can disseminate data; data is much more available to the consumer—much more so than in the past. That trend will continue.*
- *My value is helping consumers understand trends.*
- *I am a concierge to make the transaction easy for my client. Think about Lexus service for an oil change. They come to you and pick up the car and drop off a loaner!*
- *Understanding rentals is important. These used to be all mom/pop landlord rentals; now you have hedge funds to compete with. In theory, a higher level of service is needed for investors now.*

The barrier to entry to differentiate yourself will get more expensive. The little template MLS site from a brokerage has ZERO SEO value. That won't cut it in the future.

Least-valuable services you provide today and why? In the future?
Open houses. Driving customers around. Realtor broker opens. Old school. Activities that were low value that made the seller feel important.

– Mark Spain, Team, Keller Williams Realty, Alpharetta, GA (Atlanta)

Implications

Cooperation and compensation have been a critical factor in how the U.S. real estate brokerage industry evolved:

- They shielded the MLS from being viewed as simply a database of housing.
- They have facilitated an efficient market for all participants.

Sales agents can provide services to buyers and sellers. They know ahead of time how the process works and how their compensation will work. There are written and unwritten rules as to the responsibilities of each sales agent in the transaction and how much each will be paid. This also enables buyers and sellers to enjoy the benefits of a smoothly functioning market. Much of the work that is done is invisible to the ultimate consumer of the services of the market.

Cooperation and compensation are at risk. Counselor agents may resent those who are Facilitators. Newer Facilitator agents often do not live up to the unwritten rules of the agreement of who does what work in a deal. High-volume agents are frustrated with those who are less knowledgeable and experienced. Sometimes newer or part-time agents do not want to perform their functions in a transaction, and the more experienced agent ends up providing far more of the required services to close the deal. Yet they still pay a large share of commission to the less-involved agent. At least some of the growth of private-agent networks is due to this factor. This could lead to separate marketing networks for "Counselor" sales agents if left unchecked. Technology would allow this.

The Result: Realty firms will be challenged as the needs of Counselors and Facilitators diverge

The challenges are already being seen with the development of large, highly productive teams in both kinds of realty firms, those which are Counselors and those that are Facilitators. Is it possible for a realty firm to provide the right environment for both highly productive teams and individuals as well as for the less experienced? How will "Counselor" agents and "Facilitator" agents relate when they are in the same firm?

Realty firms will face increasing economic and operational challenges as they approach their own "80/20" segmentation among their agents and teams:

- Their top-producing sales agents and teams compress brokerage margins.
- How will firms generate the capital to fund the recruiting and training of new agents?
- How will firms fund the more skilled managerial talent to support more sophisticated "Counselor" agents?

- Counselors likely need less in the way of management—yet more in the way of training and accountability.
- Lower producers require much more of both, yet do not provide the splits to the company to pay for this.

Firms that try to train new agents, support cost-driven Facilitators AND give expensive, high-value training to Counselors could find themselves short of resources. They could disappoint all three groups. Higher turnover could result, placing the firm in a death spiral.

There is a 30-year history of real estate firms offering lower costs to agents. This helps high-volume agents seeking to lower their costs in the final years of their careers. It helps those who just want lower costs. Most low-cost realty models cannot afford to invest in far-reaching training and development. They welcome both Facilitators and Counselors who are more interested in lower costs than in support services from the high-service, high-cost real estate firm.

Larger sales teams may become an entirely new national business, where teams themselves start to expand to new markets. At least one large franchise is supporting this idea. There are already some multiple-office teams. Teams that specialize in supporting REO asset managers are leading the way. Once a team has a business system that has proved itself to be scalable, teams themselves may become a major new business model on a national basis.

Solutions

The summary idea for agents and firms: Make an explicit choice between Facilitator and Counselor. Many consumers believe "all agents are the same." Practice explaining your value so it is easy for the client to understand your positioning versus the general market.

If you are a Counselor positioning your choice, add more value to your client relationships. Tie clear consumer benefits to your extra skills and services. For example, on a listing presentation, you might have six marketing elements that most agents in your market do not offer. Show the client how you sell faster, get more showings and offers, and/or get a better price. If you are an owner, show

how the unique training and support you offer drives results. This could be more transactions per agent, a high average commission percentage, faster DOM, or anything tangible.

If you run a firm, your ability to add and explain value will trickle down to your agents and help them do the same with their clients. Owners can preserve margins as a result.

IF YOU ARE A HIGH-VOLUME AGENT:

- You either have, or are well on the way to, mastering the art of making contacts. Build systems to incubate these with the appropriate follow-ups to convert them to clients.
- You have already identified a unique selling proposition that makes you special in the market—and creates a perception of value with your clients and prospects. Keep up the great work.
- Continue to find ways to add more value to the transaction. This should enable you to maintain, and perhaps increase, your commission percentage.
- Evaluate your adoption of processes to drive your time-management skills and productivity. Clearly, you will be more efficient than the "typical" agent is already. However, many high-volume agents we met felt they still had much room for improvement.

IF YOU ARE A MID-VOLUME AGENT:

You can probably close a qualified client when you have one. Your challenge is finding enough qualified clients. The ideas in this chapter will help you improve your results in two areas; these should be among your areas of focus:

- Building a strong value proposition will make you much more attractive to prospective clients.
- You should consider maintaining (or perhaps increasing) your typical commission. There are two drivers:
    - Offering more value.
    - Explaining that value in a compelling way.

Both are very important. If you are a highly competent agent and you do not articulate it well, your earnings will not completely reflect your superior expertise.

To take your business to the next level, you need to find something unique you can do. You need a reliable, repeatable way of giving the message to your market. We find that most mid-level agents get most of their deals from friends and family. "Selling" the prospect to working with them is rarely required. As a result, a strong value proposition is often missing from this segment of agents.

IF YOU ARE A NEW OR LOW-VOLUME AGENT:

Newer brokers often fall into the trap of not grasping what real estate agents do all day (e.g., prospect). Many fall into the trap of working on "marketing" and "branding" when they just need to focus on prospecting. Several managing brokers have mentioned that the best way to learn is to get out with the public, talk about real estate and make a few mistakes. Do not lock yourself in a classroom for months when you start in real estate!

You have the most work to do:

1. Systemize your prospecting.
    - Get a CRM (customer relationship manager). Every high-volume agent we interviewed for this book has a well-managed CRM.
    - Commit to using the CRM several times a week on a regular basis.
    - Learn the fundamentals of time management. The most important is time blocking your prospecting time.
2. Master the deal lifecycle.
    - Stay on top of changes in real estate standard contracts. In the authors' experience with running a firm, this is more of a problem with lower-volume agents.
    - Be able to deliver a compelling listing presentation.
    - Be able to conduct a persuasive buyer consultation.
    - Learn to write effective contracts that win in a low-inventory market.
    - Strengthen your negotiation skills with clients and other agents.

3. Launch a growth plan.
   - Select what unique skills you want to build.
   - Find the marketing channels to market your message.
   - Establish follow-up systems to incubate your leads.

IF YOU RUN A BROKERAGE:

Many owners we have met have told us that newer and low-volume agents know what they should do, but are not motivated to do the work. They often attribute their results to lack of training and/or support from the firm. Usually that is not the case. These segments of agents do tend to consume many resources without much company margin. The market for real estate agents will continue to get more competitive. Many owners might need to re-evaluate the amount of resources they are willing to allocate to such agents.

Here are some fundamental thoughts to frame the discussion:

CEO of a large independent brokerage with over $2 billion in volume:

> *There are many brokerages that are just Facilitators. They do not add a lot of value in terms of education, marketing, management services, or lead generation. Nothing to nurture and grow their agents. They're just there to help agents that are doing business with a place to process it.*
>
> *If you follow the historical trail, it leads to a shift in margin (from brokerage to agent; a reduction in company dollar retained), and leads to a shift in services (brokerages can afford to do less). What is kind of messy right now is you do have some specific companies in most markets that don't consider themselves a Facilitator brokerage. In their world, they're a full-service brokerage offering all the services that any other broker has in the country. They promote themselves as providing every service that an agent could ever use and they do that better and for less money. So you have this noise in the market where no one is admitting that they're a Facilitator/discount broker with reduced services.*
>
> *No one admits it and everyone is doing it. Then you have franchise organizations; one franchise office is operating as a business practice (being a Facilitator) and another franchise in the same market is trying to follow the Counselor side of things.*

*So the noise of the future? It doesn't appear there is going to be a clear brand. It could take a while for the franchise's branding and the consumer's mind to settle on "I go to one brokerage for one set of services and go to the other brokerage for a different set."**

IF YOU ARE A BROKERAGE FOR FACILITATORS:

Your agents will eventually be under more commission pressure. They will "pass the buck" to you and pressure you for better splits. You will need to:

1. Find clear, concise ways to communicate your value as a firm.
2. Help your agents develop clear, concise ways to express their value to consumers.
3. Be ruthlessly efficient with your processes. You will need to become, or at least approach, being the lowest-cost provider in your market.
4. Find value-added services you can sell to agents to boost your retained company dollar. That might involve "unbundling" the firm offering. A la carte pricing for services might include:
   - Websites
   - CRM and lead incubation ("drip") systems
   - Developing marketing materials for prospecting
   - Developing marketing materials to promote listings
   - E+O insurance you can purchase at a large discount for the firm and resell to agents at a mark-up
   - Social media consulting
   - Paid classes (e.g., annual real estate commission classes, prospecting, negotiation, and high-impact listing presentations)

---

*This quote is from a source who wishes to remain anonymous. Throughout the remainder of the book, we've included unattributed quotes from other individuals as well. We believe their perspectives are valuable despite their request for confidentiality—and in fact, their ability to remain anonymous enabled many of them to speak with great candor.

IF YOU ARE A BROKERAGE FOR COUNSELORS:

Your agents should be immune to commission reductions from customers:

- If you are the only firm in your market that can support your agents to compete as Counselors, then you should enjoy exceptionally low turnover.
- Find ways to get to know the agents in your market at other firms who are or want to be Counselors. You should have a sustainable strategic advantage in recruiting.

What does the value-added package look like that would make your firm attractive to Counselors? This would include the list of ideas for Facilitators we presented above. In addition, you might also want to consider adding:

1. Market intelligence
   - Any title company can summarize basic real estate trends information for you.
   - You need to transcend the ordinary and develop insights to help your clients make better decisions.
   - You need to train your agents on how to use the insights in client consultations.
   - This process is labor intensive and difficult. It pays off in a competitive advantage no one else in your market is likely to be able to copy.
2. Transaction management
   - You do not have to hire and manage these professionals yourself. Consider having ties with outside vendors with solid reputations.
   - Adapt your processes (file management and review, accounting) with the preferred transaction managers to make the process seamless for agents and clients.
3. Clear standards

   If you do not already have clear standards (e.g., minimum volume levels), consider adopting them. Numerous owners have pointed out that high-volume agents want to work with and be part of a community of other producers. The lower-volume agents who are unlikely to increase their sales tend to consume more resources than they bring in.

CEO of a large MLS:

> *If you're working only on one or two transactions a year, you're likely part-time, busy doing family things and possibly have an alternative job. Regardless, from a real estate perspective, instead of a few weeks off from work, you're taking 300 days away from real estate. Therefore, your market currency is extremely limited.*
>
> *For the serious agent/Counselor, understanding and communicating trends in the micro-market is increasingly an absolute necessity. Let's call it data visualization because the analytics it depicts is not in the reams of data but in the ability to visualize and then communicate that data in a very simple, very visual manner.*
>
> *You're at a social function and the conversation goes something like this: "So how's the market doing?" The agent says, "let me show you on my iPhone. By entering a few parameters a color-coded heat map quickly tells us prices in this area are up 5%, days on market are rising slowly, inventory for townhomes is up and list price to sale price is running at 98%." For the real estate professional, this means no more off-the-cuff comments and observations. Importantly every encounter is a sales opportunity with a far better chance of closure.*
>
> *Helping the prospect visualize market trends in clear, concise, unambiguous terms with a real opportunity to engage in deeper, follow-on discussion is the result. In our market, for those that are so inclined, RBI (**R**ealestate **B**usiness **I**ntelligence) is a great tool. It's all about raising the bar versus building something for the least common denominator. We built RBI not because we thought the agent with two transactions per year was going to use it—although they probably could. This tool is designed for the fully engaged professional. Almost 2,000 agents in our market say they wouldn't even think about going into a listing presentation without it.*
>
> – David Charron, President and CEO, MRIS, Washington, D.C.

Senior executive of a large independent brokerage, $3 billion+ volume:

The companies that can maintain a culture, embrace technology, provide high-level education, restructure their physical plants where they currently have so much expense, give agents the right kind of people support they need, and stay committed to customer service are going to win. Leadership matters too. Attracting and growing your leadership team is critical. The companies that keep figuring out how all these pieces interconnect will have the greatest opportunity to differentiate themselves going forward.

– Phyllis Brookshire, President, Allen Tate Realtors, Raleigh, NC

....

By adopting these ideas, you should be able to do a better job than the overall industry in maintaining your margins.

The next chapter examines consumers who sell or buy on their own, and how their behavior might change over time.

Chapter Two

Technology enables the do-it-myself generation

Probability: Low
Impact: Moderate

The real estate industry's greatest fear is that technology will enable consumers to bypass them. This would allow consumers to assume more of the responsibility of buying and selling homes. Of course, this also cuts agents out of the process—and the proceeds. Agents and brokers have watched with horror as industry after industry has been upended by the Internet. Businesses such as travel, music, books, stock brokerage, and general retailing—to name just a few—have been reworked to such a degree as to be unrecognizable in a short period of time.

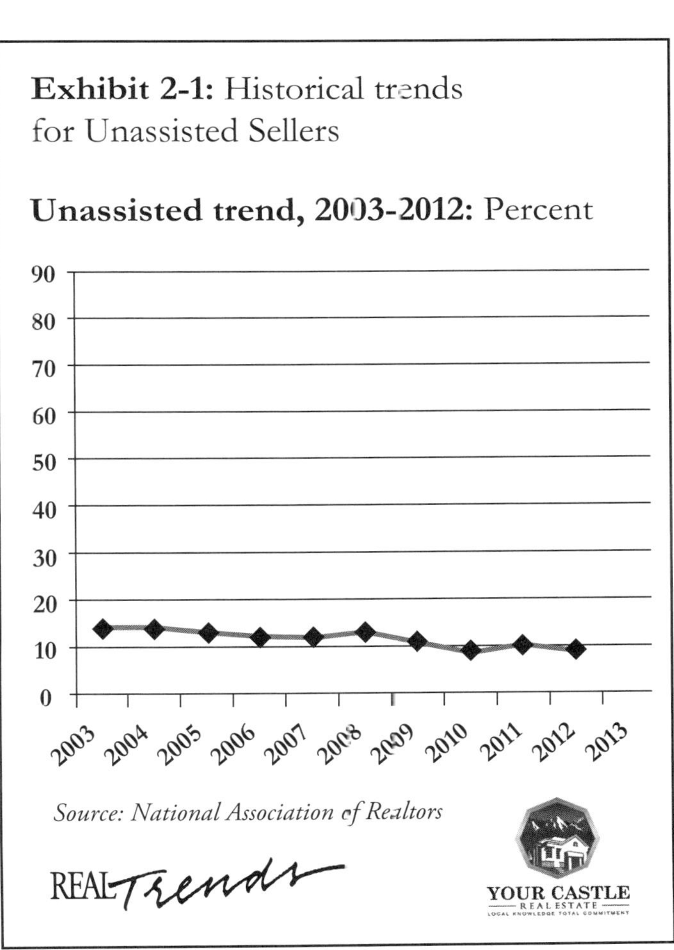

Exhibit 2-1: Historical trends for Unassisted Sellers

Source: National Association of Realtors

Housing transactions are based on access to market information and the ability to process the transaction. The Internet enables both. There has been no widespread movement away from the use of agents in the process… yet. Why? Will it remain this way? In this chapter, we'll outline possible change drivers and how to take advantage of them to capture more market share.

Why haven't more home sales gone FSBO (For Sale By Owner)?

Certain segments of consumers are comfortable doing things for themselves. Comfort varies with the product or service category and the complexity of the transaction. For instance, which would you be more comfortable with doing on your own—performing a surgical procedure or purchasing a book? The complexity of the housing transaction and its infrequency have always been bulwarks against any significant growth of do-it-yourselfers in housing sales. Exhibit 2-1 and 2-2 show this in more detail.

But the complexity of the residential real estate transaction resides mainly in the array of required forms and other legal processes, the multiple parties involved, and the erratic process of buying and selling. It is not about the actual steps involved, as they can be categorized and planned. Many steps could be organized in an online environment. Realty professionals are moving their contract processing into online and digital formats even today.

A strong portal could partner with a transaction management firm to offer a start-to-finish online process for buying or selling a home. One can imagine that viewing online materials, arranging a showing, submitting bids, accepting counters, arranging the mortgage and inspections, and moving to a closing is just a process, one that can be automated. Having a strong portal merely makes the job (and reaching consumers) easier. This portal could just as easily be a financial services company that partners with a transaction management firm. Loans are already automated online, as are closings. It wouldn't take much to move to the final step.

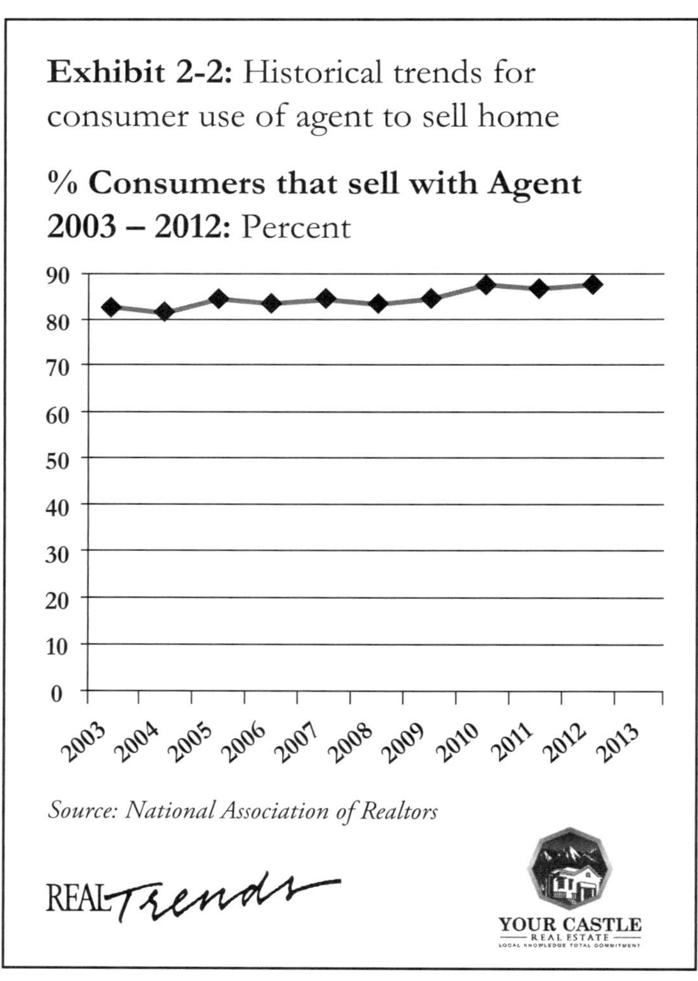

Forces that support the Do-it-Yourself Trend

In terms of what technology can accomplish, these are the forces that currently support the trend toward FSBO:

1. Millennials are much more accustomed to using technology to control what they consume. They make up a significant percentage of all purchasers in the coming decades. It is likely they will be highly aware of the cost-savings potential.
2. The technologies for creating an online marketplace already exist; they are just in different locations and have not been integrated into one platform (although there are several available that are fairly close to completion).
3. There is significant revenue potential for the first mover to create a winning platform. One could imagine that the first-to-market provider of such services could grab 5% share within five years. Even at half the average transaction cost, this would amount to over a billion dollars in annual revenue.
4. The inability of the current industry to establish consistent customer-service deliverables leaves it vulnerable to new entrants. Progress in other industries has increased consumer expectations. Agents answer less than half of their customers within 24 hours. They are vulnerable to new ways of delivering services and saving money.
5. There is a large opportunity for new forms of brokerages to capitalize on this kind of a system, with the customer at the center of the transaction as opposed to the sales agent. The potential for a more integrated approach to core services and follow-on concierge services will all come into play as this develops.

Countering the forces to increase unassisted market share

1. For the past 30 years, consumers have used real estate agents more than 90% of the time to purchase or sell a house. Even where discount firms have appeared (either flat-fee discount or rebate-based programs), consumers have not switched. Discount brokerages have 2% and unassisted consumers represent about 11% of market share.
2. The purchase of residential property using a real estate agent is seen as a no-cost option to most buyers. Most do not see that they are actually paying out of pocket for the cost of the services provided by the agent. Unless and until they

believe otherwise, their ingrained habits will not drive large shares of purchasers to do otherwise (or to pay for an online service).

3. The purchase and sale of residential property, other than for investors, is both an infrequent and complex transaction. For these reasons consumers have been reluctant to shift their buying and selling practices.
4. Thus far, no one firm has designed a truly integrated platform that encompasses all the variables of a housing transaction. Further, to automate a scaled national platform would require a firm to design in thousands of variations of the forms, regulatory requirements, processes, and notifications required to fully automate the buying and selling process. While there are robust transaction platforms available, these owners (i.e., title companies and mortgage organizations) have faced issues of channel conflict since they get most of their business from real estate agents and brokerage firms. These conflicts likely prevent them from making use of these platforms as part of a direct-to-consumer offering.
5. Providers of transaction management systems present channel conflicts that hinder traditional realty firms from adopting this service approach. A realty firm cannot likely offer both models. To adopt this form of realty service would mean the abandonment of the traditional agent-centric focus—it is an either/or choice. The incumbents have large advantages, most of which revolve around existing consumer behaviors in the purchase or sale of housing.

Comments

For the reasons cited above, it is possible that unassisted rates could increase. As you plan for your business, consider a scenario where this rate approaches 30% by the year 2025 vs. 11% today. What opportunities and challenges would that present for you?

When we interviewed real estate industry leaders, we segmented the question into two parts:

1. *Is an online transaction platform feasible?*
2. *Will the unassisted percentage increase?*

Is an online transaction platform feasible?

Regional Director of Keller Williams

Technology has changed the way consumers buy and sell homes for sure and it has been and continues to be an overwhelming development. The fear of the agent becoming redundant and substituted for a virtual tour is to say that the profession is little more than a taxi or sign service. The fiduciary value a true professional brings to their client in negotiating and packaging a transaction far outweighs the mechanics of the information and technology. Rather it supports them.

– Marian Benton, Keller Williams

Owner of a large independent brokerage:

That system doesn't eliminate the need to see property; manage disclosures; ensure compliance with all the laws. Are you comfortable with negotiation? You still need a Realtor to do this.

– David Stark, President, Stark Company Realtors (190 agents)

....

President of a large association:

It could work. However, it would require the ease of use, credibility and trust of online Turbo Tax. Could it get to the market share of Turbo Tax? Real estate is so fragmented. Even a "dominant" leader like Zillow has a small market share.

– Mike Ruzicka, CAE, RCE, President, Greater Milwaukee Association of REALTORS

....

President of a large MLS:

HAR has been providing a free transaction management solution to all of our brokers for nearly two years. It was somewhat slow to catch on, but we are definitely making progress. We currently have nearly 90,000 transactions that have gone through the platform. For us the issue isn't about whether our members should take advantage of the benefit we provide versus using someone else's product. We just want them to understand the benefits of using transaction management.

It is our job to make sure our members understand that transaction management is more than just an electronic filing cabinet. It could revolutionize their business by reducing legal claims and increasing profits, if they would only utilize it to its full potential. According to the HAR Consumer Research Panel, 92 percent of those surveyed want access to online tracking tools for their next transaction. Consumers want it, so the winners are going to be the ones who recognize that and allow consumers to have access to it.

– Bob Hale, President & CEO, Houston Association of REALTORS, Houston MLS

President/CEO of a large MLS:

Being the worldwide de facto standard for eSignatures, DocuSign has become a huge tool for real estate practitioners. It makes total sense in an industry that is bogged down with paperwork. That doesn't mean it will replace agents, unless they choose not to take advantage of the technology.

– Russ Bergeron, President/CEO Midwest Real Estate Data (Chicagoland's MLS)

Owner of a franchise brokerage:

Realtors have amazing data. Like a million census takers collecting data on homes—real time—day in, day out. We as an industry have to do something creative with this info to get consumers' attention. Let consumers know we have the most timely info—not Zillow. There's a big difference between a spy satellite and human intelligence.

– Jack Fry, RE/MAX of Reading, PA

Owner of a large independent brokerage:

This scenario is very plausible. More so in markets where buyers know what area(s) they want. Still a lot of power on the buyer side [for an agent] to advise on neighborhoods. If it is a large deal, consumers want guidance. However, this could be a big threat.

– Neal Hanks, President, Beverly Hanks Brokerage (250 Realtors)

President of a large MLS:

One-stop shopping is advocated by brokers and certainly appealing to consumers. Enabling and effectively delivering this capability gives consumers added rationale for working with a professional as opposed to DIY or a la carte. Consumers care about the number of moving parts involved in a closing only to the extent it impacts speed, cost and accuracy. Technology can surely address these issues, making the transaction more seamless and therefore more transparent, resulting in a more satisfied consumer experience. Brokers clearly want/need an end-to-end solution as it positions them for add-on business. Without it, these profitable, ancillary services go somewhere else, placing greater pressure on the company dollar derived from the transaction.

– David Charron, President, MRIS (Washington DC/ Baltimore MLS)

Regional owner Keller Williams

If the valuation capabilities of the real estate aggregators gets better, and consumers are able to get an accurate picture of the value of their home, technology could affect the listing side of things. By get better I mean they have to give a value that's within 5% of actual value or better. Right now they are probably within 20% which is essentially meaningless information. If they could get to 95% accurate on a specific house it could diminish the value for a seller. On the buyer side any agent that is a fiduciary and knows neighborhoods and communities in ways that a computer never could, is always going to be invaluable to a consumer and well worth their commission. As long as agents concentrate on being fiduciaries they will be invaluable to the transaction.

– David Osborn, Keller Williams Realty

President/CEO of a large MLS:

Having been in the biz 34 years (on both the MLS and tech vendor sides), I have heard the warnings that "the industry will change drastically" and "the transaction will be all paperless" and "consumers will be selling to consumers without Realtors"... not yet! Technology cannot replace the personal collaboration required of the practitioner with their clients, but should free them up to do more of it.

– Russ Bergeron, President/CEO Midwest Real Estate Data (Chicagoland's MLS)

Will the unassisted percentage increase?

President of a large MLS:

According to the most recent NAR consumer survey, 23 percent of Gen Y sellers preferred a limited-service brokerage rather than a full-service brokerage, compared to 8 percent for all sellers.

Additionally, only 42 percent of Gen Y sellers were very satisfied with the selling process, according to the NAR survey. You cannot continue an industry with less than half of the sellers being very satisfied with the job you're doing. We must do a better job of explaining our value proposition if we want to remain relevant and viable in the coming years.

– Bob Hale, President & CEO, Houston Association of REALTORS, Houston MLS

Owner of a large independent brokerage:

Technology will have some impact at the margin; mostly for people who were not going to use an agent anyway. Overall, technology will not produce a big change in the number of unassisted buyers or sellers. The fundamentals of real estate deal remain the same—tech helps, but is a both a distraction and an enabler. Homes are a perfectly non-commoditized asset. That doesn't lend itself to "Amazon marketplace."

– David Stark, President, Stark Company Realtors (190 agents)

President of a large MLS:

Real estate is a complicated deal. Consumers will likely always need help. Will more agents get more specialized in a neighborhood in the future? I suspect the real estate generalist serving an entire metro area will be less prevalent as a model in the future. Consumers will want more deep area expertise.

– Mike Ruzicka, President, Greater Milwaukee Association of REALTORS

President of a large independent brokerage:

You can sell a car on Craigslist, but it's not the same as inviting a stranger into your home.

– Nancy Fennell, President, Dickson Realty (250 agents)

President of a large independent brokerage:

If the consumer thinks, "I only need a Realtor to get keys," then that will gut the industry.

– Dan Elsea, President, Real Estate One (2,000 agents)

President of a large franchise brokerage:

Lots of intimidating documents—government docs—the consumer needs a guide. Consumers need help to price the house and understand the market dynamics. Technology will help way more than it will hurt Realtors in the future.

– Jack Fry, RE/MAX of Reading, PA

President of a large franchised brokerage. $5 billion+ volume:

The Internet is providing an informative consumer experience. However, the Internet will not replace the Realtor. As much as consumers think they can do it themselves, the majority really want someone to advise them and guide them. The do-it-yourselfers will always exist, but will remain a much smaller percentage of home buyers. Most consumers are busy with their families and jobs and don't necessarily have the time, energy, or effort to expend to successfully navigate the learning curve possessed by a qualified agent.

– Joan Docktor, President, Berkshire Hathaway HomeServices Fox & Roach, Realtors/The Trident Group (Philadelphia, 4,000+ agents)

Results from our Broker/Agent Survey

We surveyed over 6,000 high-production agents and teams (50 or more transactions per year) on the topic of automating transactions for do-it-yourselfers. We also surveyed the owners of the largest 1,350 brokerages in the U.S. We asked: "Currently, about 80% of transactions involve a real estate agent. Do you think this will rise, remain steady or decline over the next ten years?" [See Exhibit 2-3.]

In summary, they told us:

- Realtors (31%) are more likely to think this will increase vs. broker/owners (18%).
- A small minority of both thought that the use of agents would decline (20% for agents, 17% for broker/owners).

Exhibit 2-3: Owner and agent predictions about future market share of Unassisted Sellers.

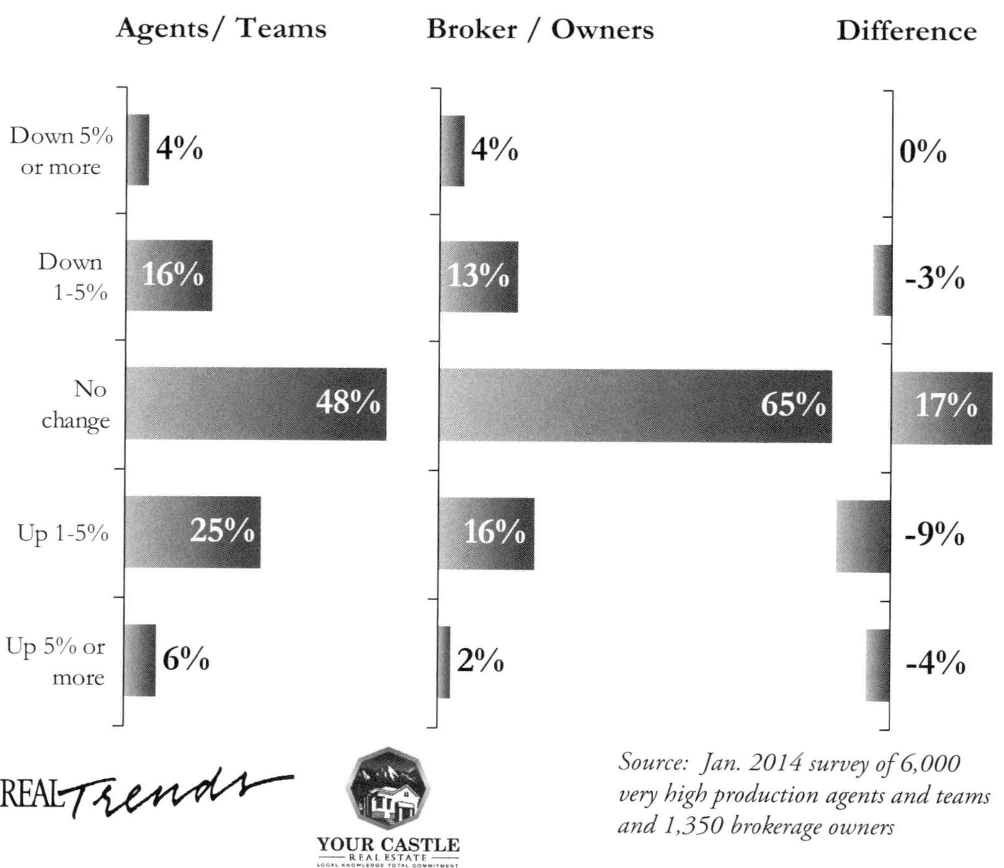

Source: Jan. 2014 survey of 6,000 very high production agents and teams and 1,350 brokerage owners

Implications

The market share of consumers who are not assisted by agents is likely to remain modest. This model will probably be similar to the discount brokerage or do-it-yourself home transaction segment that today is a small part of the market. However, should such a shift develop, it would place significant pressure on existing realty service providers to automate more transaction services. This could, in turn, exert downward pressure on commission levels. Much as existing realty service providers have had to embrace online displays of listing and sales data to stay competitive, so too would such an offering require them to delve deeper into automating their transactional capabilities and compel their agents to do the same.

Such a development would also give rise to entirely new forms of brokerages built around such systems—along with a variety of commission or fee plans for consumers. Real estate counseling on a fee basis may become more prevalent as a result.

The need to provide more automation will prompt more consolidation, both in the number of brokerage firms and sales agents. The cost of automation, including software, training, and compliance, will overwhelm all but the strongest and most adept realty organizations. It may make the value of a brokerage firm higher as a result—at least those firms that can deliver such systems for their agents and their consumers.

Realtor associations and multiple-listing systems will be challenged to deliver similar systems for their members. The need for capital and human resources skills to deliver and maintain such systems will likely be a driver of consolidation among these organizations as well. Regardless of whether it is a realty organization or a Realtor support organization, the need for capital and talent to maintain such systems and provide customer service support to real estate agents will be much higher in the future than today.

Solutions

One way for realty firms to take advantage of technology's growing capabilities is to invest much more intensively in two areas: automating their purchase and sale transactions, and training and motivating their sales agent force beyond what they're doing currently to offer a competitive service to the unassisted consumer.

A different strategy would be to emphasize the human element in the purchase and sale of housing—with less emphasis on the technological aspects. This would require many realty firms and sales agents to significantly enhance their skills, with special attention paid to the development of better interpersonal skills.

What they told us:

A significant increase in FSBO is unlikely. However, if it occurred, it could possibly drive a lot of agents out of business, as well as negatively impact profitability. A more likely scenario is that there will be growing numbers of agent teams; those who are more tech savvy will stand out in the forefront. The laggards will be crowded out, leaving a smaller number of more efficient agents.

– Joan Docktor, President, Berkshire Hathaway HomeServices Fox & Roach, Realtors/The Trident Group, Philadelphia

Agents and realty firms should focus more on serving those who do not want to "do-it-themselves"—rather than on the consumer market as a whole. Regardless of whether this trend continues to grow, a significant percentage of home buyers and sellers will continue to prefer that someone else take care of the complexities for them.

Realtor associations and MLSs may address the continuing segmentation of their membership with more of an unbundled approach to delivering services and products. The gap is growing between what full-service realty firms want, and discount, do-it-yourself realty firms want.

For example, while MLSs' role has primarily been the delivery of data (and software to access it), the future points towards more integrated data needs for smaller and medium-sized traditional realty firms. The consumer-discount segment will require nothing of the kind. One size will not fit all. MLSs will need to price their services for each group according to its needs, and not be in the business of subsidizing one group in favor of another.

Realtor associations may need to follow the same course. More differentiation among membership will likely require either a refocus on core services that everyone wants and/or mass customization of services to serve each niche of the membership. These are two entirely different strategies, not just a re-bundling of what is done today.

Chapter Three

Ratings and reviews begin to matter

Probability: High
Impact: Moderate

About 65% of consumers choose their agent because of a personal relationship or they know one. This factor has changed little in 30 years. See Exhibit 3-1A and 3-1B. Repeat and referral is one of the foundations of residential brokerage. Anything that changes how consumers select an agent will pose a threat. Ratings and reviews will have a growing, and potentially negative, impact on many agents. In contrast, a large benefit will accrue to a small number of agents—generally, Internet-savvy high producers.

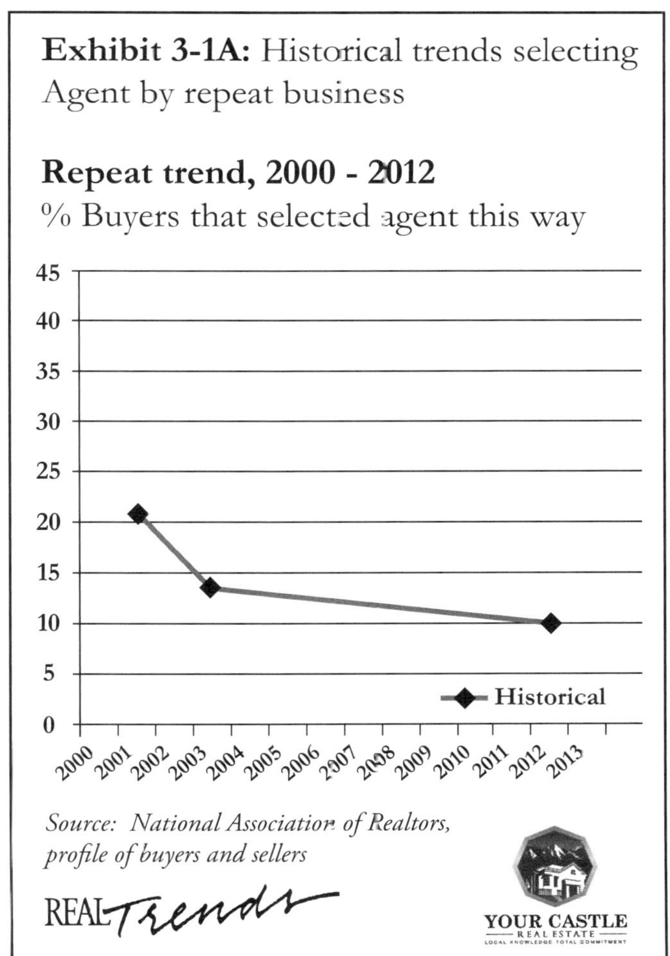

Exhibit 3-1A: Historical trends selecting Agent by repeat business

Repeat trend, 2000 - 2012
% Buyers that selected agent this way

Source: National Association of Realtors, profile of buyers and sellers

Consumers, especially younger people fluent in adopting new technology, use ratings in many of their choices. Online reviews drive decisions about what to buy, where to eat, where to travel, where to stay, and even which medical or legal advisors to use. It should be no surprise that consumers would seek this information to choose a real estate agent. The information will either fortify their selection of an agent referred to them, or drive them to select someone else. The leadership of the industry has been characteristically slow to adopt ratings and reviews. Leading agents are embracing this trend more quickly. How the incumbents adopt this change—and who provides ratings and reviews—could reshape the industry.

Consumer interest is rising

Ratings and reviews drive consumer choice in many service and product categories. Consumers use them from several sources independent of the business service or product provider. Some examples are Yelp, Trip Advisor, Angie's List, Amazon, social media rating services, and supplier sites. There are independent ratings sites for specialized services such as medical and dental, banking, home maintenance—and now real estate brokerage.

Real estate agents and brokerage firms have historically shied away from allowing ratings and reviews of either their own services or on the properties they may list for sale. While a small number of agents are promoting their reviews on independent sites such as Yelp, the great majority are not. Some agents are also allowing reviews to be posted on listing portals such as Zillow and Trulia. Reviews are generally characterized as comments posted by customers and clients, while ratings are generally considered quantitative analyses of an agent's sales and listing performance. It is the latter (ratings) that are most resisted by the industry at large.

Exhibit 3-1B: Historical trends selecting Agent by referral

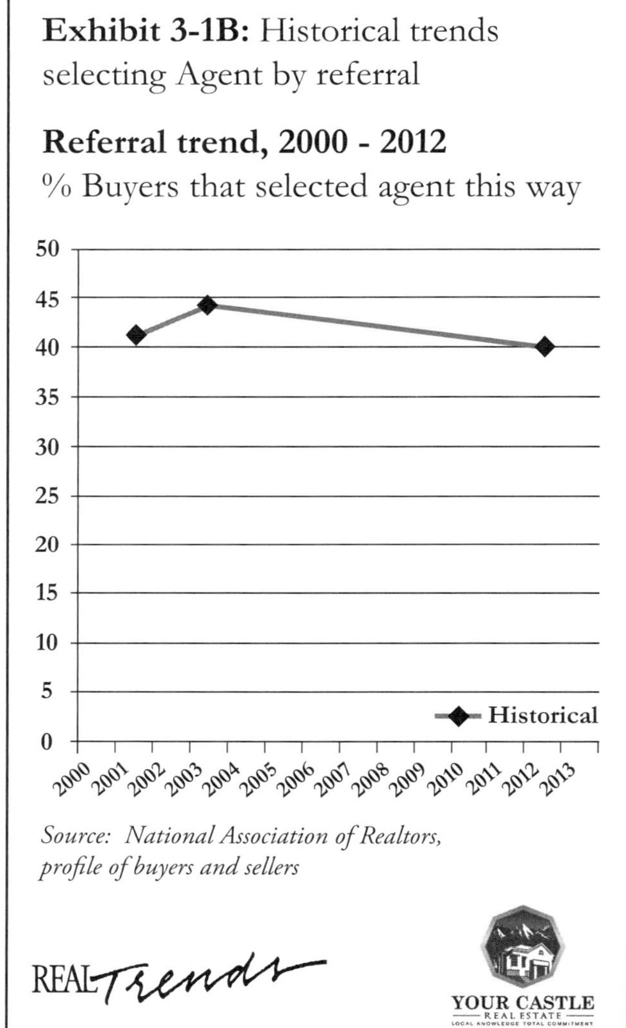

Source: National Association of Realtors, profile of buyers and sellers

Recent anecdotal evidence supports the fact that consumers are becoming more interested in both reviews and ratings of real estate agents. Both Trulia and Zillow reported recently, for instance, that those agents on their sites who have reviews posted are receiving far higher referral and inquiry traffic than those who do not allow the posting of reviews. Agents are also becoming far more interested in their ranking among their peers as shown by the increase in ranked agents on the REAL *Trends* America's Best Agents ranking report. High-producing agents obviously fear ratings less than do low-producing agents, but even high-producing agents are reluctant to allow unfiltered reviews from customers and clients.

Consumer trends in ratings and referrals

Generational differences in factors that drive consumers' choices of agents

Historically, 60-70 percent of consumers chose a real estate agent primarily through knowing someone who was an agent—or barring that, someone they knew referred them to an agent. In the following pages, we chart data from the REAL *Trends* 2001 *Room for Improvement* report and the 2014 Harris Interactive Study performed for this book. As you'll see, referrals generally occur regardless of how many transactions an agent has performed or their demonstrated skills.

Millennial home buyers are becoming a significant source of future business, and they embrace reviews and ratings. This is also true of investors who are looking for demonstrated skills. Currently, three of the largest real estate portals and several MLSs offer reviews; some are considering numerical ratings as well. At least one publisher provides data on the top-producing real estate agents. There will be more of this information available to consumers in the coming years.

Not all consumers will use ratings systems. But the evidence suggests that adoption of ratings is poised to take off rapidly. This will shift market share, probably to agents who are more productive or have more experience in a particular segment of the market. Please see Exhibit 3-2, "Important factors in selecting your agent." We hired Harris Interactive to do a study of over 1,000 consumers who recently completed a real estate transaction. We asked them what were some of the most important factors they considered when they hired their agent. Here are some key observations:

- Having a personal relationship was important for about half of consumers. There was a little variation by generation. Everyone values relationships.
- Having worked with the agent in the past increased in importance as consumers got older. This makes sense, as first-time buyers (e.g., Millennials) have not had a chance to work with an agent, while older consumers have typically completed many real estate transactions.
- Referrals were very important to all groups, especially younger consumers.
- Interestingly, "looking at websites with agent performance" had the biggest variability. The younger the consumer, the more likely they were to cite ratings as important in the decision process.

Generational differences in research performed on agents—and factors that drive choices

Exhibit 3-2: Consumers by Generation: Importance of factors when choosing agent.

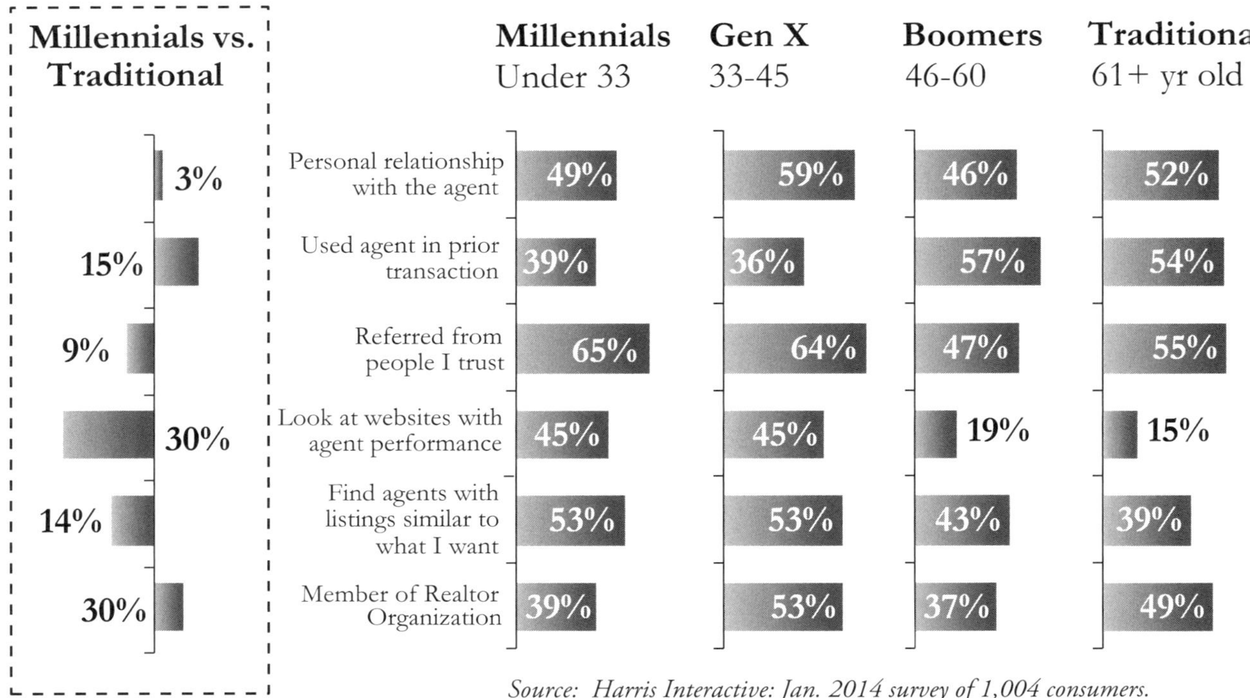

Source: Harris Interactive: Jan. 2014 survey of 1,004 consumers. Does not include 178 (18%) that didn't use an Agent.

REAL Trends

YOUR CASTLE REAL ESTATE

Exhibit 3-3: Consumers by Generation: Research completed before hiring agent.

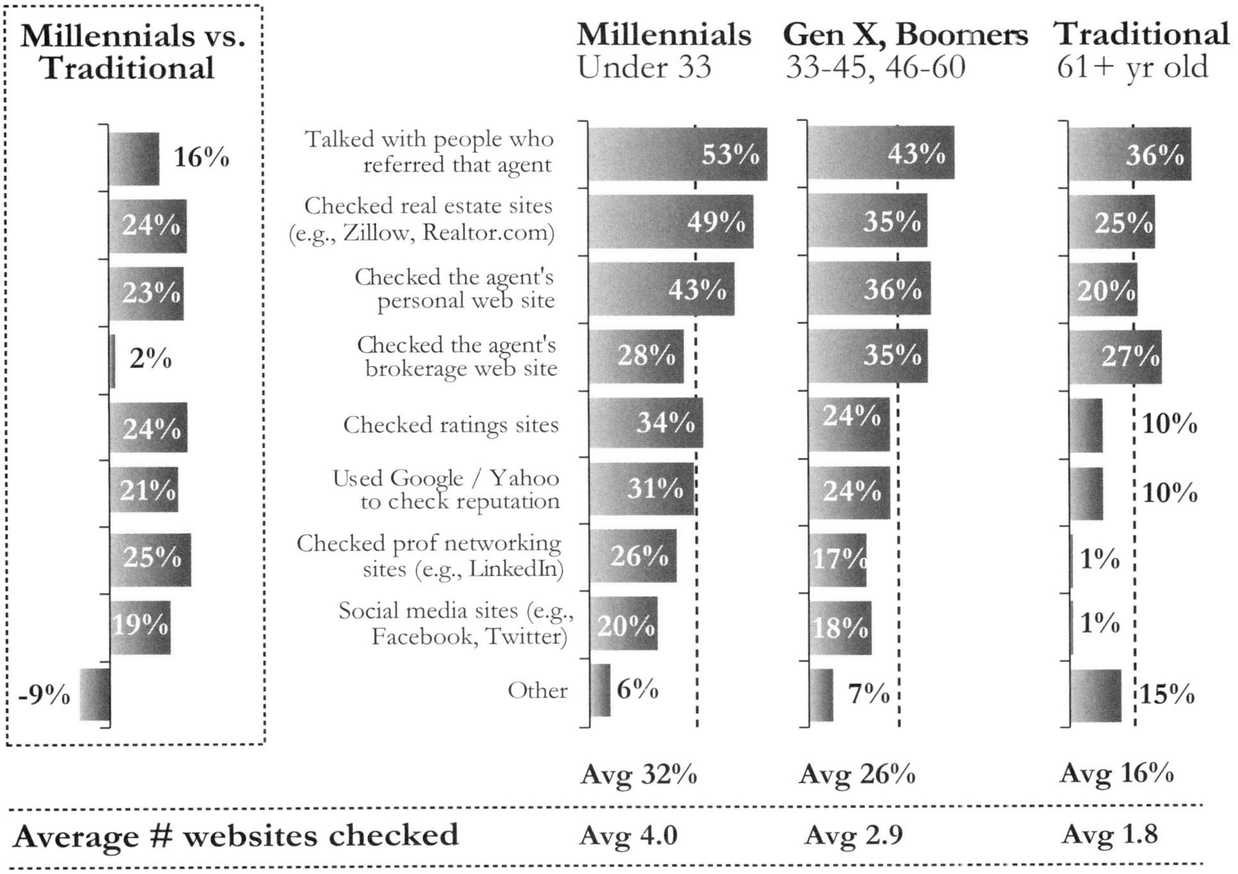

	Millennials vs. Traditional	Millennials Under 33	Gen X, Boomers 33-45, 46-60	Traditional 61+ yr old
Talked with people who referred that agent	16%	53%	43%	36%
Checked real estate sites (e.g., Zillow, Realtor.com)	24%	49%	35%	25%
Checked the agent's personal web site	23%	43%	36%	20%
Checked the agent's brokerage web site	2%	28%	35%	27%
Checked ratings sites	24%	34%	24%	10%
Used Google / Yahoo to check reputation	21%	31%	24%	10%
Checked prof networking sites (e.g., LinkedIn)	25%	26%	17%	1%
Social media sites (e.g., Facebook, Twitter)	19%	20%	18%	1%
Other	-9%	6%	7%	15%
		Avg 32%	Avg 26%	Avg 16%
Average # websites checked		**Avg 4.0**	**Avg 2.9**	**Avg 1.8**

REALTrends

Source: Harris Interactive: Jan. 2014 survey of 1,004 consumers. Does not include 178 (18%) that didn't use an Agent.

Next, please see Exhibit 3-3, based on the question, "What research did you do online before hiring your agent?" Again, we asked over 1,000 consumers about what they did as part of their decision process. Millennials checked more than twice as many sites as did Traditionals. It's particularly interesting to see what a broad array of sources were used to validate reputation and expertise.

Exhibit 3-4: Consumers by Generation: What was the one MOST IMPORTANT factor in their choice of agent.

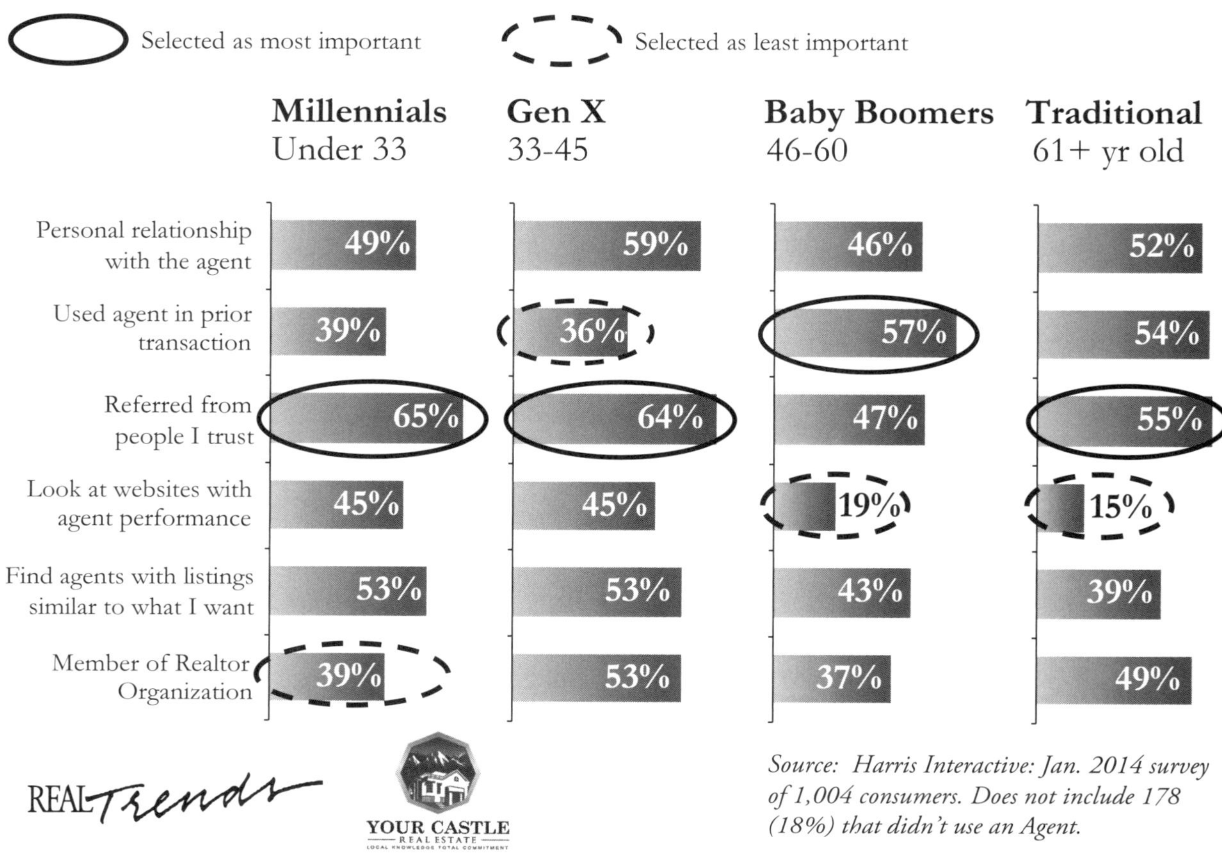

Source: Harris Interactive: Jan. 2014 survey of 1,004 consumers. Does not include 178 (18%) that didn't use an Agent.

To get the information we chart in Exhibit 3-4, we asked consumers, "Which factor was most important in the agent selection process?" Referrals are still the most important factor for all but the oldest consumers. This latter group has had much more experience with trusted advisors. The fact that "personal relationships" was most important to them makes a lot of sense. For older consumers, website performance ratings were the least important. For younger consumers, ratings websites were in the middle of the pack for influencing the hiring decision.

Exhibit 3-5: Consumers by Generation: Next time, how many more websites will you check?

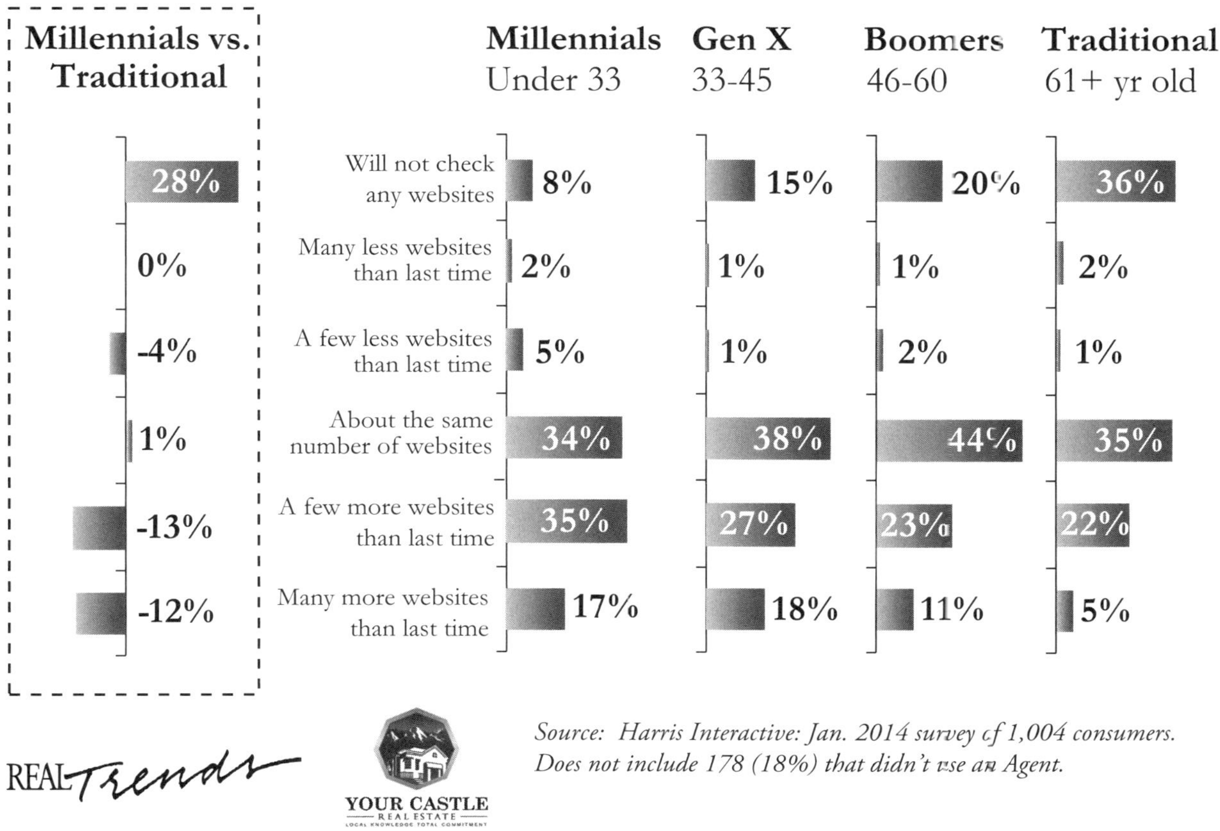

Exhibit 3-5 shows the results of asking consumers, "For your next real estate transaction, how many ratings websites will you consult?" You can see that the oldest consumers either plan to consult none, or about the same number as last time. This is consistent with their earlier responses; they have a trusted advisor and they plan to be loyal to them. For the youngest consumers with limited agent relationships (relative to older consumers), there is much more expected reliance on future ratings sites. So while Millennials are already doing more web research currently, that gap should grow dramatically in the near term.

Exhibit 3-6: Consumers by Generation: Preference for skills vs. relationship.

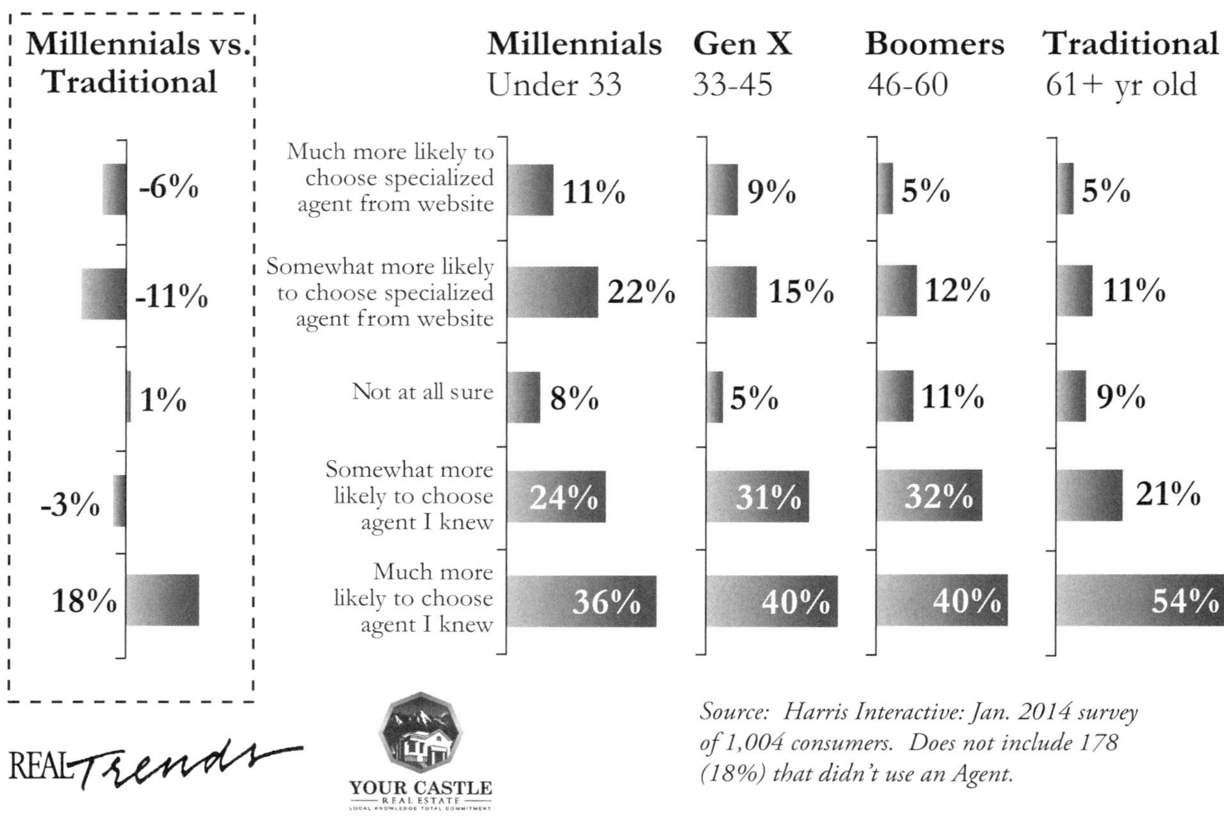

Source: Harris Interactive: Jan. 2014 survey of 1,004 consumers. Does not include 178 (18%) that didn't use an Agent.

Preference for skills vs. prior agent relationship

In Exhibit 3-6, we chart the responses we received when we asked consumers, "Would you prefer the agent you knew well or an agent with specific skills?" For all generations, "the agent I know" won the majority of the time. However, a sizable minority of young consumers (33%) were either much more likely or somewhat more likely to choose a "specialized agent found by a website."

Exhibit 3-7: Consumers by Generation: How likely would you be to use a ratings website?

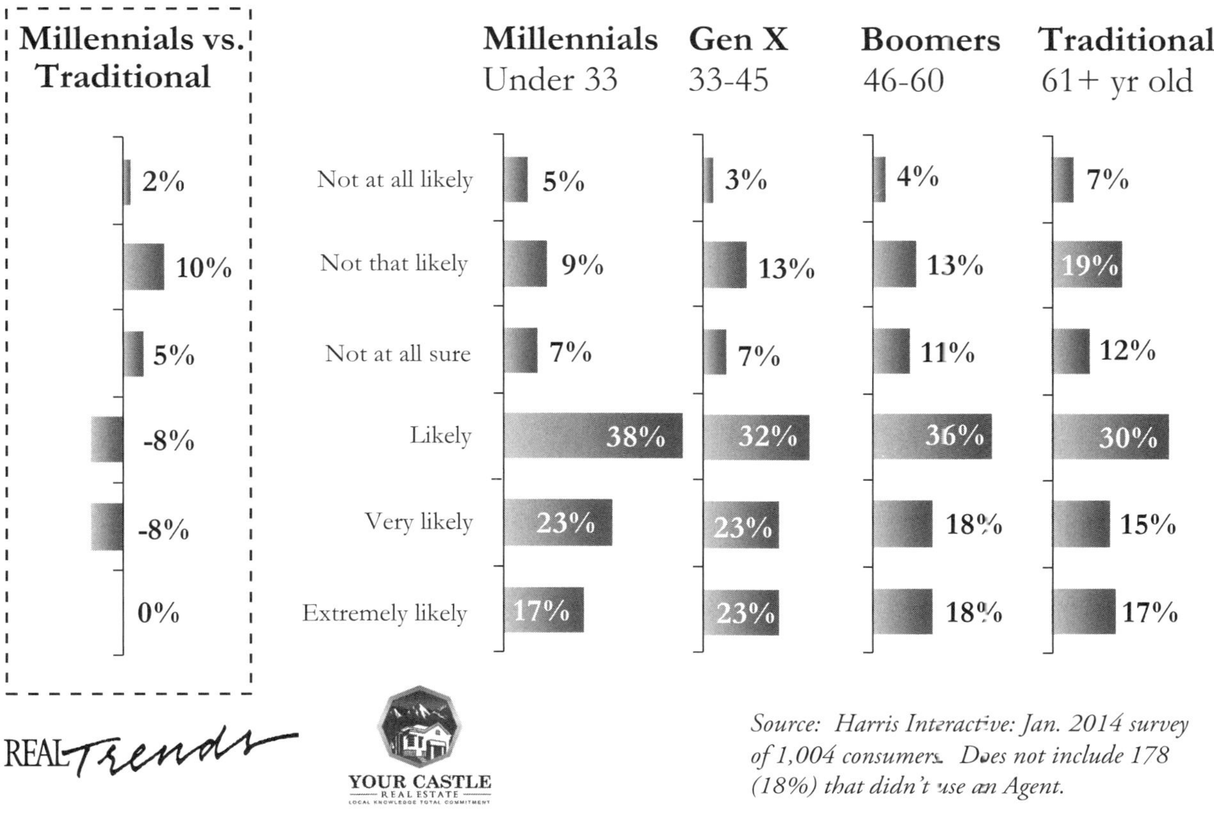

Source: Harris Interactive: Jan. 2014 survey of 1,004 consumers. Does not include 178 (18%) that didn't use an Agent.

Consumers' likelihood of using an agent-rating website

For Exhibit 3-7, we asked consumers, "If there were a website that offered ratings of real estate agents and consumer reviews, how likely would you be to use such a website?" The youngest consumers showed a clear pattern of significantly more reliance on websites—older consumers did not.

Exhibit 3-8: Consumers by Generation: How helpful to know how many deals done by agent?

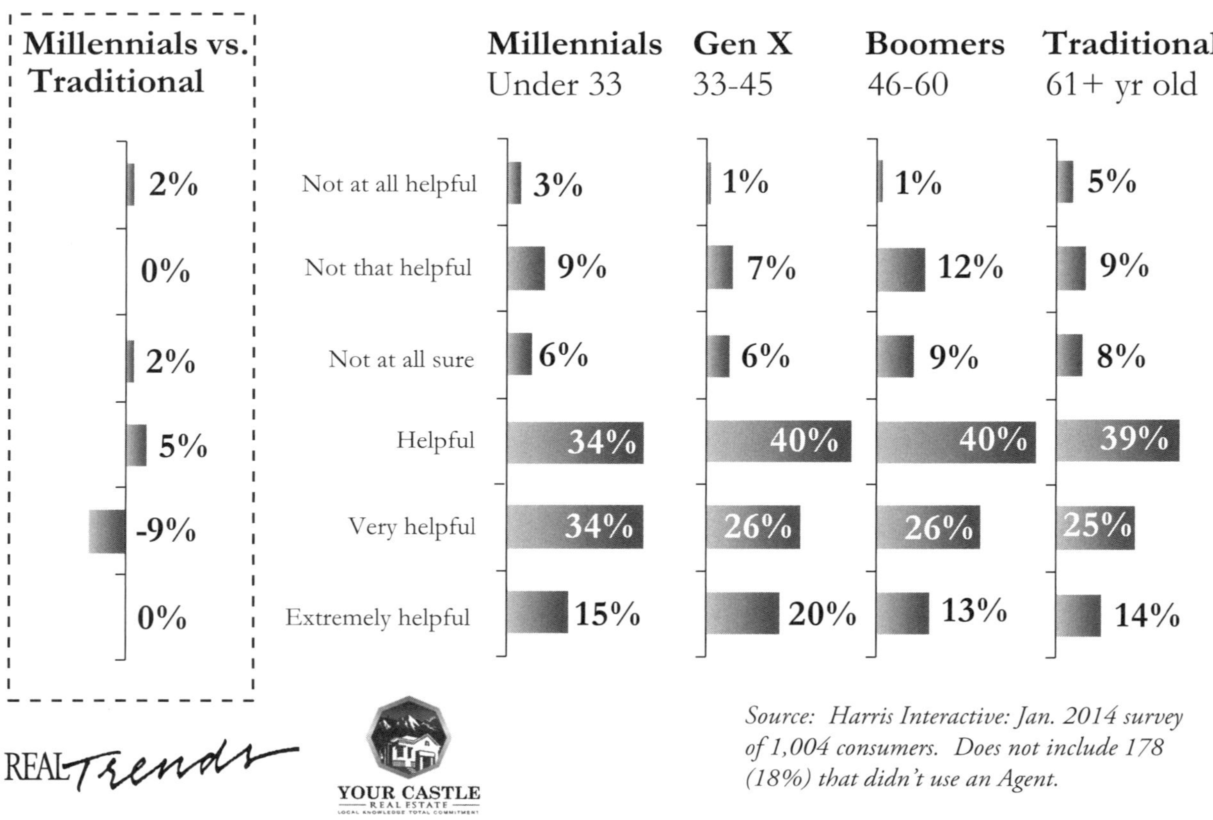

Source: Harris Interactive: Jan. 2014 survey of 1,004 consumers. Does not include 178 (18%) that didn't use an Agent.

Specific neighborhood expertise is desired by consumers across generations

For Exhibit 3-8, we asked consumers, "How helpful do you think it would be to know how many real estate deals an agent was involved in, in the neighborhood you are interested in?" To our surprise, EVERY generation tended to find this information to be helpful, even the older consumers who already have strong relationships with a preferred agent.

Exhibit 3-9: Consumers by Generation: How likely are you to use an agent for a future transaction?

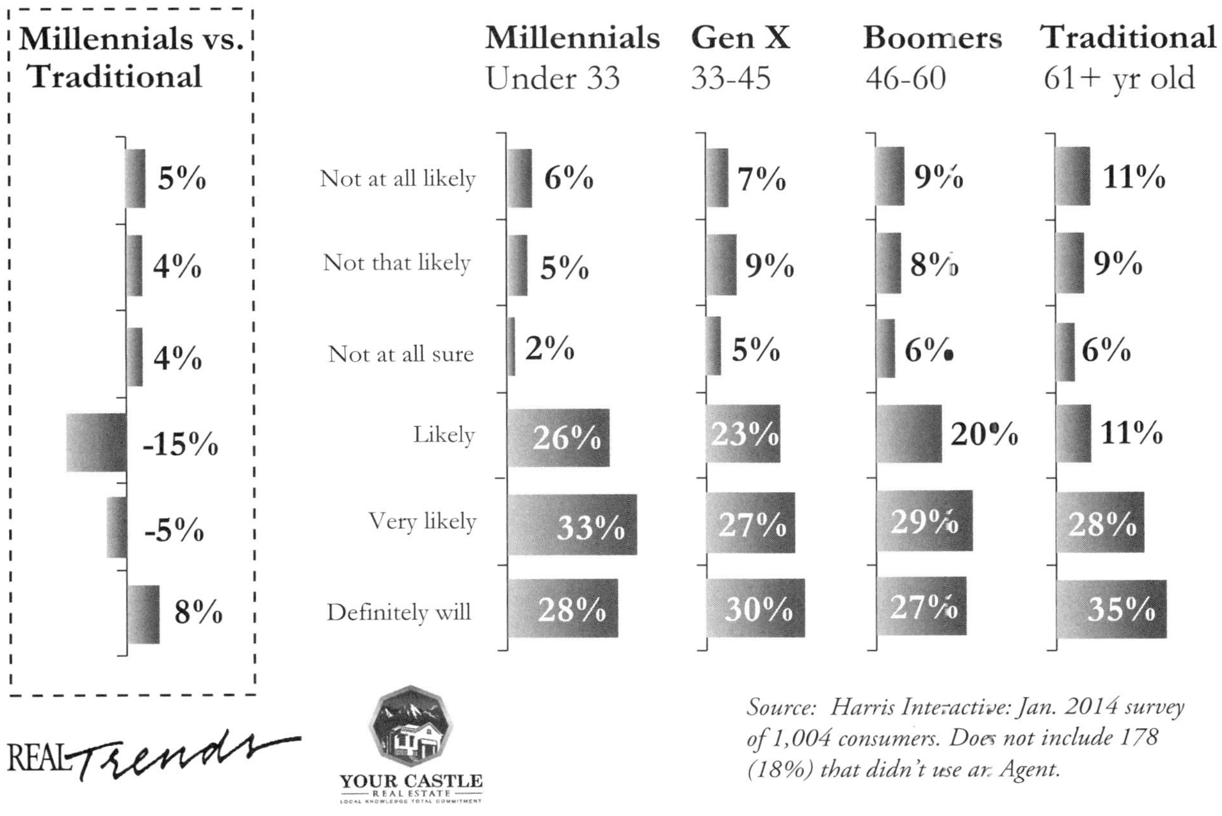

Source: Harris Interactive: Jan. 2014 survey of 1,004 consumers. Does not include 178 (18%) that didn't use an Agent.

Strength of intention to continue the agent relationship: Variation among generations

For Exhibit 3-9, we asked consumers the very basic question: "How likely are you to use your last transaction's agent again for a future transaction?" A very large number of people of all ages were happy with their agent and plan to use this person again. But again, there are some cracks forming in the wall with younger consumers. They were less likely than older consumers to select "definitely will use again"; merely "likely" was selected much more often. For this group, the strength of intent for repeat business isn't as powerful as it is for older consumers.

Repeat and referral for consumers: Conclusions

When you consider all the evidence, repeat and referral is a powerful channel for agent selection today and will continue to be in the future. This is especially true for older consumers who tend to be loyal and tend to have very established relationships with agents. However, the youngest consumers generally do not have these established connections, and a meaningful share of their transactions will probably NOT be referral based. We expect the percentage of agents selected by repeat and referral to gradually erode over time.

Exhibit 3-10: Agents and Owners: Will consumers use ratings sites to help select their Agents?

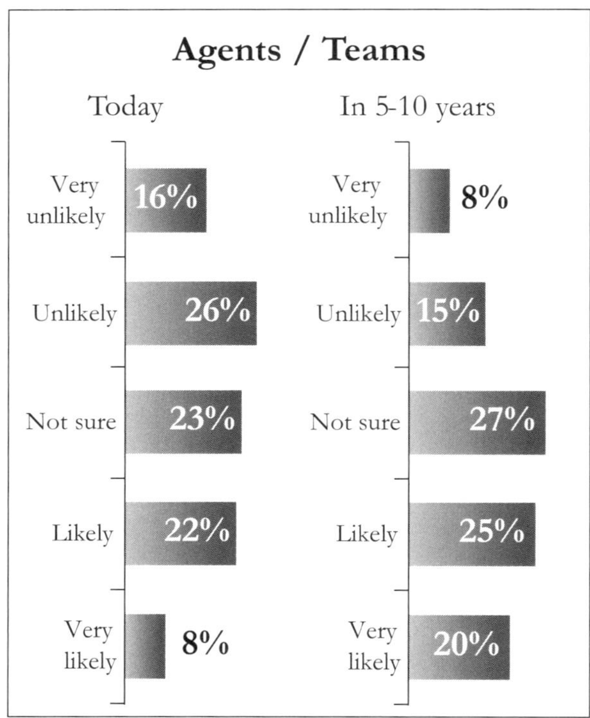

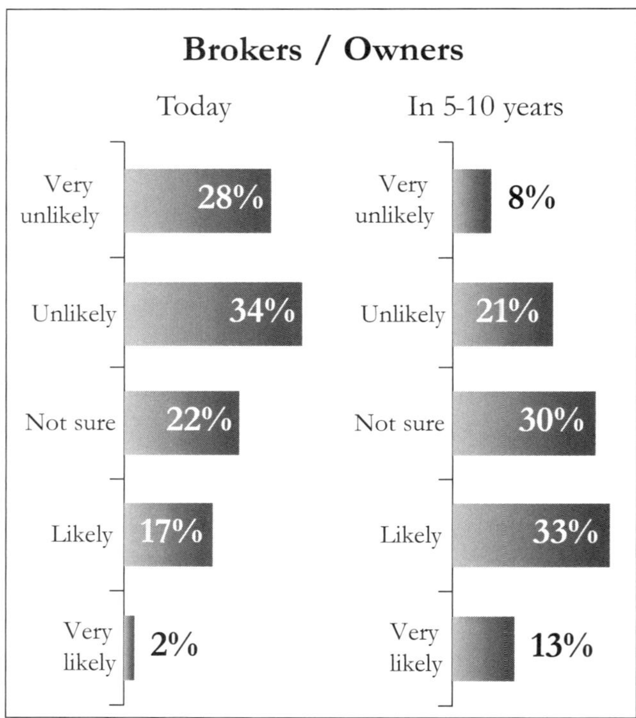

REAL Trends

YOUR CASTLE REAL ESTATE

Source: Jan. 2014 survey of 6,000 very high production Agents and teams and 1,330 brokerage owners

Owners and high producers: Their perspectives on repeat and referral trends

We also asked owners of large brokerages and high-production agents what they thought of rating sites.

Let's explore this in a little detail. Exhibit 3-10 presents the results of this question: "National High-Production Realtors/Teams—Will consumers use ratings sites to help select their Realtor?"

In summary:

- Neither agents nor owners believe that consumers would be very likely to adopt rating sites today.
- Even when asked about 5-10 years from now, only 13-20% of owners and agents selected "very likely."
- Our 50 phone interviews with owners and agents generally conveyed the sense that the real estate transaction is complex, and that consumers will continue to rely on repeat/referral in the future.

Exhibit 3-11: Agents and Owners: Will repeat and referral rate decline?

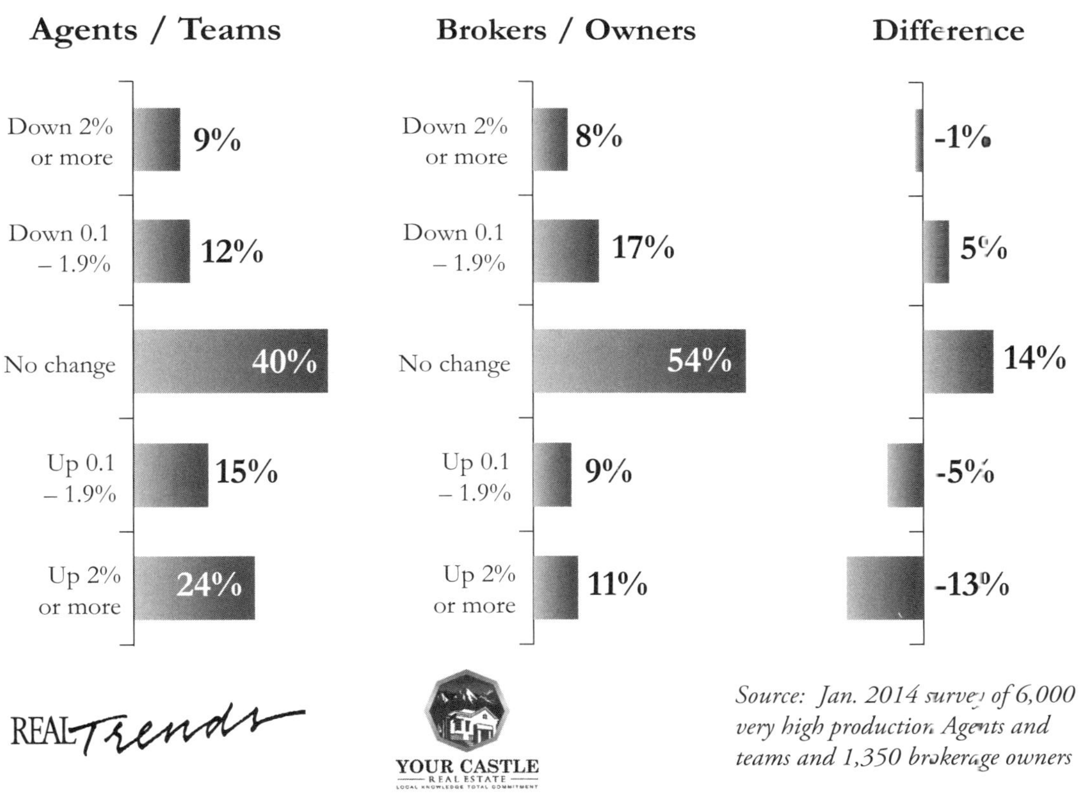

Source: Jan. 2014 survey of 6,000 very high production Agents and teams and 1,350 brokerage owners

As we discussed earlier in this chapter, consumers, on the other hand, indicated that they are more likely to adopt ratings sites to drive decisions than the industry expects.

Exhibit 3-11 displays the results of this question: "Currently, 68% of consumers find their agent via relationship or referral from a known source. Do you think this will rise, remain steady, or decline?"

The bottom line:

- There wasn't much consensus.
- Overall, there was a very slight bias towards the increasing power of repeat/referral (41% agents, 20% owners) vs. its decline (21% agents, 25% owners).
- Most expect little change.

Forces moving in favor of more ratings websites

1. Millennials are huge users of ratings sites. Growing numbers of Gen X and Traditional consumers are also using ratings for professionals and a host of products and services, such as lawyers, doctors, and hotels. As real estate agent ratings become more available, they will become part of how consumers find and select an agent. A large segment of home buyers and sellers are now investors, and their desire to select an agent with specific skills will only grow.
2. The increasing complexity of the sale and purchase of a home will require higher levels of expertise, which will lead a growing number of consumers to seek assurance that their agent truly does have the knowledge and experience to competently handle the transaction.
3. Ratings websites do not need to have perfect information. Some intelligence is better than none. For example, listing data on portals is frequently inaccurate and/or out of date, and yet commands high usage by consumers. Consumers want more information, not less.
4. High-performance real estate agents and brokerage firms will desire to be represented in the ratings systems to the extent that they can influence them. Historically, agents and brokerages promote their performance, whether it is the level of sales, productivity, or years of experience. While there will be initial resistance to ratings services that are not under the control of the industry (as there was reluctance to post listings online), ultimately those who stand to

benefit from the comparison of performance will support these ratings.

5. The data necessary to present even rudimentary ratings is available and can be easily published. Even though, in almost every case, it is incomplete and not truly representative of agent performance, it is much more information than has been available in the past. Given the interest of consumers to have more, not less, access to information in areas important to them, ratings should become standard features of the residential realty environment. This consumer interest will drive the revenue and valuations of sponsoring organizations.
6. The major listing portals already have reviews on agents who choose to permit them; these agents are receiving direct benefit from having them available. As more agents learn about the benefits of reviews and ratings, more agents will want to permit them.

Countering these forces

1. The great majority of real estate agents and brokers who will not be highly rated will not want these sites to function. They are represented by hundreds of Realtor associations and MLSs that will be pressured not to support them. Brokerage firms having both highly rated agents and those not as well rated will be pulled in both directions as to whether to support ratings sites. At the least, brokerages will be prone to be passive in their responses. The same is true of the position of the existing national real estate organizations.
2. Agents and brokerages are the primary source of revenue for the listing portals (not consumers' direct spending). Portals will have to be careful in approaching how ratings and reviews are implemented. While publishing raw sales data, derived from MLS information, may be acceptable to some agents, allowing unfiltered consumer content on listing portal sites may hurt revenue. Further, since MLS data is not the complete subset of sales by real estate agents, providers of ratings may be challenged in numerous ways to insure that their data is accurate (particularly as ratings become more and more important in the selection process).
3. The historical manner in which consumers choose an agent will not change rapidly. Due to the infrequency and complexity of the housing transaction, personal relationships may still matter far more than ratings. If this occurs, the value of ratings to their sponsors may not offset the other challenges faced in providing the information.

Based on the pros and cons cited above, we believe it is likely that:

- Ratings sites for agent performance will become more available over time.
- Consumers will be eager for the information.
- Younger generations are much more likely to use the information to influence their decisions.
- Those agents who embrace reviews and ratings will garner greater share of the available business opportunities.

Comments from the industry

When we asked industry leaders for their perspectives, we segmented their responses into:

1. *Will consumers use ratings sites, and will it impact their decisions?*
2. *Will repeat and referral decline over time?*

Owner of a 2,000+ agent independent brokerage:

> *Agent rating systems currently are in the arena of dog groomers and restaurants. Yelp has not gotten to high-end service (yet). Within the travel industry, TripAdvisor is massive, so we can see that ratings can drive an industry. In real estate, top people will capture more business, as a result of agent rating sites. Ratings will help consumers discover and select between Kmart vs. Nordstrom service-level agents.*
>
> – Dan Elsea, President, Real Estate One

Owner of a large franchise brokerage:

> *Agent rating sites—are coming. Ratings are a super good thing for the industry. Ratings keep agents accountable to deliver a higher level of service.*
>
> – Jack Fry, RE/MAX of Reading, PA

Regional Director, Keller Williams

Agent ratings have always mattered but now technology has enabled consumers to research agent's performance as it relates to the client's needs more accurately. Just as a consumer would search for information on a doctor or a lawyer so it is with agents. However our industry needs to guard against having a stated ratings system as a measure of an agent's worth. Putting such "hotel/restaurant" like rating on our professionals is not by itself a valid approach. It can be misleading and may degrade our profession.

– Marian Benton, Keller Williams

....

Owner of a 150 agent independent brokerage:

Agent ratings: lots of ways to game the system . We should disaggregate reviews vs. performance (# of closings), which is broker metrics-style, quantitative info.

– Staige Davis, CEO, Lang Mclaughry

....

President of a large MLS and REALTOR organization:

Consumers research virtually everything based on ratings—cameras, hotels, restaurants, etc. HAR surveyed 7,000 real estate consumers last year, and 90 percent found agent ratings to be helpful in their decision of which real estate professional to hire. Yelp, Redfin, ZipRealty, Coldwell Banker brokers, Better Homes & Gardens brokers, Trulia and Zillow (400,000+ agent ratings) all offer consumers some form of agent ratings. HAR offers agent ratings on a voluntary basis and currently 4,200 agents are being rated with 83,000 clients surveyed responding favorably about their experience with their agent.

– Bob Hale, President & CEO, Houston Association of REALTORS, Houston MLS

....

Owner of an 1,800 agent independent brokerage:

Will Gen Y use rating sites instead of repeat referral? No, credibility of personal referral is more important. People (consumers) may not trust the rating—and then there is the challenge of happy people not posting and unhappy people speaking loudly.

– Merle Whitehead, President, Realty USA, upper New York State

---

Owner of a 250+ agent independent brokerage:

I think the consumer is going to love it [ratings], and Realtor.com will not be able to do it because 50, 60, 70% of the agents don't want ratings because it favors the top producers. Therefore, they [NAR, associations, MLSs] won't be able to get it done and somebody from the outside will.

Less repeat and referral increases the value of lead generation. If you are a lead gen company OR a Realtor rating/agent match firm, your strategy is to break the bond of repeat and referral and insert yourself between Realtors and consumers.

Most people know 10 realtors—which one to pick? Look online for ratings—who sells the most homes in my neighborhood. Even if you are referred to three Realtors, what is the tie breaker? Ratings.

– Neal Hanks, President, Beverly Hanks Brokerage

Team that did $90+ million in volume in 2012:

Consumers do not use agent ratings more than referrals… yet. People who are 40 and over and have done a deal with them are a client for life. The younger prospects are much more at risk. They have not experi-enced the team's service yet. Younger consumers use Zillow, Redfin, Trulia a LOT more than older consumers.

– Emily Sachs Wong, Team, @properties, Chicago, IL

Team that did $100+ million in volume in 2012:

> *Yes, no question consumers will use ratings sites. They use Amazon reviews to buy everything. People use TripAdvisor, Yelp to pick a restaurant. The days of hiding behind "units sold" are going away. Your track record will be more transparent. I was surprised Realtor.com shut down agent ratings.*
>
> *Why hide? Your service is what it is. It has happened already on a small scale—we can manipulate everything to say "I am #1 Realtor"... Zillow should reflect that. I sold 50 and my nearest competitor sold 10, and I have 40 reviews, my reputation is "out there."*
>
> – Mark Spain, KW, Atlanta, GA

....

Individual agent with $250 million in volume:

> *It is going to change, and the change process has already started. Lots of people that reach out to me (buyers viewing my listings) don't know me. You don't pick a doctor or hairdresser from the Internet. You get personal referrals.*
>
> – Deborah Grubman, The Corcoran Group, New York, NY

....

Implications

As ratings become a meaningful tool for consumers in their selection process for agents, the following may occur:

1. There will be a shift of market share from the less productive and experienced to those who are the most productive and experienced.
2. This would make it harder for new agents to get a career started. This will put more pressure on both gross and net margins for brokerage firms due to lower gross margins from high producers.
3. These ratings trends may prompt an increase in the market share of agent teams. For many brokerage owners, teams do not generate high gross margins for the brokerage, especially relative to newer agents and mid-level producers.

4. An increased reliance on ratings would likely cause a decrease in membership and participant levels for Realtor associations and MLSs.
5. Training systems that are geared to personal networking and farming, while still paramount, will share attention and time with those who manage reviews and ratings successfully.
6. Much more attention would need to be focused on improving the productivity of new and existing agents to improve their ability to compete.
7. Some agents could take advantage of the trend by focusing on developing expertise in certain market segments—as opposed to being generalists—as they seek to be highly rated in those segments. This would lead to a shift in training, technology, and marketing spending among agents and brokerage firms.
8. Realtor associations and MLSs may have to display their own ratings systems to remain viable as a trusted source for consumers. This will change the relationship they have with their memberships; they'd also be under pressure to support a higher level of data integrity than now exists.

Solutions: Brokerages and Agents

In many markets, 20% of the agents do 80% of the transactions. As ratings become more important to consumers, lower-producing agents would be impacted the most. The outcome could be fewer agents and brokerage firms, with the survivors having far-higher market shares.

Training and an emphasis on productivity is clearly the best answer. Focusing agents to develop expertise in relevant and definable market segments is another. Gathering input and ratings back from customers and clients to post online will also help.

Insuring that ratings data are accurate is important. But: We don't consider accuracy critical. There is so much consumer interest in ratings that they will use whatever information is provided to them. The earlier versions of the listing portals included home valuation estimates and gained enormous viewership before the accuracy improved. Industry professionals criticized the accuracy of the automated valuation. Consumers didn't listen. Consumers loved having more information. Ratings will be the same way.

This information doesn't have to be (and likely can't be) perfect at all times but that should be a goal of every organization that wishes to publish ratings and reviews. This also applies to how these are organized and presented. For instance, how geographic areas, service specializations, variances of list to sell, time on market, and other performance data are being rated are all important to the end user as well as those being rated.

Solutions: Associations and MLSs

Reviews and ratings will become an important part of the residential real estate landscape. While associations are not the likely source of reviews and ratings, MLSs are. MLSs will remain the prominent source of ratings data; their ability to provide the widest possible range of searchable data about performance is unmatched by any other sources. Consumers will want to evaluate the performance data from many angles—and there is simply no other source that can provide that and keep it updated and current.

Chapter Four

The not-so-safe harbor

Probability: Low to Moderate
Impact: High

The industry has enjoyed the independent contractor arrangement for more than 40 years. This has been blessed by the IRS and embraced fully by all industry players. It creates low barriers of entry for those wanting to try real estate sales, low marginal costs for brokerage firms to employ new people, and a large supply of members to local, state, and national Realtor associations and MLSs. Few in the industry desire any of this to change.

Yet government regulation and litigation are now attacking the very heart of the independent contractor agreement. These current attacks are likely only the first wave. Growing numbers of agent teams hire their agents as employees. Many have seen significant production and profit improvements. The brokerage leaders we interviewed see new opportunities their firms would enjoy if agents' status as employees became more commonplace. In this chapter, we will explore the reasons why this trend could develop.

Where we stand today

Most real estate agents are independent contractors. This minimizes the cost of entry for agents and for participants in realty organizations (e.g., Realtor associations, MLSs, brokerage firms). The costs of adding an independent contractor are significantly lower and less complex than those related to employee agents. Everyone benefits—except the government agencies that miss out on payroll taxes.

Because the cost of adding an agent to a brokerage or a Realtor association is low, the industry is structured to add as many as possible:

- The MLS and Realtor associations get paid based on membership headcount.
- Low-production agents are typically on commission plans that are more favorable to the brokerage than those offered to high producers, which increases the average company dollar retained.

However, the system has led to some challenges:

- The industry has a very low per-person productivity.
- Low-production agents never get very proficient. They don't have the experience to be able to provide a high level of service and competence.

As a result, the overall reputation of real estate agents is low.

Changes could be underway. Currently, many agent teams have a mix of independent contractors and employees, whose duties are not as well defined as the IRS statute may require. With larger offices and more requirements for compliance and disclosure, it may be that in some cases brokerage firms cannot comply without crossing the line of the safe harbor provisions. This is not to say that this is happening, only that the likelihood is higher than it used to be.

Several industry leaders feel that having agents be employees instead of independent contractors would lead to a huge disruption in our business. But, after the initial turmoil, this shift would also offer positive elements. While a brokerage's costs would certainly go up, so would productivity on a per-person basis, as part-time agents depart the industry. And so would the level of customer service and professionalism. While the number of agents in the industry would likely drop substantially, this does not mean that agents couldn't still have their own businesses. Some think that this kind of transformation would dramatically improve the overall caliber of the agents that enter the business.

Forces moving in favor

The federal government, along with local and state governments, are hungry for additional revenue. At the federal level, social security and Medicare shortfalls are looming; income tax bites have been on the rise. At the state level, as many states have struggled to balance their budgets, several states that levy an income tax have sought to squeeze more revenue out of taxpayers; unemployment taxes and worker's compensation taxes have also been impacted. Finally, at the local level, unemployment and income taxes are a factor. Momentum is certainly building to place pressure on the safe haven of independent contractors:

1. Independent contractors have more latitude in how they report income than employees. They certainly get to deduct business expenses (real or imagined) to reduce their tax exposure.
2. Many states do not collect unemployment or worker's compensation taxation from independent contractor real estate agents.
3. It would be easier to regulate agents if they held employee status. Currently, real estate agents are licensed and governed by state laws. The residential real estate transaction is now significantly regulated at the federal level through the Real Estate Settlement Procedures Act (RESPA) and the Consumer Finance Protection Bureau (CFPB). There are other federal-level regulations that directly affect lending to housing, thus indirectly affecting realty services. As with the mortgage lending industry, it would not be unusual for regulators at the federal level to institute licensing requirements for residential real estate agents, especially where federal lending is involved.
4. There are numerous new-model brokerage firms that have entered the industry in the last 10 years that have attempted to employ real estate agents as employees rather than as independent contractors. Most of these attempts have not worked, as the intended benefits of greater control and accountability of the real estate agent did not offset the additional expense of full employee status. While in most of these cases the employment status of the agents didn't achieve the desired results, this does not mean that some evolved form of real estate brokerage would not achieve success.
5. There are several existing traditional brokerage firms and many teams that employ sales agents under an employee status. The duties and daily practices of these agents, while more structured, differ little from those of independent contractor agents in the same company or on the same team. As the lines between these employee agents and independent contractor agents blur, more employee-status agents will emerge.

Countering these forces

1. The Realtor organizations would fight any change to the current independent contractor status with every means at their disposal. So would most national real estate branded firms. Should agents become employees, with even low hourly compensation, the numbers of agents would fall dramatically. Some believe that the number of agents would fall 50-70 percent. Such a decline would decimate the Realtor organization and create a significant challenge to every large national real estate firm in terms of franchise numbers and franchise earnings. We would expect that each of these firms would leverage its political strength to stop any such effort.
2. The cost of converting a brokerage firm from independent contractor agents to employee agents would overwhelm the traditional residential realty industry in the near term. While small realty firms—those fielding fewer than five sales agents—may be able to shift to an employee model, those with more than 20 agents would see a significant diminution of their financial viability. Were realty firms required to compensate agents on an hourly basis, they would hire far fewer than they do under the independent contractor arrangement that exists today. The need for office space would diminish. Virtually every existing brokerage in the country would oppose change. Collectively, these firms have enormous influence in the political arena. This opposition to change is likely true for most of the productive sales agents in the industry as well, as their freedoms under the current arrangement (e.g., tax management) are significant.
3. Numerous industries employ independent contractors both in sales and in other facets of private enterprise. The federal government would face an enormous challenge in re-regulating all of these businesses—or discriminating towards one over the other—in applying any new treatment of independent contractors. This would be ruinously expensive for every business, not just real estate brokerage, to convert from independent contractor to employee status. The small-business lobby and other interested parties alone would be likely to stop any such action in its tracks.

For these reasons, we believe that it is not likely that real estate agents will be required to be treated as employees—and lose their status as contractors. However, if this did occur, it would result in a significant disruption of the current ways in which we conduct business in this industry. As you plan for your business, you might want to consider what opportunities and challenges this kind of change would present for you.

Comments

In my market, we'd go from 700 to 150 agents … $5MM producers and up would make the cut. Many of the lower producers would be forced out.

– Anonymous

President of a large independent brokerage:

Independent contractors are a double-edged sword for us. All industry systems hang on it. This doesn't mean that it has to be that way. Would we be better off without it? It encourages a lack of productivity. As an industry, we can hire tons of people, and the commissions get spread over too big of a group. You don't know how many will make it—so you hire too many. If your bottom quartile does 1-2 deals, sometimes it still makes sense economically. You would need less office space, less overhead, less admin support. However, it would really change the MLSs and Associations—membership would drop a lot in a hurry. Competition for good agents would really pick up.

Owner of a large franchise brokerage:

That would be a huge shift. Accept it—it would thin our ranks. For the most productive brokerages, it might cut headcount in half. You'd have to be serious and productive and performing to stay.

The brokerage would be more liable for what Realtors do and say more so than today. For example, fair housing, steering, sexual harassment. There is a very comfortable cap now with the independent contractor status. I'm on the hook for anything from a brokerage standpoint and fair housing, steering, but those people could go out and sexually harass somebody and as the broker of record I'm not on the hook, they're an independent contractor. But, if they're an employee, I'm going to be on the hook for that type of action.

Also we'd have to provide health insurance. We would adapt. There would be lots less people in the business. 50-70% decline in members to NAR, CAR, local associations.

Owner of a large independent brokerage:

> *Might have to be a LOT more selective in hiring. "I can't make it to training" would certainly be less common.*
>
> – Staige Davis, CEO, Lang Mclaughry Real Estate (150 agents)

Senior executive of a franchise:

> *If that were to happen and work its way through the states very quickly, it would restructure the entire industry within a period of months, not years. However, the best operators would leverage the opportunity created by change, adapt to the new landscape where others couldn't, and eventually prosper with an evolved model.*
>
> – Budge Huskey, President & CEO, Coldwell Banker Real Estate LLC, Madison, NJ

CEO of a large association:

> *We would probably lose two-thirds of our members, but it would be a far higher quality of member and most likely far more involved in what we are doing. We may lose members but to those who remained we would likely be far more valuable.*

Implications

As we discussed above, a change from agents' current ability to define themselves as independent contractors under tax law would doubtless result in far fewer people employed as real estate agents. Some estimates are as high as 70 percent of all current independent contractor agents exiting the industry. And there would be far fewer brokerage firms willing and able to employ them. The costs of employing agents would go up considerably, especially in adhering to minimum wage requirements, along with health care and other costs. At the very least, these costs would require brokerage firms to quickly remove unproductive sales agents from their payrolls.

Some leaders of realty firms believe, however, that while the transition to employee-status sales agents would be very difficult, it would ultimately have a positive impact on the overall management of the business. Although there would, in all likelihood, be far fewer agents, those remaining would tend to offer a far-higher level of professionalism. The average agent production would certainly skyrocket after all of the low/no producers were eliminated.

These same leaders believe that under this scenario, they could deliver more consistent and higher-quality service to housing consumers. While realty firms would be smaller and fewer in number, they likely would be more profitable due to higher per-person productivity. Smaller firms, even one-person realty companies, could still thrive, given that they would still have access to the information and tools needed to compete.

Different brokerage models would be impacted in different ways. Those brokerages carrying the highest number of agents with the lowest per-person productivity would suffer the most; those with fewer agents but with higher per-agent productivity would suffer the least. The industry would consolidate significantly. The capital required to compete would be far higher and the ability to grow from small to large would be prohibitive. With fewer agents and brokerage firms, the largest firms would be likely to adapt over time. Smaller firms would not have to face much change. The team model has already established how this might be accomplished. Those realty firms in the middle tier would probably face the most difficult burden.

The main drivers of consolidation would be the decline in the number of sales agents, which would result in the need for fewer offices and fewer companies. The cost of employment would go up substantially; along with federal and state minimum wage, health care and other requirements, medium-sized and larger firms would face enormously higher costs than they do now. The best example of this is the millions of dollars in costs that were saved by ZipRealty when it converted from an employee model to independent contractor status several years ago.

Employee status requires at least minimum-wage compensation. In that environment, brokerage firms would employ far fewer people in their sales ranks.

Realtor associations and MLSs would have far fewer members. There could be significant consolidation among these organizations, leaving fewer-but-larger MLSs and local associations. Most of the consolidation would take place within local Realtor associations, but there could come a point when several state associations merged as well. For example, this could also take the form of office/administrative and financial systems being handled at the state level, with governance and mediation remaining at the local level.

Some leaders of these groups believe, however, that while they would have fewer members, those remaining members would be required to pay more for access to the services that these organizations provide.

The environment conducive to the formation of agent teams would certainly be enhanced. There are already many teams that have licensed individuals in both selling and non-selling activities as employees. New small brokerage firms could be formed that resemble today's teams.

Solutions: Brokerages

Were the federal government to compel a change in the status of real estate agents from an independent contractor to an employee status, realty firms, realtor associations, and MLSs would each need to reassess how they are structured, how they would finance their businesses, and what changes they would make in which agents they would retain as employees. While there would be fewer agents, as well as fewer medium-to-large brokerage firms, far more small realty firms with less than five agents could arise. Many of these would be formed under a model similar to those of today's teams.

Realty firms would be compelled to be much more selective of the agents they take on, as the cost and investment would be much higher. Office space requirements would shrink substantially. New training and coaching systems could be built with the goal of providing the new employee-agent with a disciplined process by which they could build their income. In return for hiring and investing in new agents, the realty firm could expect far higher levels of production from the employee-agent in return for the compensation they received.

Realty firms would, in turn, build integrated platforms that incorporated market and customer data that would be required inputs from the employee-agent.

Solutions: Agents

If you are a production agent today, this change would be the best thing that ever happened to you. It would force most of the non- and low producers out of the market. You would capture much more market share.

Solutions: MLSs and Associations

Due to membership loss, these organizations would face a significant challenge. They would likely reap some minor cost savings in the form of reduced support teams and training schedules. However, those savings would not be enough to offset the dramatic decline in revenue. These organizations would need to cut costs (if they had anything left to cut after that last recession!) and raise rates.

This type of dramatic industry transformation would drive enormous consolidation at all levels of the association and MLS environment. The solution would be for associations and MLSs to pursue mergers with other groups that made geographic sense—and to build a new understanding of what each level provided to the market. Local-level associations would offer services different from the state level; both would provide different levels than those offered at the national level. Such a change would save enormous amounts of money and allow greater specialization among the three levels. It would also rationalize the unwieldy current situation: About 54 percent of U.S. associations have fewer than 500 members.

MLS organizations would have to consolidate along some kind of rational regional or other localized geographic basis. It is likely that this kind of shift would support lower costs along with higher levels of technological innovation, as costs could be spread over a larger number of users.

Chapter Five

The homeownership rate declines

Probability: High
Impact: Low

Over the past 30 years, roughly two-thirds of Americans have owned their own homes. The desire to do so is virtually ingrained in young and old alike. Government regulations, tax policies, and financial markets have created highly favorable conditions for homeownership. In fact, the drive to enable more families to become homeowners was the single biggest contributor to the housing downturn of 2005-2011. Too many were chasing homeownership without the means to support their dream.

Since 2004, the homeownership rate has declined by five percent. This adds up to six million more individuals and families who rent versus own. First-time homebuyers historically make up about 35 percent of the market. They are notably absent from the current housing recovery. Although their desire to become owners remains strong, they are inhibited by substantial student loan debt and a weak job market. Stricter mortgage underwriting standards have had a chilling effect. Each of these factors may well drive homeownership to new, and perhaps permanently, lower levels. What opportunities and threats do these pose for the industry?

Exhibit 5-1: Historical trends home ownership rate

Source: Census Bureau

Many factors are contributing to the current drop in homeownership rates

As you can see from Exhibit 5-1, the homeownership rate peaked in 2004 at 69 percent, and declined to nearly 64.7 percent at the end of 2013. It is likely to continue to fall in the coming years due to a combination of factors.

Over the past 30 years, the homeownership rate averaged approximately 65.8 percent, with a high of 69.0 percent in 2004 and a low of 63.8 percent as recently as 1988. The run up to 69 percent took place in the early 2000s as greatly liberalized mortgage under-writing standards, record-low interest rates, and soaring home prices all combined to drive housing sales to an all-time high. With the housing crash of 2006-2010 and the resultant rise in foreclosure activity, the homeownership rate fell back to below its 30-year average.

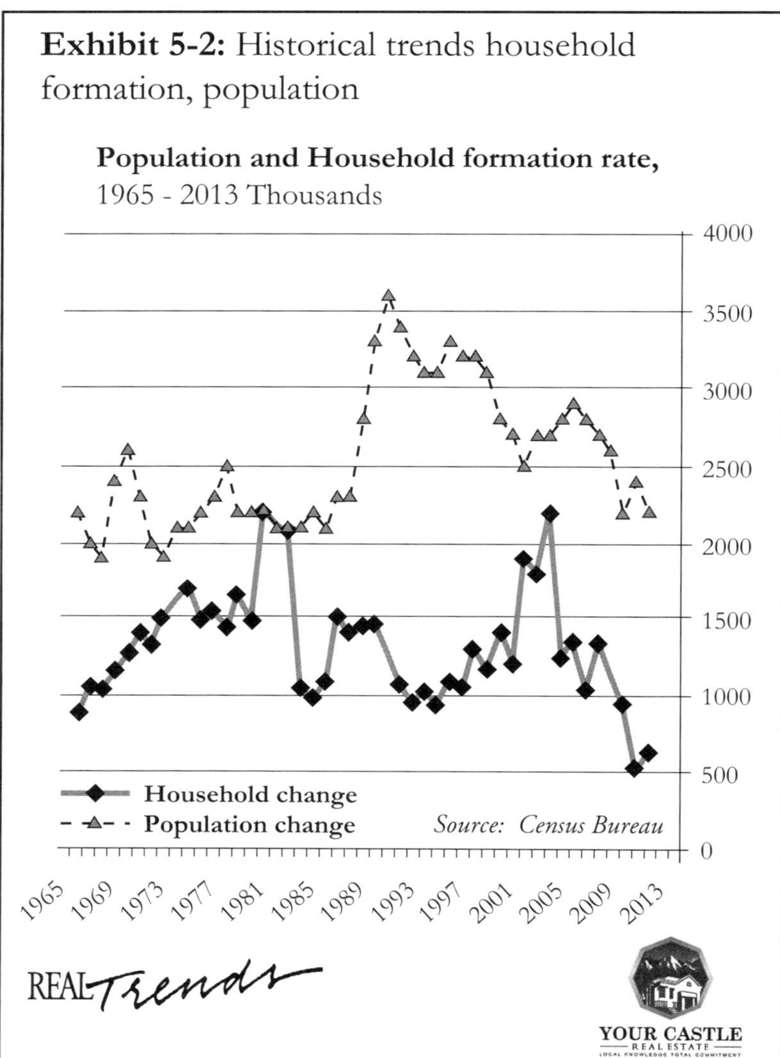

The effects of the housing downturn are still being felt three years after the beginning of the housing recovery in 2011. Nearly 12 percent of all homeowners have negative equity in their homes, and the number of mortgages still in some form of distress comprises nearly seven percent of all mortgage holders.

While most major surveys indicate a continued preference for homeownership, the factors that created an almost-25-year boom in housing sales are not nearly as robust as they once were. Several of the forces that are contributing to the current decline are listed below.

The homeownership rate could continue to fall for these and other reasons such as demographics, financial stress, and the desire for mobility. One other large issue is the mismatch between the demand from Generation X and Millennials, and the supply of housing left behind by the Boomer and Traditional generations. One example. Younger families tend to desire housing near urban cores while their predecessors prefer suburban detached homes.

Forces driving continued declines in the homeownership rate

1. The tightening of underwriting standards for mortgage finance.
2. The flattening of employment and income growth in the U.S.—especially among the Millennial generation. These potential homebuyers make up nearly one-quarter of the population of the U.S. and most of the first-time homebuyer segment.
3. The Millennial generation's indebtedness, with college debt alone surpassing $1 trillion. This impacts this generation's ability to meet underwriting standards.
4. The uncertainty of housing market appreciation and the transactional costs associated with a relocation to secure employment.
5. The imbalance between demand and supply for both Generation X and Millennials. There are too few affordable homes with access to the amenities sought by these two age cohorts—and too many unaffordable suburban homes that are distant from the amenities they seek.
6. The likelihood that tax benefits associated with homeownership will become less favorable (e.g., the mortgage interest deduction and exempting capital gains taxes for personal housing).

Countering these forces (in favor of a stabilized homeownership rate)

1. The strong desire for homeownership, as evidenced by numerous consumer sentiment surveys.
2. The ability of the Traditional and Boomer generations to finance the purchase of real property for their children and grandchildren. Various estimates place the wealth held by these two generations in excess of $10 trillion. Some part of this wealth is being used to assist young family members in the purchase of a home.
3. Continued pressure at the federal level to support homeownership, especially for low-income families. The government's policy tools continue to control the majority of the nation's housing finance mechanisms.

Despite the three counterbalancing forces cited above, we believe it is likely that homeownership rates will continue to fall. As you plan for your business, you might want to consider a scenario where this rate approaches 55 percent by the year 2025. What opportunities and challenges would that present for you?

Comments from the industry

Owner of a large RE/MAX with $3.6+ billion in closed sales volume in 2013:

If homeownership rates declined to 55% by 2025, the biggest challenge may be our message. How can our industry continue to sell the dream of homeownership and wealth creation to a generation that may not care?

Fortunately, studies have shown that Millennials do want to own their home, but clearly face headwinds preventing them from buying and selling as soon and as often as generations before them (i.e., student loan debt). The sheer size of Generation Y will hopefully prevent this percentage decline from actually occurring. Fewer Millennials may be able to purchase a home, but because their numbers are so great, the impact may not be all that threatening.

The opportunity, if homeownership rates decline significantly in the next decade, will be in working with investors, overseas buyers, and institutions that will own a larger majority of homes in the U.S.

– Chad Ochsner, President, RE/MAX Alliance, Denver, CO

President of a 1,000+ agent brokerage:

While surveys show Gen Y is very interested in purchasing homes, will they be able to, or will there be delays? This generation is experiencing challenges in current under-employment and historically high (student) debt. And lending is more difficult than it has been historically.

– Phyllis Brookshire, President, Allen Tate Real Estate

Large 250-agent independent brokerage owner:

The perception of volatility—my Millennial sales manager thinks this is a problem. When I buy—am I at the top of another bubble? Should I buy now? Millennials worry about this.

– Nancy Fennell, President, Dickson Realty

CEO of a Realtor association:

There is a threat of over-regulation. If it's harder for a consumer to buy a home, will the homeownership rate decrease? Further, will there be a "black market" for buyers who don't meet the higher regulations—that creates another layer of the market that is unregulated? Sounds possible to me.

– Janice McCrary, CEO, Greater Albuquerque Association of REALTORS

Owner of a large 190-agent independent brokerage:

Every home has an owner. A decline in the homeownership rate just means more investor owners. Investors sell homes more often than owner occupants. Change means the buyers of homes change (owner occupants vs. investors) so agents need different skill sets. It's mainly a training issue.

– David Stark, President, Stark Company Realtors

Large franchised brokerage leader with 4,000+ agents:

During the economic boom, housing was a key "way to grow one's wealth." But since the downturn, that has changed. Nonetheless, the pursuit of homeownership is still the cornerstone of the American dream, as it demonstrates a source of security, a place to raise your kids, and roots in a community.

– Joan Docktor, President, Berkshire Hathaway HomeServices Fox & Roach, Realtors/The Trident Group, Philadelphia, PA

Results from our Broker/Agent Survey

We conducted a survey of more than 6,000 high-production agents and teams (50 or more deals a year). We also surveyed the owners of the largest 1,350 brokerages in the U.S. We asked, "Will homeownership rates change in the next 10 years?" Exhibit 5-3 maps out the results.

Exhibit 5-3: Agents and Owners: How will homeownership rates change over the next 10 years?

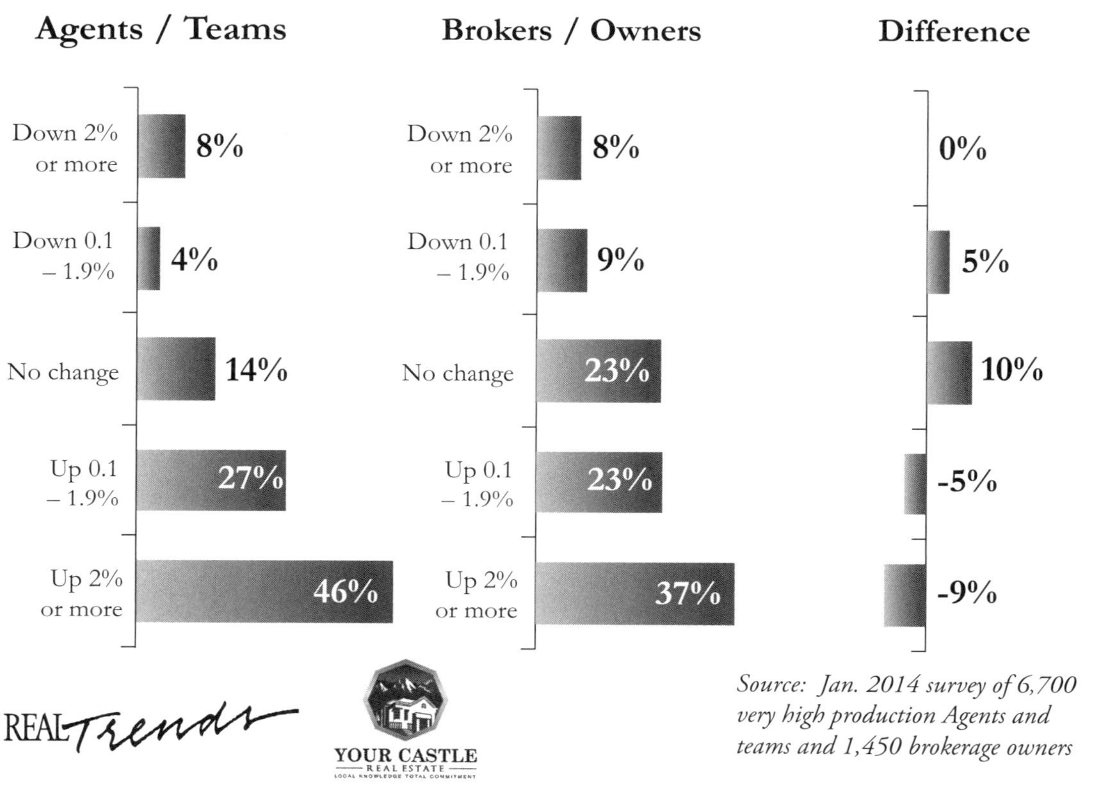

Source: Jan. 2014 survey of 6,700 very high production Agents and teams and 1,450 brokerage owners

In summary, these patterns emerged:

- Broker/owners are more likely to believe the homeownership rate will be stable or continue to decline (17 vs. 12 percent).
- The majority of Realtors surveyed expect the ownership rate to go back up (73 vs. 60 percent for broker/owners).
- In our phone interviews with broker/owners, we were given no clear consensus on where the market was likely to go next.

Implications

The population of the U.S. continues to grow. According to the Joint Center for Housing Studies of Harvard University, approximately 1.1 to 1.3 million net new households will be created each year through 2025. These families and individuals will need a place to live. Whether they are in a position to purchase a home or will choose to rent, they will seek housing.

Countering this growth in households, many agents and brokerage owners have stories that suggest Millennials are not as interested in homeownership as prior generations were.

Here's a perspective that stood out to us:

Owner of a brokerage with 1,150 closed transaction sides in 2012:

> *My biggest concern is the change in attitude toward homeownership and the endless barrage of media towards this next generation about the importance of homeownership. It might override their parents' generation's strong interest or encouragement of homeownership. In my opinion, it is no longer important to much of this younger generation that they own a house. We need to do a better job in re-educating this next generation that it's worth the risk of purchase.*
>
> *The importance of building a nest for you and your family—that is equally important to the baby boomers' making a ton of money off their house. I think it will have modest appreciation, keeping up with construction costs, and costs of living, but I don't think the huge surge will be there. But I'm more concerned with teaching this next generation about the importance and habit of investing for your future and building a nest for your family, whatever that nest is.*
>
> *I worry that this homeownership rate will dip, but it's more than that—I'm worried about a longer-term trend. I'm concerned that over the long term it goes to 50% … It doesn't scare me for our industry, it may scare me personally, but it doesn't scare me for the industry because 100% of the folks need shelter.*
>
> – Frank Norton, Jr., CEO, The Norton Agency, Gainesville, GA (metro Atlanta)

Investors have proven to be up to the task of purchasing and managing single- and multi-family rental properties. Large, well-capitalized investors (such as hedge funds) have entered many markets recently. Even with this new institutional entrant, the majority of rental homes, condos, and small apartment buildings are bought and sold by private individuals.

These investors tend to buy and sell more frequently than traditional homeowners. They tend to use the services of professionals to do much of the buying, selling, and managing of their investments. While they tend to not pay retail (e.g., full commission) for such services at all times, they are comfortable using financial metrics to determine their use of such services. Where a real estate agent can assist in effecting a quicker sale at an acceptable price, investors will tend to continue to use these services.

The implications for real estate agents, brokerage firms, and others are that training, marketing, and service systems will need to be retooled to capture market share in this segment. Under most scenarios, we expect investors to represent a larger share of transactions in the future. The question is: *How much of a shift?* One brokerage owner said, "We'd have to re-train our staff's mentality. We're in the housing business and we need to be equally focused—on selling rental houses as well as residential homes."

Regardless of whether homes are purchased as rentals or for homeownership, the total aggregate of commissions in the industry will not be affected significantly. The big impact of this trend is: *Which agents and which brokerages will receive the benefits of this shift in market share?* That will depend mostly on their ability to understand and serve the requirements of this market segment.

A large U.S. brokerage recently did a study of their 2013 transactions. They found that owner occupants and investors had exactly the same average commission percentage.

As you would expect, the average investor deal was about 20% smaller than the average owner occupant deal.

Another perspective worth sharing:

Owner of a 2,000+ agent independent brokerage with 2012 closed volume of $2.6 billion:

> *If homeownership drops to 50%, the impact will be a dramatic clearing-out of a significant chunk of the industry. It will probably be like it was with the recession. It will not just be the bottom-quartile talent that will go away. In the past few years, we lost as many third-quartile agents as we did bottom-quartile agents. If you're making $80,000 a year and your lifestyle spend is $70,000 and if you lose 20% of your business, you're going to leave the business. As we've seen in the recession, it will just drive more business to the top.*
>
> *I think homeownership probably will shift down; but I don't know if it will hit 50%. Either way, I think the investor component to our world will be permanently higher than it ever traditionally has been. I think it will be with us for a long time.*
>
> *Business will shift, property management will start to become more significant, and the sophistication to handle investor needs will become critical. You can't just be a facilitator and "take the order." Successful agents will be a counselor for investors. It will be interesting to see how that continuum works on the investors. The good news for the real estate industry is, somebody will still own property. The investor segment in our Michigan markets has probably tripled since 2005.*
>
> – Dan Elsea, President, Real Estate One, Detroit, MI

Skill sets for successfully working with investor owners

As we saw in an earlier chapter, agents can grow their skills to provide high-value services—becoming counselors instead of "show property, then take the order" facilitators. Counselors capture more share and higher commissions. Investors tend to be more sophisticated and have much more real estate experience than owner-occupants.

Subject knowledge: Rentals

- Be familiar with the common financial metrics investors use to measure returns (year one cash-on-cash, simple ROI, cap rate, average five-year after-tax IRR, etc.).

Be adroit enough to adapt scripts on the fly to mirror the investor's "preferred language."

- Be able to conduct high-level cash-flow analyses for different types of rental and lease-back scenarios.
- Have access to and knowledge of the key assumptions that drive investment-planning results in your unique market. This would include but not be limited to:
  - Typical rents and how they vary by property type and location
  - Typical vacancy rates and how they vary
  - How different asset classes in your market are impacted by economic cycles. For example, an investment that provides a great return today but has been historically highly volatile might not be the best choice.
- Know the interest rates, amortization periods, and interest-rate lock horizons that are probable for a given asset class. The client won't expect the agent to be a CPA, but the agent should have a general grasp on the trade-offs:
  - For example, should I buy rental houses where I can lock rates for 30 years—or an apartment building with an interest rate that floats after five years?
  - What impact does the interest rate have on a property's valuation?
  - How would that fit with the client's overall portfolio?
- How do cap rates (rates of return) vary by neighborhood and asset class in the counselor's area of specialty?
- What are the historical rates of appreciation in different buy-and-hold areas? Given current supply-and-demand characteristics in different submarkets, where are the best opportunities for appreciation?

Subject knowledge: Fix and flips

- What neighborhoods have the best gross margins?
- Do some F&F areas tend to have higher ROI and/or require greater marketing time than others?
- You should have a network of sources and/or marketing channels to find properties that are not in the MLS.
- You should be able to conduct at least a rudimentary cash-flow projection to screen projects.

Client education and support skills

- For less-sophisticated investors with an incomplete mastery of investment economics, you should be able to educate them and show them the trade-offs between their alternatives.
- You should be able to rapidly identify other stakeholders and influencers in the planning and decision process. As well, you should have the ability to "bring the buyer/investor along" in the process, so you can efficiently move towards a consensus to act.
- You should know and be able to clearly articulate why investment real estate is, for many investors, a superior alternative to stocks and bonds.

Transaction Skills

You should:

- Understand the fundamentals of 1031 tax-deferred exchanges.
- Understand how a purchase contract and disclosures differ between owner-occupant homes and investor properties. And be able to include proper due diligence action steps in the additional provisions.
- Possess excellent negotiation skills.

In addition, you should have a trusted network of referral partners, and be able to skillfully orchestrate their activities during the due diligence period. These partners should include:

- Title companies that can handle the unique needs of investors, such as hold-open policies for fix-and-flip investors
- 1031 exchange facilitators
- Commercial mortgage brokers
- Residential mortgage brokers who can work with non-warrantable properties (e.g., condos whose HOA do not meet FHA guidelines)
- Property managers for different types of asset classes (e.g., apartment buildings vs. rental homes)
- Sophisticated property inspectors who can handle commercial as well as residential properties
- Contractors who can help with renovation work

- Attorneys who can handle unique zoning issues for investment properties in your market
- Accountants who specialize in the tax handling and optimization of investment real estate
- Financial planners who can integrate an investor's long-term financial goals with stocks, bonds, AND real estate.

As you review the list, you might think that only very high-net-worth individuals would be concerned about these topics. To our surprise when we did our research, we found a large brokerage with a significant investment real estate practice that focused mainly on investors with just a few properties. This brokerage provides most of the support features listed above to its agents, along with training and support. These agents have captured a lot of market share with small-time investors in a limited number of properties.

When these small investors have to choose between their brother-in-law who only does owner-occupant work, and the counselor with the tools above, experience trumps relationships almost every time.

Solutions: MLSs and associations

Please see Chapter One, Facilitator vs. Counselor, for a set of ideas that applies to this.

Solutions: Brokerage firms and agents

For brokerage firms and agents, it is a matter of deciding whether to specifically address and capture a part of this market. The requirements for success are well known and not overly complicated. However, the majority of agents specialize in serving owner-occupants, and are not comfortable—let alone competent—to assist investors. Specialized training, marketing, and service systems will need to be developed and deployed to successfully service this segment of the housing sale and purchase market.

For brokerage firms, there is an additional opportunity—to enter the market for property management. State regulations (if any) that govern this vary dramatically from one state to the next. In Colorado, for example, property management is scrutinized by regulators and is the leading source of consumer complaints to the commission. Brokerages are required to document essentially every interaction with a tenant. In this environment, property management might not be a desirable (or profitable) line-of-business addition. In Georgia, on the other hand, regulators are currently not providing oversight. As a result, there is less risk to the brokerage and more potential for profitable expansion.

During our interviews, many brokerage owners expressed interest in expanding into property management—if only to make sure they retain that client when the time comes to finally sell the property. For brokerage owners that are either in states where the regulatory requirement is not conducive, or that conclude that it is not a core competency, there is another option. One brokerage has partnered with a property management company that solely manages, and does not buy or sell. They have become referral partners for each other.

Here are two more perspectives on the investor owner market from market leaders:

Large franchised brokerage leader with 4,000+ agents and 2012 closed sales volume of $7.9 billion:

> *The Philadelphia market has never had the ups and downs in pricing that some markets have experienced. Therefore, we have not attracted as many investors. We do, however, have some who purchase and hold properties for rent. Their portfolios have grown over the years and we are now seeing an increase in property management businesses.*
>
> – Joan Docktor, President, Berkshire Hathaway HomeServices Fox & Roach, Realtors/The Trident Group, Philadelphia, PA

Western U.S. Brokerage, $500-900 million volume:

> *Have your closing department start flagging commission disbursements to track if these are investor or owner-occupant transactions. Start figuring out which agents in the market are working with investors. Talk to those agents. Ask, "Would it make sense to have mastermind sessions with those investors to share best practices?" Run a few sessions and summarize the results. Now you've got a white paper you can share*

*as a marketing piece to attract more investors and you've got the research to back it up. You can recruit investor-focused agents (or agents that WANT to focus but need the tools) from other firms, too.**

Possible action steps for owners and agents

- Set up training so your agents can be counselors, not just facilitators.
- Offer this training to investor-focused agents outside your firm as a recruiting opportunity.
- Sponsor (or organize) investor groups in your market. Become known as the firm with expertise.
- National REA is a trade association for small investors based in Cincinnati, Ohio. Members must own at least four rental units; these are generally small mom-and-pop properties. Why not sponsor your local group?
- IMNREO is an annual rental conference. IMN (Information Management Network) is a national organization. Major hedge funds such as Blackstone and Colony often attend. Attending the conference could provide an opportunity for you to network and become a resource to the institutions in your market.

Chapter Six

Competition drives commission rates and gross margins down to new lows

Based on national averages, the mythical six percent commission has been just that—a myth—for nearly 20 years. With the exception of a moderate rise during the downturn, the average commission has fallen every year since 1991. Given industry economics, consumer pressures, and intense competition for listings, commissions will continue to decline. We discuss how this will influence the industry in the first part of this chapter.

In the second half of this chapter, we examine firms' gross margins. Real estate agents have benefitted enormously from:

- The explosion in brokerage firms that offer more favorable commission sharing with their agents.
- The availability of technology and marketing tools from a wider variety of sources.
- The trend towards teams.

Each trend has reduced brokerage gross margins. This has forced significant changes, both on these firms and in the economics of the brokerage business in general. How can brokerage firms adapt and thrive in this environment?

Declines in the commission rate

Probability: High
Impact: Moderate to high

From 1991 to 2005, the average commission rate charged to housing consumers fell from a national average of 6.1 to 5.0 percent (see Exhibit 6-1). With the downturn in housing sales in late 2005, the average commission rose again to 5.4 percent. However, once housing sales turned up in the 3rd quarter of 2011, the average commission rate began to fall again; as of the end of 2013 it's projected to be less than 5.3 percent. There are high-priced markets where the average rate is already under 5.0 percent—and declining—as well.

The current low levels of inventory, combined with rising numbers of sales agents, indicate that commission levels will continue their downward trend for at least the next few years. Right now, average U.S. inventory levels are at less than four months. Many markets are measurably below that level. At the same time, the number of Realtors has risen nearly 90,000 since the recovery began in 2011, according to NAR membership numbers; many association leaders are indicating that U.S. growth in the next year will be in the 30,000 – 40,000 level.

Exhibit 6-1: Average commission rate in the U.S.

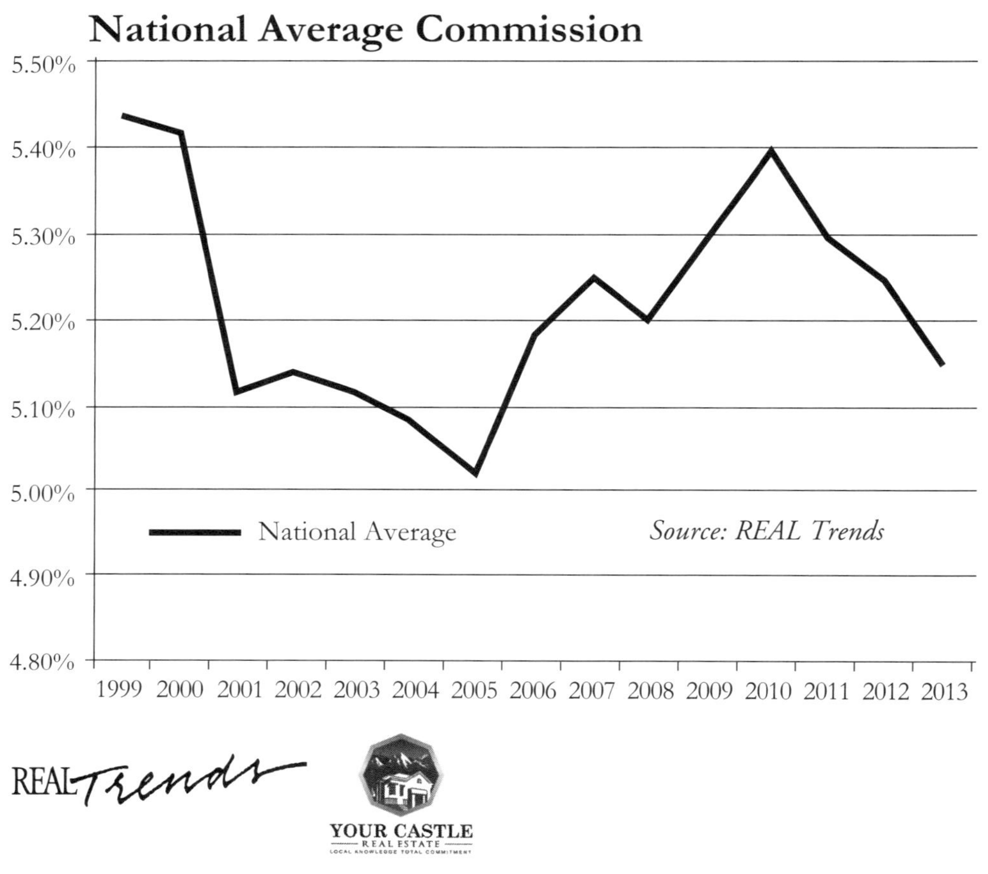

The lack of substantial growth in single-family home construction compounds the inventory problem (Exhibit 6-2). Despite strongly favorable conditions for home building, single-family permits and starts remain well below their previous highs—and below long-term averages. In the short term, this means that housing inventory levels will remain below the historical averages and keep pressure on commission levels for the foreseeable future.

Millennial clients have different needs. Since they do more of the work in finding and assessing housing choices, they also believe that the value of the real estate agent is diminished to some extent. This may play out with home buyers going direct to the listing agents of listed homes—and requesting a portion of the commission—due to the lack of a cooperative payment to another agent.

Exhibit 6-2: Number of new home construction starts, by year (in thousands)

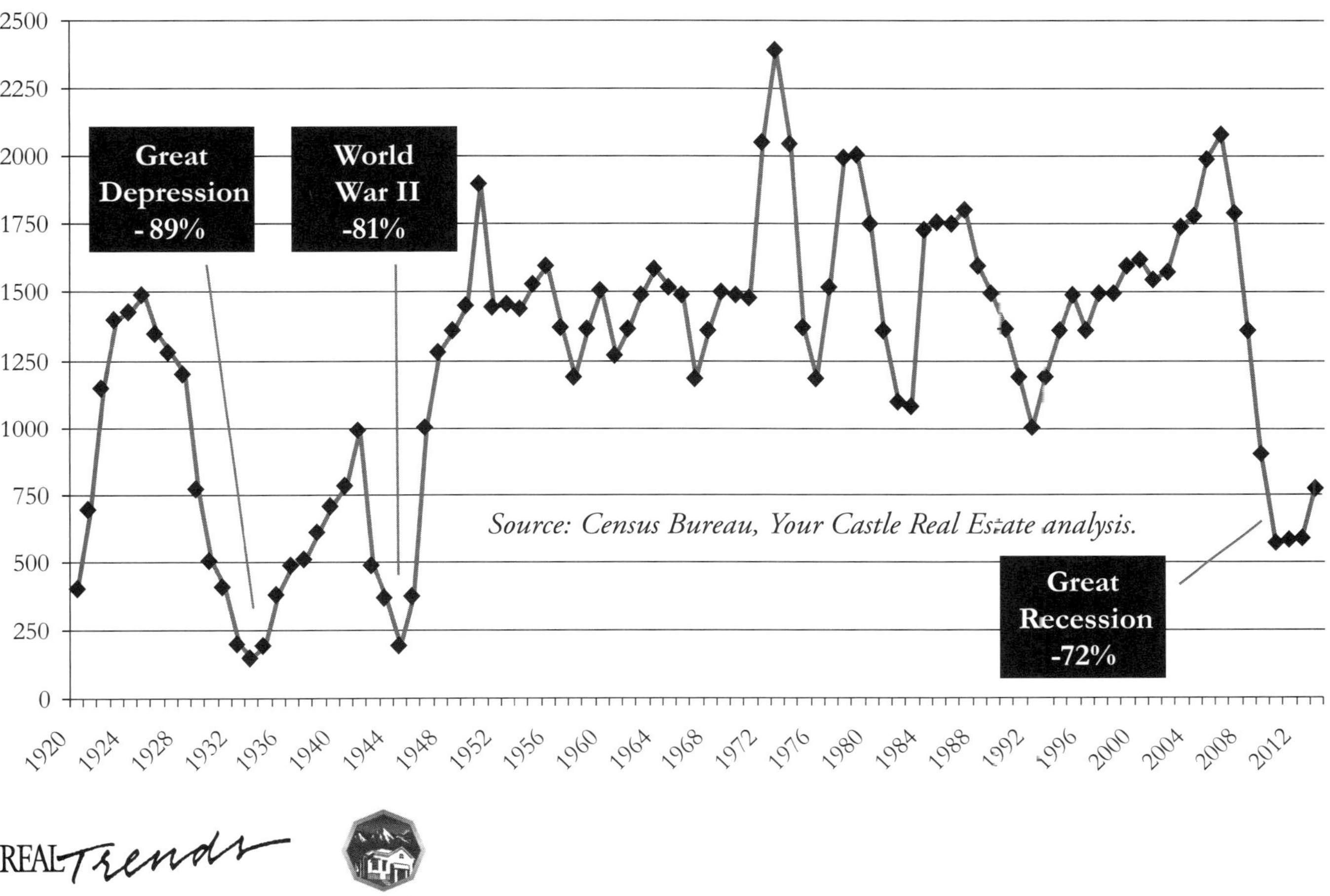

The two main drivers of the changes in Exhibit 6-3:

- The relative inventory of homes for sale, versus
- The number of real estate agents active in the market.

The lower the number of homes for sale in a given market compared to real estate agents, the lower the commission level. Also, most high-priced markets have lower commission levels. Thus, as inventory stays level and the number of agents rises, the average commission rate will trend downward.

Exhibit 6-3: Impact of Members and Inventory on Commission Rates

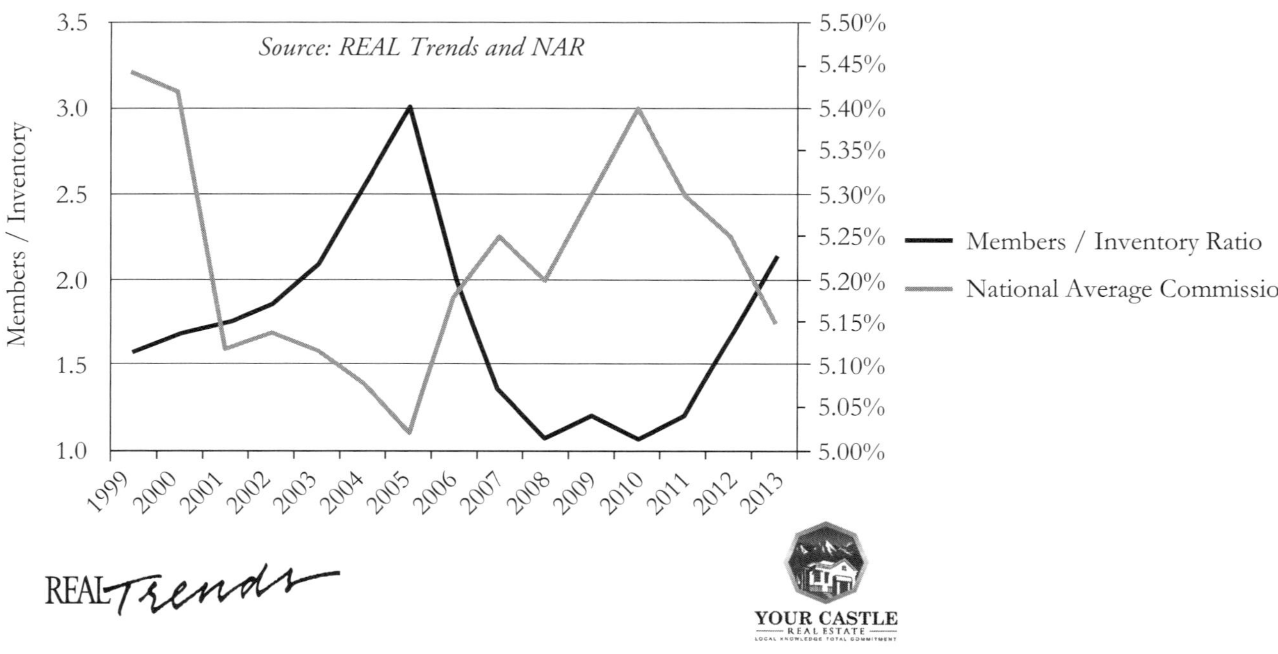

As you can see from above (Exhibit 6-3), when the number of agents relative to the number of listings climbs the national average commission rate declines. There is a strong correlation.

Other factors that affect the average commission rate are:

- The increased consolidation of transactions among fewer sales agents
- The percentage of sales agents associated with brokerage firms that do not have a financial incentive to influence these agents what their charges to consumers should be

Another factor: More brokerage firms have no financial incentive to police commission rates. In 2013, the total percentage of agents working with brokerages that lack the incentive to enforce a commission level probably exceeded over half of all agents working in the industry.

Forces moving in favor

1. As the number of sales agents grows faster than inventory, there will be downward pressure on commissions.
2. The number of sales agents working in brokerage firms where the firm charges a flat or capped fee has increased. More than half of the agents in the U.S. now work for firms where there is little brokerage incentive to enforce discipline over commissions. Sales agents tend to want to offer special pricing to repeat customers, on double-sided transactions, and for their friends and family. For many agents, this can add up to more than half of their total business.
3. Consumers are more aware that commissions are negotiable than they were in the past. There are numerous firms that offer either discounts or rebates to consumers. Some of these firms are local limited service businesses. Some market through the web. Information about consumers' ability to save money on their commission through entities like these is abundant.
4. More than prior generations, Millennials have been raised with the tools to comparison shop. A higher percentage of these younger buyers and sellers will use that knowledge to lower their costs.

Countering these forces

1. Consumers still show a strong preference to use full-service real estate agents to buy and sell housing. And they still prefer to work with an agent whom they

know or to whom they've been referred. The infrequency and complexity of the housing transaction tends to drive consumers to use real estate agents. When working with someone familiar to them, consumers, especially Boomer and Traditional generations, tend not to negotiate commissions.

2. While a shrinking percentage of brokerage firms have agent commission plans where the firm has a financial incentive to maintain discipline in their overall commission schedule, there remains a significant segment of brokerages that employ agents through a fee structure where both the firm and the agent are incented to maintain commission levels. As pressure mounts on brokerage gross margins, so too will brokerage pressure on their sales agents to maintain the gross commission level. Many traditional firms (and some that are flat-fee) strongly encourage their agents to maintain their commission rates for the financial benefit of both parties.

Comments from the industry

Senior executive of a large independent brokerage with 1,000+ agents:

The industry has always struggled with a "lowest common denominator" mentality. The barriers to entry for getting a real estate license have always been very low. If you are a solid entrepreneur —you can make a great living. Everything (e.g., CRM, marketing tools) is available to all agents, whether you sell 0 or 100 homes per year. From a consumer point of view, "all Realtors look the same." It's a small leap, then, for the consumer to think, "If all Realtors are the same, then I can pick the $500 agent vs. the full-commission agent and save myself some money."

– Phyllis Brookshire, President, Allen Tate Realtors

President of a large independent brokerage with 1,800 agents:

High-production agents can afford to invest more in tools, marketing and services than mid-to-low-production agents. 50% of our customers are personal referrals and because of more transactions, they have more referrals. This creates a feedback loop where the productive agents continue to expand market share.

– Merle Whitehead, President, Realty USA

Owner of large franchise brokerage with 800+ agents:

While downward pressure on commissions may continue into the next decade, hopefully with a continued increase in home values, the impact on Realtors may not be that significant. There will always be a place for flat-fee and discounters, but the savvy consumer will still adhere to the adage of getting what you pay for. There will be Realtors that have the knowledge, technology and tools to justify their fees, and those that won't be able to invest in their business that will be forced to discount their services.

– Chad Ochsner, Owner, RE/MAX, Alliance, CO

President of a MLS:

Commission pressure will come on the listing side first.

– Steve Sullivan, CEO, Metropolitan Indianapolis Board of Realtors and BLC Listing Service

President of a large independent brokerage with 200+ agents:

Commissions will decline where listings are commoditized or "cookie cutter." It is already happening in my market. Special homes that need special marketing or services won't have as much commission pressure. In an extreme case of commoditization—could we get pressured to flat fees? "Flat fee RE" in this market is gaining share already. *

Results from our Broker/Agent Survey

We conducted a survey of more than 6,000 high-production agents and teams (50 or more deals a year). We also surveyed the owners of the 1,350 largest brokerages in the U.S.

We asked, "Where are average commission levels heading?" For the results, see Exhibit 6-4.

Exhibit 6-4: Agents and Owners: How will average commissions change over the next ten years?

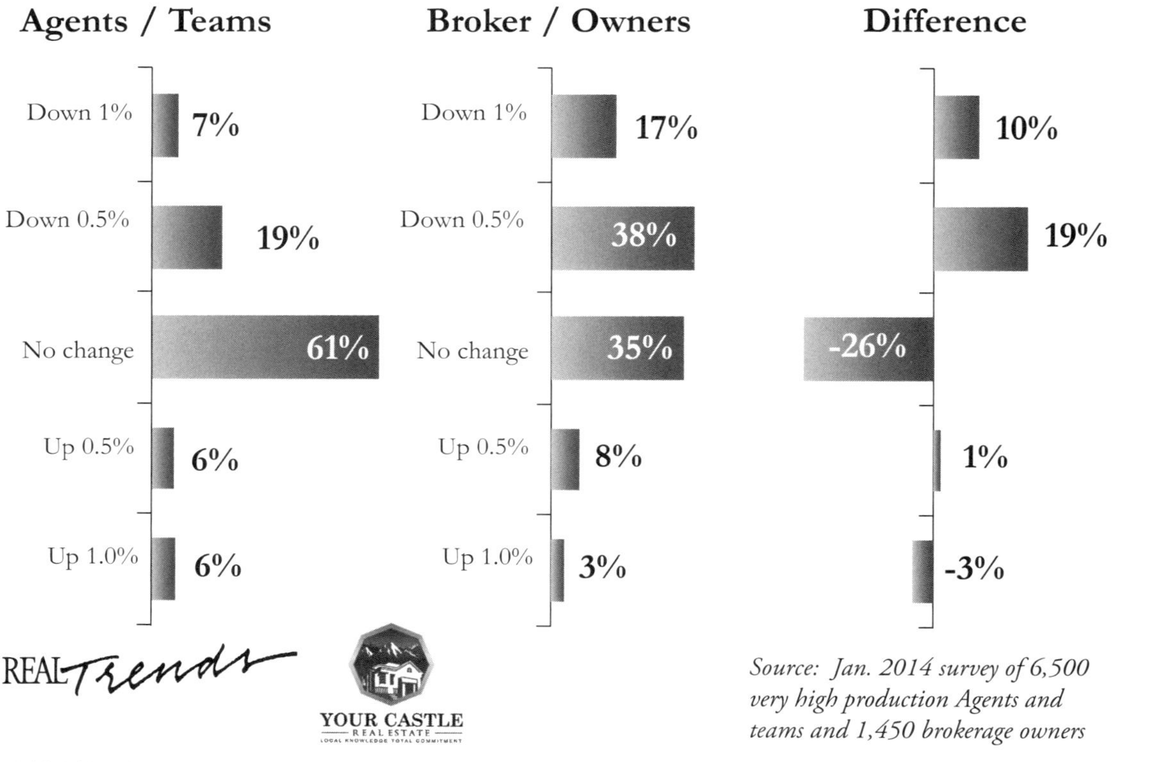

Source: Jan. 2014 survey of 6,500 very high production Agents and teams and 1,450 brokerage owners

In summary, they told us:

- Broker/owners (55 percent) are much more likely to think that commissions will be under pressure than agents (26 percent).
- Only a few respondents (12 percent) expect commissions to increase.
- The majority of agents (61 percent) expect commissions to stay about the same, versus only 35 percent of the owner/brokers.
- In phone interviews with broker/owners, most expected commissions to drift down over time. They expected more pressure on the listing side than the buyer side.

Implications

Based on 2013 new and existing homes sales, total U.S. gross commission revenue was approximately $54 billion. For each 0.1% decline in the commission rate, the industry loses $1 billion in commission revenues. Should the average commission rate drop from its current level of approximately 5.2 percent (U.S) to 4.6 percent, that decline would result in $6 billion in reduced revenues.

Solutions

- Implementing the ideas in Chapter One (facilitators versus counselors) is the best defense for agents and teams to maintain—and perhaps improve—their commission income. That chapter offers an extensive checklist of ideas.
- If you decide that the facilitator approach is right for you (it will be a good choice for many!), then you should focus on:
  - While you might not want to fully adopt all of the counselor ideas, you could selectively implement a few. These alone might help add enough additional value to enable you to retain your commission rates while others in your market are forced to discount more.
  - Get as operationally efficient as you can. You don't need to be the lowest-overhead provider as an agent, but it'd help if you were closer to the low end of the range.
  - Leverage technology to become more efficient. Avoid shiny objects and fads. Technology useful for you might be more along the lines of:
    - A robust CRM (customer relationship manager) that you use almost every day to stay in relationship with your SOI (sphere of influence)
    - If you run online or direct-mail marketing campaigns, a drip email system to incubate leads over time
    - Electronic (paperless) contract management, if it is available in your market
  - You will probably need to do more transactions, more efficiently, and at a lower (or hopefully, steady) commission to maintain your income. Develop a plan to grow your transaction volume.

If you run a team, then all of the concepts for individual agents apply to you. Most of the teams we interviewed for this book are taking a counselor approach. This seems to lend itself well to the process discipline that most successful teams have.

Declines in gross margin/company revenue percentages

Probability: High
Impact: Moderate to high

In our survey of high-production agents, teams, and owners, we also asked: "The average retained company revenue for brokerage firms (all sizes and business models) is 26 percent. Do you think this will rise, remain steady, or decline in the next 10 years?" The results are in Exhibit 6-5.

In summary, here is what we heard back:

- Realtors/teams were likely to report 'no change' or some decline.
- Most broker/owners chose 'decline.'
- Few owners thought this percentage would rise.
- Based on phone interviews with broker/owners, most expected that the decline in the average company dollar retained would continue.

Exhibit 6-5: Agents and Owners: How will average gross margin/company revenue change over the next ten years?

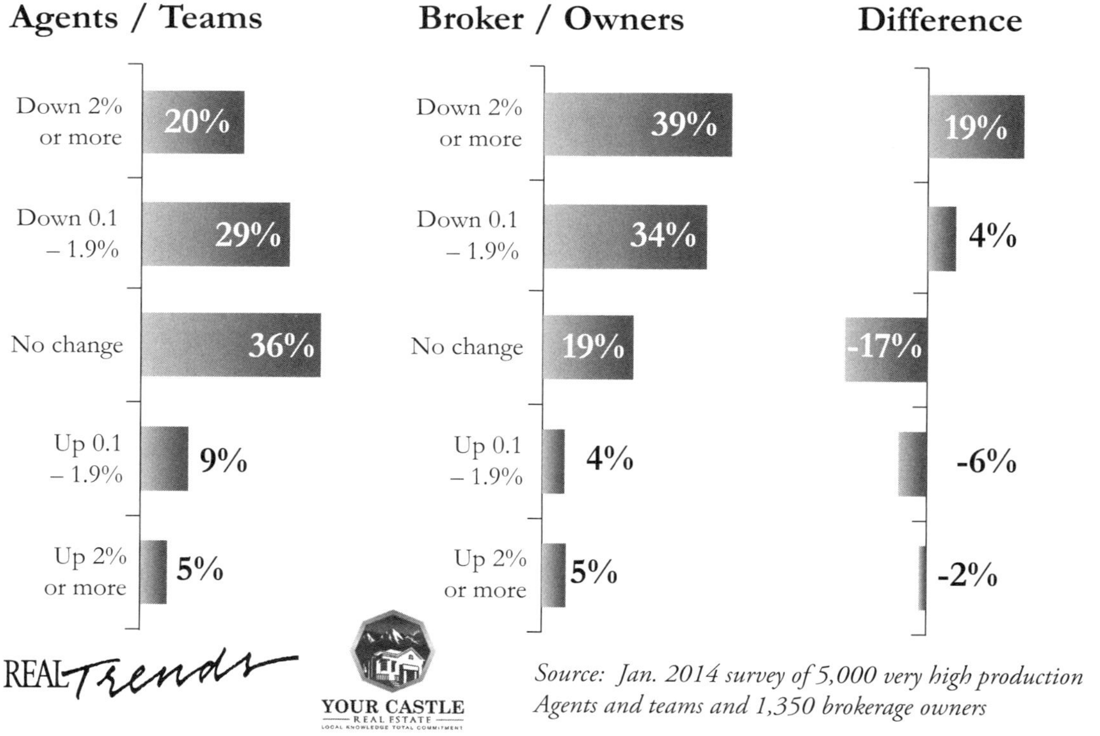

Source: Jan. 2014 survey of 5,000 very high production Agents and teams and 1,350 brokerage owners

The gross margin (also known as company revenue) for brokerage firms has been shrinking for the past 20 years. There are two forces at work. First is the desire by many firms to grow the number of agents as well as their organization's sales production, which has led to competition for both experienced high-production agents as well as new entrants. We refer to this as the pursuit of growth in share over growth in profit.

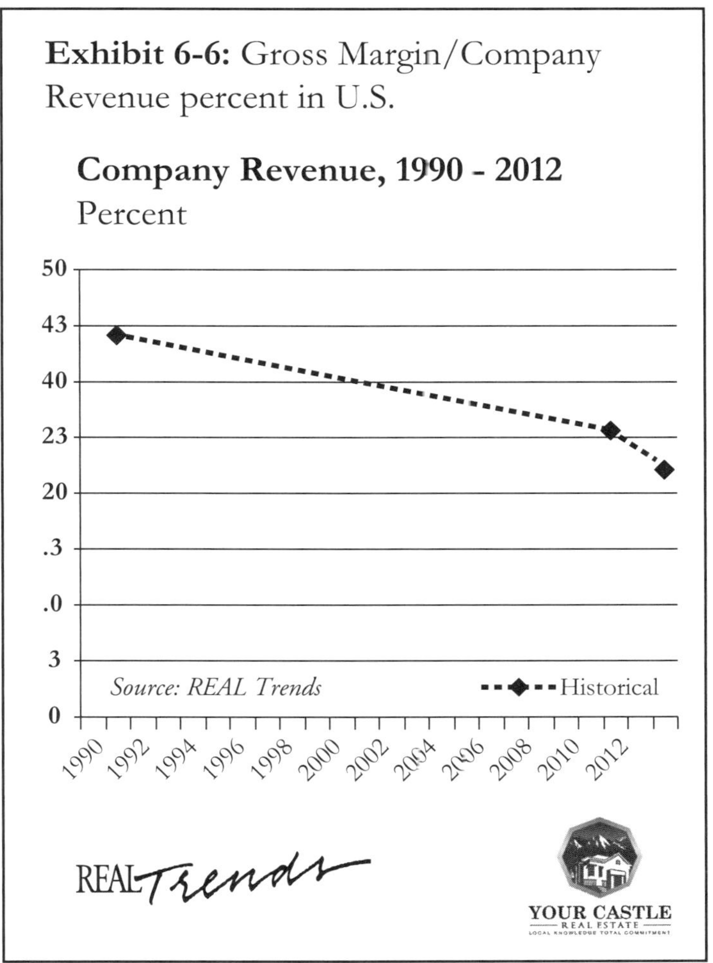

Exhibit 6-6: Gross Margin/Company Revenue percent in U.S.

Second, the types (and numbers) of brokerage models that offer lower costs that are now available to sales agents have multiplied enormously in that time. Not only have high-commission brokerage firms (which generally have low gross margins) multiplied, but the capped company revenue model firms and virtual brokerage firms that offer a flat fee for agent services have also grown significantly.

One other change that is impacting brokerage gross margins is the abundance of technology, marketing and educational services, tools, and products that are available a la carte from an increasing number of sources. Realtor associations, MLSs, and private firms have flooded the market with many of these tools and services. These were once the domain of the brokerage firm—and at one time the value these provided to agents was considered a competitive advantage.

The decline in gross margins has recently accelerated—as an annual study done by REAL *Trends* shows. In a survey of 180 brokerage firms of all models and regions from 2011 to 2012, the decline was nearly 15 percent in one year. This was caused by a rapidly rising market. Agents on either graduated commission plans or capped company revenue plans were able to "max" out their contributions to the brokerage—and increase their retained percentage of gross commission.

Forces moving in favor of declining gross margins

1. Brokerage competition for agents will continue to drive gross margins downward. The challenge of recruiting new sales agents and getting them into production is more difficult than ever, and brokerages will strive to recruit those who are already producing. They will compete with their services, such as in technology, marketing, and management assistance. They will also compete with the cost of these services. With the advent of ever-lower-cost realty business models, the bar of what is "reasonable" in terms of a commission split or fee program for the agent also gets lower.
2. The availability of services needed by sales agents to operate their business also contributes to this erosion. In the past, brokerages were the exclusive providers of technology, marketing, educational, and other services desired by agents. Now, virtually all of these services are available from other sources (e.g., third-party suppliers, national networks, the Realtor organization, the local MLS). Much of the value that was added by a brokerage has been diminished by agents having access to multiple sources for the services and support they need to operate their business.
3. Brokerages' pursuit of market share above other goals (e.g., maximizing profit) drives gross margins down. Many realty firms believe that growth in market share will lead ultimately to profit, so they pursue growth in production via recruiting. (They could focus on growing the production of their current agents, which might be more profitable.)

Countering these forces

At some point, realty firms will have to radically change their approach to recruiting and retaining sales agents and teams so that they can remain viable. While firms are certainly lowering their overall cost to deliver services, they are also starting to charge back for some services—which tends to raise the gross margin somewhat.

Industry comments

Senior executive of a large independent brokerage:

> *The brokerage is being disintermediated over time, but at a slow pace so it is hard to notice. Drivers include:*
>
> - *MLS, trade association—public MLS websites for consumers. They provide a lot more training than they did in the past. Some also provide CRM and marketing tools and support.*
> - *Portals (e.g., Zillow) sell leads direct to agents. The brokerage used to provide the majority of the leads to agents (e.g., relocation).*
> - *Tools directly sold to agents—CRM, marketing tools, electronic contracts*
> - *Technology gets cheaper and more powerful. Equipment and services that used to be prohibitively expensive for the individual—e.g., fax machines, color printers, fast Internet connections—are now cheap and commonplace.*
>
> *As a result, a Realtor's competitive differentiators that used to be only available from a sophisticated brokerage office are now easily available to solo agents. Collectively, it erodes the value of the brokerage, and you see that in the declines in the company dollar retained over time. The brokerage owner has to provide great service, great marketing, great support to great agents—you will win. It will slow GM erosion, but it doesn't solve it. It only slows it down.*
>
> *In Canada, RE/MAX and Royal LePage have 50% share—so economies of scale really come into play. They use the franchise training, web sites, support, etc. much more in Canada than they do in the U.S. Collectively, this shifts costs from the brokerage to the franchise. This enables Canadian brokers to make money on lower margins. As you might predict, there are only a few large independents in Canada—generally one per large market. This might be where the U.S. market is going.**

....

Senior executive of a large non-franchise brokerage with 1,800 agents:

Many of the problems in the real estate industry are a reflection of problems in society. For example, the "rich getting richer." The same is true with sales associates. In the past, an 80-person office would have dozens of $3 million producers. Today, we'll have a $15MM, a $10MM, some at $3MM, and many agents with low/no production. Since the highest producers cap, my blended company dollar retained goes down.

I'm not worried about consolidation in the industry. Many of the big franchise companies are publicly traded. Am I concerned about Warren Buffet (Berkshire Hathaway)? He wants to run a profitable business. I want to compete with someone that is profit driven. I don't want to compete on price. Pressure for profitability from Wall Street helps me. However, there is a big difference between publicly traded franchises and a privately held brokerage.

– Merle Whitehead, President, Realty USA

CEO of a large independent brokerage:

If you add a lot of agents at the margin on a 99/1—it all goes to bottom line. But eventually they talk and the margin goes away. You have to be really small or really big (economies of scale in back office)—no one will survive in the middle. What is "really big"? The % of revenue I could afford to invest in occupancy so it can't go over X%.

Big problem of current brokerages: managing from fear. Managers never call the bluff of agents and always give ground on commission split.

*Pressure comes from "core services": Mortgage JV gone. MSA (Marketing Services Agreements) are under similar pressure. Brokerages gave too much margin to agents when they had these revenue streams. Now they are gone. Has been lots of consolidation in other industries; it is coming to real estate.**

Owner of a large franchise brokerage with 1,400 agents:

> *Huge brokerage consolidation opportunities—you have to be good and really know your model. Be market centric—different models in different cities. You now have to be a solid business person too.*
>
> *Each market will have a critical mass required for the dynamics of that unique city—but you will have to hit that threshold to truly be successful and profitable on any reasonable level. Have a unique model approach to business—do NOT follow the pack.*
>
> – Mark Stark, CEO, Prudential Americana Group and Prudential Arizona Properties

President, large MLS:

> *All of the stakeholders in this business have focused far too much effort on attracting and retaining the least common denominator. It starts with minimum thresholds for licensing, to brokers who are only too pleased to invite a newly licensed agent to join the firm, to associations and MLSs that generate revenues regardless of levels of agent production. With this type of baseline, how can we be surprised that pressure on profitability remains front and center? Market and business consolidation [discussed in the next chapter] may well occur. But unless they are accompanied by dramatic and measurable performance thresholds, the listing side of the pie will simply get smaller, faster.*
>
> – David Charron, President, MRIS, Washington DC/Baltimore MLS

Implications

Based on the current level of approximately 22 percent gross margin for brokerage firms ranked as the largest 1,350 in the U.S., the revenue accruing to realty firms was $11.9 billion for 2013. The average gross margin for all firms declined nearly

15.4 percent from 2011 to 2013. The revenue loss was $2.2 billion in gross margin. Should the decline in gross margin continue downward, this would mean less revenue for investment in technology, management, training, and the myriad of services and support that brokerage firms historically have provided agents, especially in traditional full-service realty firms.

Solutions

1. Realty firms could measurably increase the percentage of company-driven business through making use of online marketing. Company-generated online business can produce far-higher gross margins when managed effectively. This fact has been established both at the brokerage level as well as among real estate teams. However, many brokerage owners lack the technical skills to implement this strategy.
2. Realty firms could focus on developing new agents as their firm's primary focus. Providing support for these new agents to develop their businesses can generally be accomplished at lower costs to the brokerage firm. Although there will always be departures over time, a firm that can become adept at developing new agents as an ongoing mission can raise its gross margin.
3. Firms can change course away from the pursuit of market share at all costs. Instead, they could focus on developing agents and teams who respect the tools, resources, and culture of the firm—while gracefully allowing those who value higher splits to depart. There are examples of firms currently operating that do not view market share as the most important measure of success; instead, theirs is a more balanced approach between growth and profitability.
4. A somewhat radical idea would be for brokerage firms to begin to charge a percentage of the sales price of the home rather than a percentage of the commission as their fee for services. This would tie the brokerage revenues to the sales prices of homes being sold rather than the commission that is being charged by the sales agent. One benefit to agents would be that they could then charge whatever they feel necessary or driven to offer to gain assignments. For the brokerage, absent any significant drop in homes prices, there is little downside (other than the cost of converting to such a system). At least one national franchise firm now charges its franchise fee in this fashion.

Further thoughts:

- Implementing the ideas in Chapter One (facilitator versus counselor) is a great place to start. That chapter has an extensive checklist of ideas, depending on which economic model you are running.
- As with the agent categorizations, do not feel that as a firm, you are limited to being just a facilitator or just a counselor. If you are primarily going to follow the facilitator path, implementing a few ideas from the counselor list could help boost your agents' commissions and your margins.
- Beyond the ideas from Chapter One, consider what your primary business goal is. Are you trying to capture more market share? Or are you trying to optimize profit? Many owners often believe that getting more share will lead to more profits. Often, that is not the case.

Chapter Seven

Consolidation comes to MLSs and associations

Probability: Low to Moderate
Impact: Moderate

The number of associations and MLSs in the U.S. has changed little over the past 10 years. Since the market peak, NAR membership has declined 30%, or by 350,000 agents. This is a $150-$170 million reduction in dues revenue. As a result many boards are seeking non-dues revenues, lowered costs, or both. At the same time, other housing marketplaces are now available (e.g., Zillow, Trulia) and gaining consumer acceptance. With the value of the board so closely tied (in most markets) to the MLSs, it creates uncertainty about the future.

Consolidations of MLSs and associations are just a matter of time. Executives of associations, MLSs, and brokerage leaders all acknowledge this trend. It could take place via mergers or shared service arrangements. How this will affect the industry at large? Will it impact the highly efficient housing marketplace?

Marketplace facilitators—or gatekeepers?

There are an estimated 1,400 Associations of Realtors in the U.S. Over 54 percent of them have fewer than 500 members—and there are hundreds with fewer than 250 members. At the same time, there remain approximately 800 MLS systems operating in the country; again, more than half have fewer than 500 users. In most major metropolitan areas where MLSs may have consolidated, there are several to dozens of associations, each with their own staff and board.

MLS research done by Clareity Consulting indicates that the approximate total of expenditures by MLS participants in 2013 was nearly $700 million. For the same period, the total estimated expenditures by these MLS operators for the actual software that runs the MLSs was approximately $100 million. So the annual overhead for space, personnel, additional technology services and marketing for

MLS operators is $500-$550 million. The average monthly cost to a typical customer of an MLS is about $39 per month.

According to research, most members of associations indicate that the main reason for joining an association is: a) an agent joining a brokerage firm that is a member must become a member of the association; and b) in many markets, an agent must join the association to gain access to the MLS. In some markets where access to an MLS is not dependent on joining the association, the percentage of practitioners who join it has fallen significantly. This is furthered by the growth of large realty firms that do not require their agents to join.

As one industry follower has pointed out *"whereas the MLS used to be the marketplace, it is now becoming the gatekeeper—the institution that assembles and cleans the data before forwarding it on to the emerging marketplaces operating as listing portals, such as Realtor.com, Zillow, Trulia, and Homes.com. With the competition from these new marketplaces and with association membership to some great extent dependent on the MLS as the foundation of value for many members, it seems plausible that a diminution of the MLS could have a material effect on the association and its business model."*

Forces driving consolidation

1. In Chapter Four, we discussed the possibility of real estate agents being required by the federal government to become employees of brokerage firms. If this were the case, the number of people with a real estate license would collapse by 50-70 percent. Membership in the MLS and Realtor organizations would follow.
2. In some areas, there are multiple MLSs in a rational geographical market place (New York, San Francisco, Atlanta are examples). In other areas, MLS regions overlap and agents have to list properties in both systems to ensure maximum coverage (e.g., Atlanta). Agents, brokerage owners, and consumers would all realize efficiencies by consolidation.
3. Associations and MLSs are offering many more services to members than they did in the past. A few of our interviewees referred to this as "mission creep"—an effort to provide more value and garner more non-dues income. Unfortunately, from the viewpoint of the full-service brokerages, these extra services level the playing field between high-cost, high-value brokerages and low-value, low-cost brokerages. This has been a factor in brokerage gross margin erosion (see Chapter

Six for a full discussion). The full-service brokerages may increasingly push back on association creep. That might promote some loss of membership, thus providing the incentive for consolidation. Lastly consumers still consider the MLS a highly valued part of the service that they receive from an agent.

4. As MLSs are faced with new forms of competition and their numbers decline, so too would the numbers of associations decline.

Countering the forces that are driving consolidation

1. Associations and MLSs have historically held a strong independent mindset. Without a compelling financial argument, it seems unlikely that this consolidation would take place on its own.
2. In many resort markets, the MLS is a wall to keep out other agents. In Vail, Colorado, for example, joining the board and MLS is a laborious and relatively time-consuming process. It is clearly designed to keep Denver metro agents from selling properties in that market. The incumbent agents, brokerages, and local association all have a large economic interest in keeping this wall in place.
3. While the percentage of housing consumers who find their agent or the home they end up purchasing online has increased, the major marketplace for selling homes remains the MLS and not the listing portals. Most consumers still choose an agent or team because they know one or are referred to one. Most agents will use the MLS to find the homes that consumers want. They will not use the listing portals as their primary provider of housing information.
4. The political power of the associations and MLSs among owners, elected officials, and users is powerful. Most practitioners do not easily give up the autonomy of having their own locally controlled association and MLS. Regardless of economic issues, this one factor is the most important in restraining any large-scale move towards substantial consolidation.

Comments

President of one of the largest MLS systems in his region:

In my experience, teams charged with both creation and support invariably see the former suffer when challenged by the latter. When the crisis arises, the entire team moves into triage mode. Innovation comes to parade rest. It invariably takes a back seat. Said another way, those charged with creating the future (consolidation) likely have too great a stake in maintaining the status quo (isolation). There is less risk and potentially continued reward for intransigence.

As a result, consolidation, if it is to occur, must be driven and repeatedly reinforced by engaged, enlightened brokers. After all, it is their business.

– David Charron, President and CEO, MRIS, Washington, D.C.

President of a large MLS with 6,000 members:

The industry is fractured—needs to be more consolidated; more focused. Too many associations. Association Creep is taking place at the local, state and national level. National and state-level NAR/IAR groups doing what the local boards have historically done. Their efforts to be a point of info for property—compete with local listing services and have added no significant value, just cost duplicity. State associations want to produce value in providing duplicative "state-wide services." Instead of consolidating back-room operations, we are duplicating the program side. This is a worst-case scenario in many regards, economically. "Mission creep"—broadens reach in an attempt to increase a perception of value. This creates (or will create) conflict, especially with brokerage owners.

– Steve Sullivan, CEO, MIBOR, Central Indiana's REALTORS

Owner of a franchise brokerage and MLS chairman:

*Major problem (especially on the east coast) of Overlapping Market Disorder — MLS systems that overlap. The fiefdoms do not benefit the consumers. These artificial boundaries hurt everyone except the MLSs that will not consolidate.**

President of a large independent brokerage:

> *All too often, as it relates to the struggle between brokers and MLSs, brokers are challenged to have any substantial influence on MLSs because they have difficulties coordinating with one another. In my opinion, the big brokers have shown an inability to work together and compromise on common ground.*
>
> – Jeff Detwiler, President/COO, Long & Foster Companies, Inc. (Mid Atlantic)

Association Executive of a large Realtor association:

What should MLS do with data?

- *Big syndication debate—crazy—brokers have to decide where listings go.*
- *There are challenges: how to sell the value proposition for the association to the Realtors.*
- *We created order out of the Wild West (e.g., ethics, standards). Associations and MLSs create order in a world that would look like the wild, wild west if we didn't exist (e.g., ethics, standards, rules, etc.).*
- *Now we are adding technology—perhaps a service not desired by all of our brokerages.*

Brokerages want to do the consumer-facing listing promotion to generate leads for their agents. They don't want associations providing services that level the playing field for recruiting or retaining agents. Associations need to consider scaling back their offerings based on their own brokers' desires; this varies from place to place.

Weaknesses: Our reliance on history when making decisions—default thinking is that the future will be like the past —is not true. I have been in the industry a long time and have seen a lot. We are at a crossroads this time—there is potential for SIGNIFICANT changes in the business. Industry history won't be enough for predicting what will happen next.

Many in leadership are OK with changes—big changes—but we are still often held back by so many who want to rely on that past history for future decision-making.

– Diane Ruggiero, Association Executive, Kansas City Regional Association of Realtors

President/CEO of a large MLS:

Technology has allowed us to do amazing things with the data. From an MLS standpoint, the biggest opportunity is to try to consolidate MLS databases, not necessarily consolidate MLSs. For example, if we had a Midwest Real Estate Database into which all listings were entered from Ohio, Illinois, Iowa, Michigan, Minnesota, Missouri, etc.—and if we all had the same rules regarding that data—most of the issues that the brokers have with MLSs would disappear. I assume you could take it to the national stage as well, but it would be good to at least create a regional capability first.

If we could accomplish this, it sets us up for what I call front-end of choice. In that an MLS, a broker, even an agent could decide what software or app they wanted to use to access this database. It would obviously have a great impact on MLS system vendors who would have to adapt to new models but that is not necessarily a bad thing. Look how software companies and app developers get swallowed up by bigger companies today. No reason a traditional MLS vendor couldn't become a warehouse of apps that could be used by the agent and broker in the field.

STRENGTHS: At MRED we have size on our side. Serving 90% of the Realtors in Illinois gives us a distinct advantage and the recognition we have received locally and nationally proves that out. There are certain economies of scale that we can take advantage of.

However, the recent push to unbundle services from the MLS may very well destroy that advantage. If we were to take a product that we provide as part of the bundled package that might be used by 10,000 of our members, and all of a sudden start charging a fee—no matter how small—the use of that product would plummet. Then you enter the vicious death spiral—fewer subscriptions, raise the price, fewer subscriptions, etc. And a good product bites the dust because it cannot be sustained.

Hanging onto traditional models of ownership and governance. It just takes too long to get things decided. NAR is a good example. They have been trying to define social media/marketing and while they have tried the world has passed them/us by. Agile and nimble are not words that are used when talking about realty organizations and MLSs. I have to applaud Illinois Association of REALTORS for their recent decision to reduce their board of directors from 100 people to just 28.

This also points out the Realtor relevancy issue. When 70% of your members aren't really in the business full time you can't expect them to be involved at the association level, so your pool of involved people is minimalized.

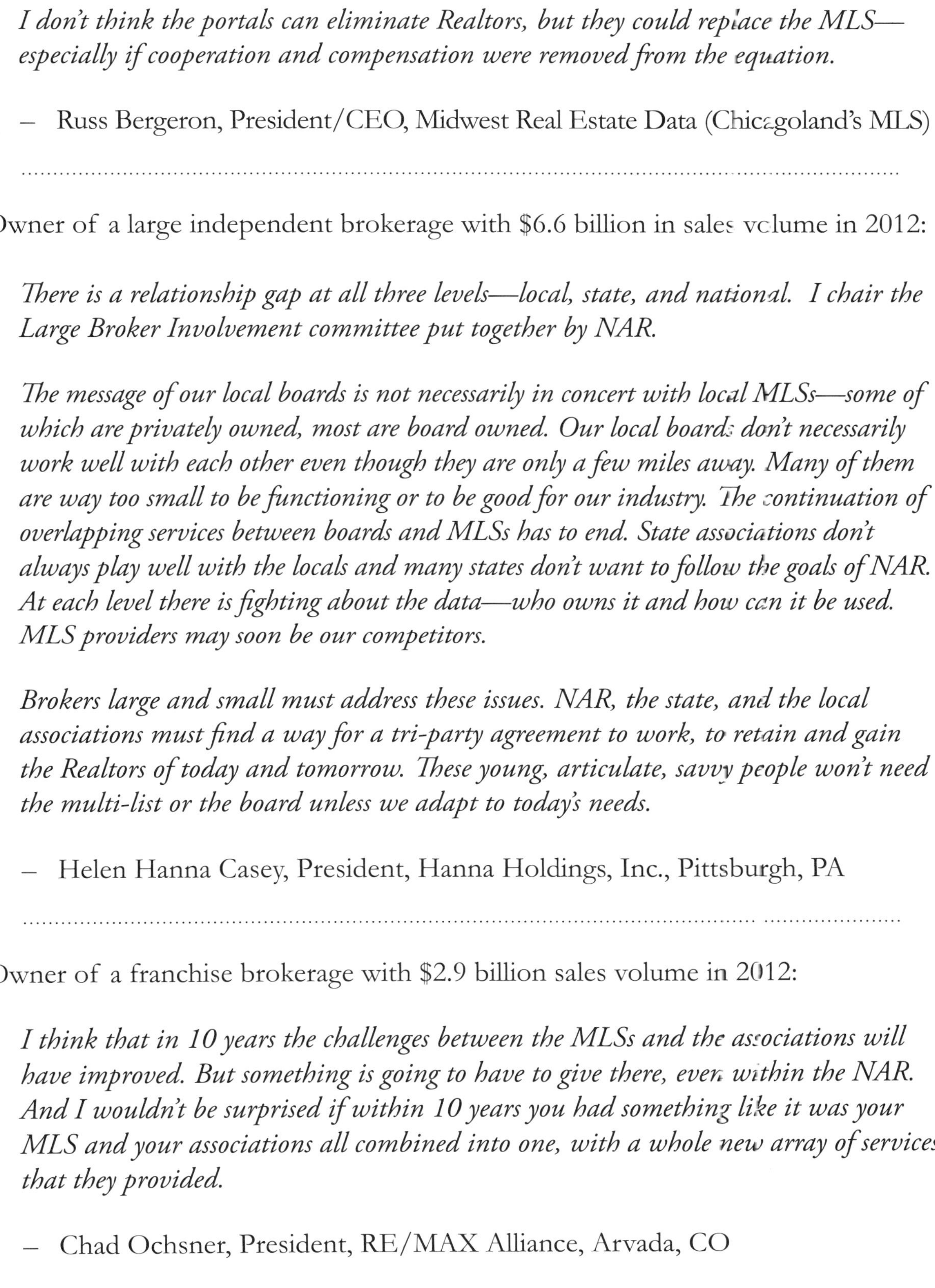

I don't think the portals can eliminate Realtors, but they could replace the MLS—especially if cooperation and compensation were removed from the equation.

– Russ Bergeron, President/CEO, Midwest Real Estate Data (Chicagoland's MLS)

Owner of a large independent brokerage with $6.6 billion in sales volume in 2012:

There is a relationship gap at all three levels—local, state, and national. I chair the Large Broker Involvement committee put together by NAR.

The message of our local boards is not necessarily in concert with local MLSs—some of which are privately owned, most are board owned. Our local boards don't necessarily work well with each other even though they are only a few miles away. Many of them are way too small to be functioning or to be good for our industry. The continuation of overlapping services between boards and MLSs has to end. State associations don't always play well with the locals and many states don't want to follow the goals of NAR. At each level there is fighting about the data—who owns it and how can it be used. MLS providers may soon be our competitors.

Brokers large and small must address these issues. NAR, the state, and the local associations must find a way for a tri-party agreement to work, to retain and gain the Realtors of today and tomorrow. These young, articulate, savvy people won't need the multi-list or the board unless we adapt to today's needs.

– Helen Hanna Casey, President, Hanna Holdings, Inc., Pittsburgh, PA

Owner of a franchise brokerage with $2.9 billion sales volume in 2012:

I think that in 10 years the challenges between the MLSs and the associations will have improved. But something is going to have to give there, even within the NAR. And I wouldn't be surprised if within 10 years you had something like it was your MLS and your associations all combined into one, with a whole new array of services that they provided.

– Chad Ochsner, President, RE/MAX Alliance, Arvada, CO

Association Executive of a Realtor Association:

> *Will organized real estate, along with MLSs and associations, continue to exist in their current structure? There is a lot of in-fighting and not a lot of focus on what the threats are outside the industry. We only must look to Europe where there is no organized real estate and ask ourselves "is this what we are to become?" We are stronger together than we are apart, but there is not a lot of buy-in to the concept.*
>
> *The industry must overcome complacency. The industry must look at itself and ask: Are we an industry of part-timers or are we dedicated real estate professionals with high business literacy? Fundamentally, we are not responsive enough to consumers—and we must face the fact that if we are not responsive, someone will be. That is why we now have Zillow and Trulia. While the industry was still arguing about can it be done, should it be done—it got done.*
>
> *The associations are facing challenges as well. What is the role of the association? Do brokerages mistrust the association as associations struggle to find their role? Most of the services provided by the association are needed by the "small" brokerages and not needed by the large ones. Is this helping to erode the competitive advantage of the brokerages that are able to provide those tools? If organized real estate is to thrive, the association must look outside its walls and find its relevancy. Many MLS leaders (e.g., directors) are more concerned about competition down street than outside industry.*
>
> – Janice McCrary, CEO, Greater Albuquerque Association of Realtors

---

Senior executive for a franchise:

> *There is a kind of energy in our entire industry. All the players will expend it on internal struggles rather than using that energy to focus on enhancing the customer experience and relationship. It's brokers versus associations and MLS organizations; it's associations against each other; it's associations against MLSs; it's content generators versus content aggregators; it's independents versus franchise; it's agent versus broker. It is a great distraction and I think it's a disservice that we all are responsible for to the industry.*
>
> – Budge Huskey, President & CEO, Coldwell Banker Real Estate LLC, Madison, NJ

Leader of a large real estate team with 650 sides in 2012—and past president of a local Realtor association:

> *Despite being a past president of the association, I am disenchanted with all of it. Our MLS is independent and for-profit and in many ways not responsive to Realtors. Some of the new MLS policies don't make sense and there is less influence at the Realtor level; sometimes I wonder if they remember who the customer is?*
>
> *There are frustrations with the associations also. The quality of agents is lacking and there has been a dramatic change over recent years in poor business practices. Ignorance; lack of training; poor ethics. The industry needs to do something creative and new to train agents better. Many agents I speak with think that the boards are not as vital as they used to be and a main sentiment is that it is only needed for them to have MLS access.*
>
> – Jeff Perry, individual agent, Prudential Results Realty, St. Cloud, FL

Leader of a large real estate team with $109 million in sales volume in 2012:

> *We need to provide better education to members. Lots of education now is by third parties—"certifications," "designation," with no controls—some are great; many are … not as well thought out. I have a CPA and worked at PricewaterhouseCoopers before real estate. I understand professional education. CPA world for CE is a lot different than Real Estate. A two-day class and you are a short sale "expert." And the consumer can't tell the difference. (At least the unsophisticated ones.) All of this negatively impacts the reputation and perception of the professionalism of the industry. There is a great need to standardize the training/certification process.*
>
> – Marie Chung, individual agent, Modern Realty Co., Cerritos, CA

Implications

In a brave new world of fewer and larger MLS systems and associations, all would have far more resources to focus on their core missions. The redundancy of staff and administrative overhead would be significantly reduced, freeing resources toward those areas that have the highest value to membership. Whether the core mission is training and education, legislative advocacy, or standards, each would benefit from consolidation within rational regional boundaries.

Using one benchmark, the Clareity study of MLS revenues and expense, one can see that overhead for the nation's 800+ MLSs is nearly $600 million. Were the MLSs to consolidate within rational regional or state-wide boundaries, to, say, less than 150 MLSs, and without cutting charges, there would be on the order of $150-$250 million that could be used for new technologies, training and education, and online systems that could make the entire market work more efficiently. The same is true in the association arena, where the 1,400+ associations could at the very least consolidate within metropolitan areas. The revenues saved from eliminating duplicative administration could be applied in the same areas.

The implications of consolidation further the conflicts that exist between the various local, state, and national Realtor organizations, as each fights to expand its revenues and influence. Rather than being able to invest in the most highly valued member services, most associations will have to spend on overhead, which often adds little value from the member's point of view. This is especially true of those associations that also control the MLS in their market area. Often, some mandate exists: that to use a particular MLS, a firm and its agents must also join the controlling association. This increases members' costs and the complexity of doing business. Mission creep, or the pursuit of services and products not closely related to the mission of a particular association, will continue, causing friction among the various levels of the association—and needless expense.

MLSs have similar challenges. While it is clear that fewer and stronger MLSs makes sense from an economic point of view, the failure to do so will increase the friction between MLSs and their participants. There remain far too many brokerage firms and agents that are compelled to belong to, and pay excessive fees to, multiple MLSs to participate in their marketplace. It also increases complexity, as each MLS has its own login and system functionality requirements. In many cases, the rules of the MLS differ. This creates significant inefficiencies for far too many brokerage firms and sales agents. One danger is that a new organization, using available technologies, could develop a less-expensive, more-efficient MLS system that eliminates most boundaries that now exist. This could occur at the regional market level, the national level, or both.

Solutions

First, associations at all levels need to define marketplaces and then rebuild associations around those markets. It makes no sense, in markets where there is one MLS, to have a half-dozen or more local associations. Then, a plan of consolidation could be devised to use this as a model for other areas around the country. These new local associations could then be defined by the metropolitan areas that they serve.

Second, since there are many administrative services that can be most efficiently handled on a larger scale, many of these services should be consolidated at the state or regional level. Finance, accounting, dues billing, meeting logistics, human resources, and a few others can all be done on a scalable basis at higher levels with shared services and costs.

Third, at each level of the association, specific responsibilities should be assigned to the most effective association. For instance, determine whether it is at the local, state, or national level that education is delivered. Then, that level of association and only that one is responsible for its delivery. While this cannot be done perfectly in each case due to size and membership population differences, it would work in most cases. Legislative advocacy and standards of performance can also be assigned appropriately.

MLSs should organize first around rational metropolitan areas and then determine where there are opportunities to consolidate even further. Is it really necessary for a state with a population of fewer than six million, and only three metropolitan areas each with over 400,000 populations, to have more than 15 MLSs—many of them with fewer than 500 participants?

MLSs should also consider only those services that serve their participants and their ability to conduct their business—and not intervene between the members and the housing consumer. While this is a controversial topic, and is related to the maintenance of membership, it is not rational that an MLS should act as a consumer service. That is clearly the role of the sales agent and brokerage firm.

Chapter Eight

The listing portals lock up the consumer relationship

Probability: Moderate
Impact: Moderate

A study done for REAL *Trends* by Harris Interactive indicates that consumers are nearly as familiar with the largest online real estate portals like Zillow and Trulia as they are with traditional "brick-and-mortar" real estate brokerages like RE/MAX, Coldwell Banker, and Keller Williams. The level of trust consumers feel towards portals and major brokerage brands is almost the same. While portals are newer to the industry, they already have had an impact on consumers, and have changed the way they shop for homes.

Will listing portals be content to stop at being providers of information and operating with an advertising model? Will they dive deeper into the relationship with the consumer? Will portals use their influence to move into the commissionable transaction and/or field their own agents? Should brokerages and agents see the portals as friend or foe? Will portals become the disrupter of real estate, as other industries have been reconfigured by their portals (e.g., travel, books, stock brokerage)? These are the kinds of questions we'll be asking—and addressing—in this chapter.

"Portal power"

As Dr. Phillip Evans said in his book *Blown to Bits,* the Internet will change everything. Every relationship between parties, whether in commerce, government, or education, is without boundaries. He also said the Internet will eliminate the trade-offs between "richness" and "reach." A marketer will be able to deliver high-quality content to an infinite number of customers for that message. For residential real estate this means:

- High-quality photography and video can be delivered as easily as a simple text description of a home for sale.
- Sales agents and brokerage firms can reach an infinite audience with whatever message or format works best for the sender and the receiver.

In the past 10 years, new kinds of content firms have arisen in residential real estate. We shall refer to them as "listing portals" or "portals." They are much more than the listing content they display. That is what causes so much consternation in the industry. The largest firms in terms of audience are Zillow, Trulia, Realtor.com, and Homes.com. There are many others, but these are the current giants.

A survey of over 6,000 top-producing agents and 1,350 brokerage owners in January 2014 reflected current concerns about how these portals' influence will affect incumbents. For more specifics, please see Exhibit 8-1. These respondents' greatest fears were:

- 47 percent said portals would send more referrals to those agents who paid them the most.
- 39 percent said portals would compete for the relationship with the housing consumer.
- 31 percent said that the portals would enter the brokerage business.

Exhibit 8-1: Owners: Listing portal (e.g., Zillow, Trulia) challenge assessment.

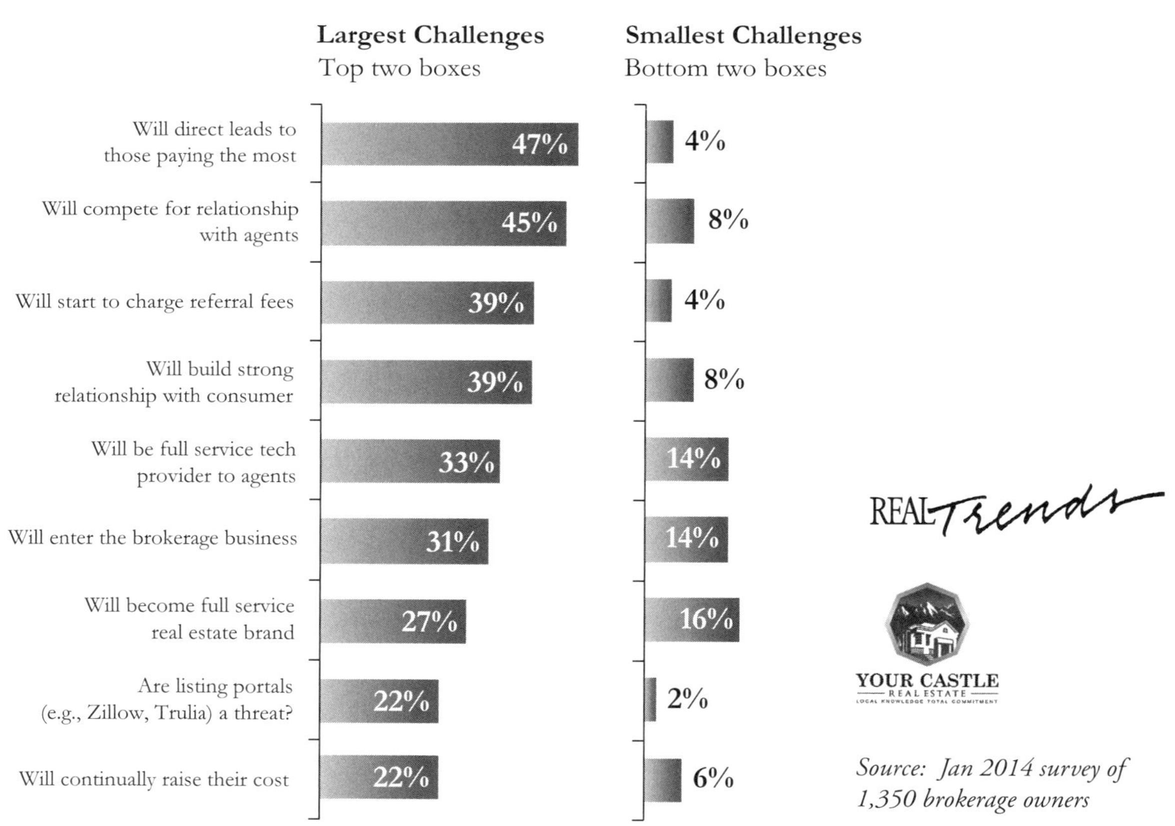

Reactions were strong and mixed:

- One industry leader said, "In the past, a brokerage with many listings drove many phone leads. With the strength of the portals, that is becoming less and less the case."
- Another leader said, "They have 60 million consumers a month visiting their site and 400,000 agent ratings and growing. They have over 20 individual mobile web apps. No broker has that or is ever going to have that. We have heard that they intend to start charging referral fees as well."
- One top agent commented, "I spend tens of thousands of dollars a month on the portals and make a significant profit doing so. I plan to increase that spending because it makes sense for my business."
- Another top agent said, "I have found it is the most effective manner of reaching new, younger customers whom I don't know personally yet. They are the future of my business."

The portals' business model currently focuses on selling advertising to real estate agents and brokerage firms. Some are also branching out to the rental, mortgage, and other homeownership product-and-service categories. These various advertisers are seeking access to the significant audiences the portals have accumulated: tens of millions of unique visitors each month. This dwarfs the online audiences of the more traditional real estate brand's web sites. The combination of the large audience and the growing brand influence with housing consumers and agents is a significant source of concern among established industry players.

Our study revealed two great fears. Portals may:

1. Become dominant; they can potentially charge much higher advertising or referral fees than they do currently.
2. Enter the brokerage business, hire their own sales agents under their own brand names, and close their own leads. This could bypass existing brokerage organizations.

Forces moving in favor of the portals' expanding influence

1. Portals have rapidly built powerful brands. They are nearly as recognizable as legacy brick-and-mortar brokerages. Our January 2014 study found that:
   - Fifty-eight percent of recent buyers and sellers said they were at least somewhat familiar with five large existing brick-and-mortar brands.
   - Fifty-four percent said they were at least somewhat familiar with the four largest portals.

   Our study also found that 62 percent of consumers at least "somewhat trusted" the five large existing real estate brands, while 54 percent had the same feeling toward the four largest portals.
2. The average age of the legacy real estate brands in the study was 30+ years. The average portal age is under 10 years. Portals have rapidly demonstrated their ability to build recognized and trusted brands.
3. Three of the four largest portals are publicly held. They trade at significant premiums to the general market. Their premium is very high relative to that of traditional firms like RE/MAX and Realogy. To maintain their stock price, portals must find ways to significantly grow their top-line and bottom-line results in the next few years. They will have to expand their penetration of the residential brokerage business in terms of customer count and per-customer revenue. They must expand into other home-related businesses with their advertising models. In short, they need to grow their businesses much faster than the home sales growth rate to sustain their stock prices.
4. Growing numbers of leading sales agents and teams are spending an increasing amount of their advertising budgets online. There are more than 100,000 sales agents with monthly portal ad spending of more than $180. Many agents spend that much with each portal. As long as lead generation is the key driver of agent behavior, portal ad spending will continue to increase.
5. As consumer awareness grows and portals deliver more content, consumers may begin to view the portals as the de facto MLS. Many agents already ensure that their listings are in one or more portals due to competitive pressures from other listing agents. Agents and brokers find themselves in a position similar to 1970 when they "had" to have newspaper classifieds. The sellers' beliefs forced the placement of advertising regardless of the effectiveness of the ad or the medium's ability to deliver quantifiable results. One great difference today is that with the portals, brokers and agents can track the effectiveness of online

advertising. Research and our interviews found that many agents find the investment compelling.

6. Lastly, portals are expanding the content they provide to consumers. Our research (described in Chapter Three) verified that consumers strongly value agent ratings. They will use ratings to guide their selection of an agent. This interest in ratings spans all generations. When portals provide ratings, consumers read them. Portals are also building stronger consumer ties with rental information. Thirty-five percent of households rent rather than own. This is another area where portals can move to cement their appeal.

Countering these forces

1. Our research indicates that consumers, across all demographic segments, continue to strongly favor the use of traditional real estate agents when buying or selling a home.
   - Seventy-nine percent said having a personal relationship with the agent they selected was important.
   - Sixty-two percent said that having used an agent in the past was important.
   - Rated at the top of the list, at 86 percent, were consumers who said having a referral from someone they trust was important.
2. Thus, personal relationships still matter to housing consumers in how they select a real estate agent. The portals' influence over consumer selection of agents is currently limited.
3. Much of the portals' appeal lies in their broad housing market information. This includes active listings, sold comparables, and related data. They currently enjoy broad access to the raw data they need. This vital listing data is updated frequently and voluntarily by agents, brokerage firms, and multiple listing systems. Many factors could lead these parties to terminate their data updates to the portals (some brokerages and MLSs already have).
4. If enough industry incumbents cut off the portals' data access, it would diminish their appeal as a "one-stop source" for consumers. The potential for such action by large suppliers of listing data does limit the portals' maneuverability to some extent.
5. Several competing portals are chasing the same housing consumer and the same advertising revenue. Portals' total unique visits greatly exceed the total number

of buyers and sellers. This indicates that consumers are looking at multiple sites. Research indicates that the average consumer visited 3.6 web sites in 2013 before settling on a course of action.

6. There has been consolidation among brokerages and agents (see Chapter Six). We expect this to continue. Advertising revenue is limited and controlled by fewer agents and firms. We anticipate commission rates will fall (also in Chapter Six) in the years ahead. This further limits the revenues available for portal models. Any of these factors could put pressure on the portals' financial results.

The forces in favor of portals' expanding influence currently appear to have the upper hand. We believe it is likely that portals will:

- Continue to strengthen their brands and consumer trust
- Continue to extend their offerings and refine their current sites, which consumers enjoy
- Capture an increasing share of brokerage and agent ad spending

As you plan for your business, what opportunities and challenges would this environment present for you?

Industry perspectives

Here's what we heard from industry leaders about the evolving relationship between the portals and industry incumbents:

President of a large franchise brokerage with 4,000+ agents:

> *There is a plethora of real estate portals on the Internet. Because of the ubiquitous use of technology, consumers are more sophisticated about buying and selling. This could put pressure on commissions. However, if we continue to create value for the savvy consumer with state-of-the-art technology, combined with the personal expertise and guidance of the broker, we will meet and exceed the consumers' needs.*

– Joan Docktor, President, Berkshire Hathaway HomeServices Fox & Roach, Realtors/The Trident Group, Philadelphia, PA

....

President/CEO of a large MLS:

Third parties (e.g., Zillow) so far are just ad models, really. It's an update on the newspaper model. Some consumers ask Realtors to have their listings on the portals... just like they used to ask for newspaper ads.

I don't think the portals can eliminate Realtors, but they could replace the MLS, especially if cooperation and compensation were removed from the equation.

– Russ Bergeron, President/CEO, Midwest Real Estate Data (Chicagoland's MLS)

President of a large independent brokerage with 2,000 agents:

Aggregators are taking customers and are shrinking our margins.

– Gino Blefari, CEO, Intero Real Estate

President of a large independent brokerage with 250 Realtors:

Aggregators (e.g., Zillow) will siphon a lot of profit from agent and brokerage—could lead to more brokerage consolidation.

– Neal Hanks, President, Beverly Hanks Brokerage

....

President of a large independent brokerage:

I think they're accelerating. Zillow and Trulia get a lot of press in our industry, so we get drawn into thinking how big they are. You talk to an average consumer and they are only casually engaged with them. So it really hasn't taken hold yet but it will, in terms of lead generation for our industry.

The next generation (the Millennials) will certainly be more used to going online to gather all their information, as well as their friends, clients, and social conversation. So I think the reason it took so long for web leads to grow is because we had control of the information.

The consumers had to come to us for information and that also made us a little bit lazy as an industry. Our service was providing information, which meant you didn't have to have a skill set as high as you might if the client came to you with the information. Going forward we will have to be the interpreter and the manager of information.

It happened to stockbrokers the same way. Stock data became available online so consumers could get that information quickly. I think technology has facilitated that change, but it's access to information that is the real driver. Access to information greatly changed the relationship between agents and brokers back in the 70s as well with the creation of the MLS. So this is just the next phase, shifting the information access from the agent to the consumer.

– Dan Elsea, President, Real Estate One, Detroit, MI

Results from our Broker/Agent Survey

We surveyed the owners of the largest 1,350 brokerages in the U.S., asking them a number of questions about portals.

In summary, they told us:

- Their largest concerns about portals centered on their giving leads to the agents that pay the most (vs., perhaps, the most qualified agents), along with competition for agent relationships.
- Least frequently mentioned as largest concerns were the portals' overall threat level and cost inflation.
- Items most frequently cited as smaller challenges were portals: becoming a full-service brand, entering the brokerage business, and becoming a full tech provider.

When we sorted interviewees' responses by brokerage size, we noted:

- As with other questions, the smaller brokerages were somewhat less likely to view this industry change as a challenge.
- Larger firms were more concerned about consumer relationship erosion as well as the potential for portals to expand in order to offer technology services to the firms' agents.

- Smaller firms were more concerned than the large firms with regard to the potential for portals to develop national brands and enter the brokerage business.

When we sorted their responses by owners' ages, we noted:

- When asked "are the portals a threat?," older owners were about twice as likely (26 percent) as younger (15 percent) to highly agree.
- Younger owners were more concerned about portals:
    - Becoming brands (40 percent vs. 19 percent)
    - Becoming brokerages (40 percent vs. 26 percent)
    - Competing with their brokerage for agent relationships (50 percent vs. 42 percent)
- Older owners were more concerned about portals:
    - Raising costs (29 percent vs. 10 percent)
    - Starting to charge referral fees (42 percent vs. 35 percent)
    - Competing with their brokerage for consumer relationships (42 percent vs. 35 percent)

Implications

The residential real estate industry generated approximately $54 billion in commission revenues in 2013. Brokerage firm and agent advertising are estimated at $4-5 billion. Portals currently garner less than 15 percent of the total ad spending by brokers and agents. As the portals continue their momentum in strengthening consumer relationships, they should be able to command a higher share of all ad spending. The "price to play" for agents and brokerages would increase. This is barely different from the days when newspapers could routinely raise their residential real estate ad rates.

If their relationships with consumers become strong enough, portals could initiate a "referral fee" method of garnering revenue. They could *collect referral fees from homebuyers and sellers* who are referred to these portals' preferred agents—or those who sign up for such a system. Assuming customary referral fees, this increases potential revenue to a much higher level than a simple ad-based model. Portals could enter the brokerage business through owned and operated brokerage businesses or through a franchise arrangement.

As one commentator has stated, the MLS is the marketplace for real estate agents, while the portals are the marketplace for consumers. At what point do those who control the marketplace for consumers become the marketplace for real estate agents? And should that happen (as in many parts of the world) then the portal becomes the de facto MLS for agents and consumers alike. For those who have been promoting "off-market listings," this is already occurring. Some portals in Europe are the de facto MLS—and their charges and earnings are significantly higher than those of the major portals in the U.S. and Canada. It is entirely possible that this shift would take place.

Increases in portal ad spending that are not offset by advertising spending cuts elsewhere would result in lower margins for brokerages and agents. If the portals start to charge referral fees, the incremental commission income would more than offset the costs. However, the market share of agents not using portal referrals would decline. This would likely force some lower-production agents out of the industry.

In all cases, other advertising channels would lose share. Consolidation among brokerage firms and sales agents could accelerate. Portals will direct more business to those who have the means to pay for it. This shift could also lead to the formation of more teams of agents, as they are often best positioned to build systems to incubate and monetize large numbers of online leads.

Portals could replace the existing multiple listing systems as well. Consumers have already indicated with their online viewing that: a) they don't require the level of accuracy inherent in today's MLS and b) they don't require the level of detail on each property available in the MLS. The portals could easily develop the import of data direct from real estate agents and/or direct from consumers for display to their viewers. Portals would become the de facto supplier of listing and sales data to the industry and to the consumer.

Finally, portals with strong consumer brands could extend their reach into transactional technologies. They could become the entire backbone of the process of buying and selling. While it is unlikely that such a system would replace most agents and brokerage firms, it would serve to expand the FSBO (for sale by owner) segment of the market. FSBOs currently comprise just fewer than 11 percent of all sellers. Because of consumer preferences for the use of agents, such a move may not expand the FSBO market—but it may result in commission compression.

Solutions

For most of its history, the residential real estate industry operated a closed information system. Agents and brokers deposited all of their listing and sales data into the MLS. It was accessible only by other members of the local real estate association. There was little competition among participants for the display of such information, other than through public advertising through acceptable media channels.

The MLSs and most brokerage websites are still built mainly with the real estate professional in mind. The industry is mostly online to remain competitive in terms of recruiting and retaining sales agents, and not for the convenience of housing consumers. The portals, on the other hand, are built solely to attract and service housing consumers—and make no mistake, this is a big difference.

The advent of the Internet has changed the entire landscape. However, the mindset of most industry participants has not changed and adapted to this new environment. Until that mindset changes, the industry will have a difficult time dealing with, let alone competing with, the portals. The industry still sees itself as the owner of the listing data and the housing consumer. This is true to a great extent for all industry participants, whether brokerage firms, sales agents, associations of Realtors, or MLSs. It is "our" data and "they" are using "our" data to sell us "our customers" back to us is a common refrain.

Choose to compete

Realty organizations at all levels need to grasp that their online presence must be built solely for the convenience of their customers—and not for the benefit of their sales agents. This does not end with the website, but goes to the entire customer response systems that the brokerage should have. Even the portals say that one of their largest challenges is the substantial lack of response and follow through by sales agents when customers request assistance.

Listings are not anyone's property except the seller/consumer. Consumers aren't owned by anyone. The housing consumer should be supplied with the services they want, when they want them, and in a format that is easy for them to use. Once brokers, agents, associations, and MLSs grasp this, then the solution is simple—compete to become the preferred supplier of information ***and service*** to the consumer in all things related to housing. This is not what the industry wants, but this focuses on what the consumer wants.

The industry has a firm hold on consumers when it comes to the actual process of buying and selling homes. Our 2014 consumer research shows that 81 percent of all consumers who bought or sold a home in 2013 used an agent and found their service valuable and relevant to their needs (the NAR number is 89 percent.) That is not in doubt, and will not be challenged by the portals as they exist at this time. ***Where the industry needs to compete is online.***

Competing with portals means mostly that the realty industry must choose to compete on the basis of what the consumer wants and not what the incumbents are willing to share on a limited basis. Consumers want sales data and will go where it is provided. They don't care if it is totally accurate. Some information is much better than none. Similarly, agent ratings are a growing consumer requirement. Whether the industry likes ratings or not, consumers are going to seek them. They will go to sites that have at least some data about agent performance. It doesn't have to be perfect but it has to be available.

Chapter Nine

Which brokerage services do clients value?

As part of the research for this book, we commissioned national opinion studies. We asked consumers, real estate agents, and broker/owners to rank the importance of a series of commonly understood housing services. We also asked consumers about their recent experiences with agents in buying or selling a home. As to which services are most valuable, the three groups did not always agree:

- Gaps exist between what consumers value and their perception of the service they received. These shortfalls create opportunities for agents and brokerages that can remedy them.
- There are gaps between what agents and owners believe is valuable. Some brokerages might be providing too much support in some areas. This might present an opportunity for cost savings. In addition, brokerages might not be doing enough in providing other services.

This chapter outlines these opportunities, as well as generational differences among consumer groups concerning which real estate services matter most.

What we asked

We asked clients, agents, and owners the same questions about the value of a variety of real estate services:

- Help negotiate the best price to sell or buy a home.
- Provide clients with a marketing plan for the sale of their home.
- Provide CMA (comparative market analysis) of comps on the sale or purchase process.
- Educate clients on the process of buying and/or selling their home.
- Refer services—inspectors, title, closing services, etc.
- Refer the client to a lender to get financing.

- Provide online information on homes that meet the client's criteria.
- Provide useful websites so clients can look at homes.
- Provide information: neighborhoods, schools, crime, etc.

The groups that we asked in January 2014:

- 6,000+ high-volume agents (at least 50 closings per year).
- 1,350+ brokerage owners in January 2014 (at least $500 million in sales).
- 1,000+ consumers who closed a purchase and/or sale in the prior six months.

Client results

We hired Harris Interactive to survey 1,000 consumers who recently bought or sold a home. See Exhibit 9-1. Overall, clients who used an agent to help them with their last deal (about 80 percent of the people surveyed) found these services to be the most valuable:

- Help negotiate the best price to sell or buy their home: 82 percent.
- Provide useful websites so clients could look at homes: 69 percent.
- Provide CMA of comps (sale or purchase process): 68 percent.

The big surprise was "provide websites." Clients certainly have plenty of choices for MLS-type access online. They can use the portals (e.g., Zillow, Trulia), agent-specific sites, or a number of other options. We would guess that when clients get deep into the search process, real-time data is very useful. In the current market, clients need to know if a home they want is still active or not. This is true in most markets with tight inventory. The portals and many other online sources are not as "real time" as the MLSs. Agents may feel they have nothing to offer clients for web-listing access, but clients do not share that opinion. This is an opportunity for agents and firms.

Exhibit 9-1: Consumers: How important were different real estate services?

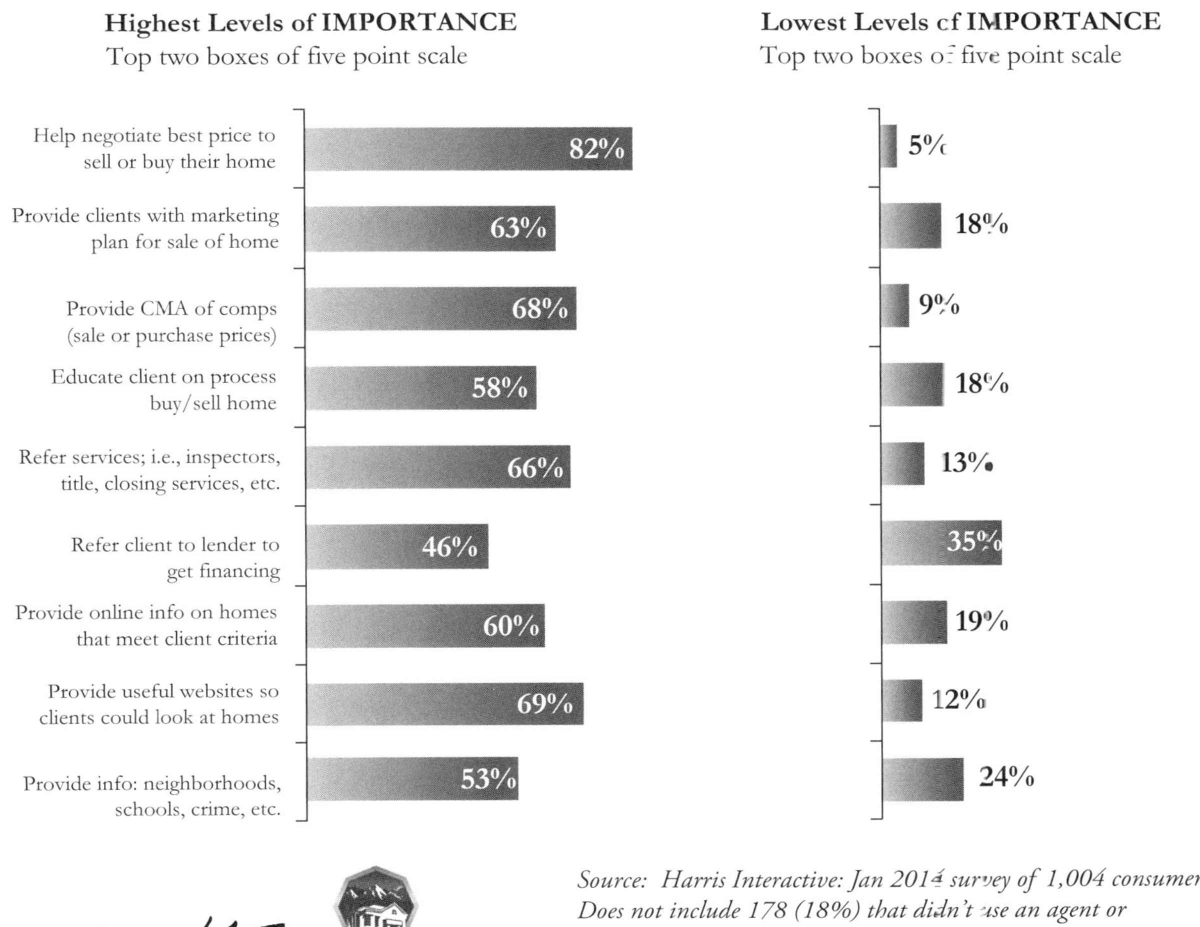

Source: Harris Interactive: Jan 2014 survey of 1,004 consumers. Does not include 178 (18%) that didn't use an agent or consumers that selected "Not applicable" for a given question (e.g., first-time buyers and "marketing plan for my home")

The right side of Exhibit 9-1 shows the services clients found to be least helpful. Most cited were:

- Refer client to a lender to get financing: 35 percent.
- Provide info on neighborhoods, schools, crime, etc.: 24 percent.
- Provide online info on homes that meet client criteria: 19 percent.

From talking with sales agents, it appears that many clients start the real estate search process by meeting with a lender to find out how much they can afford.

Exhibit 9-2 examines client needs in more depth. The middle of the chart shows how important consumers thought each of these services were.

Exhibit 9-2: Consumers: Service importance vs. satisfaction gap analysis

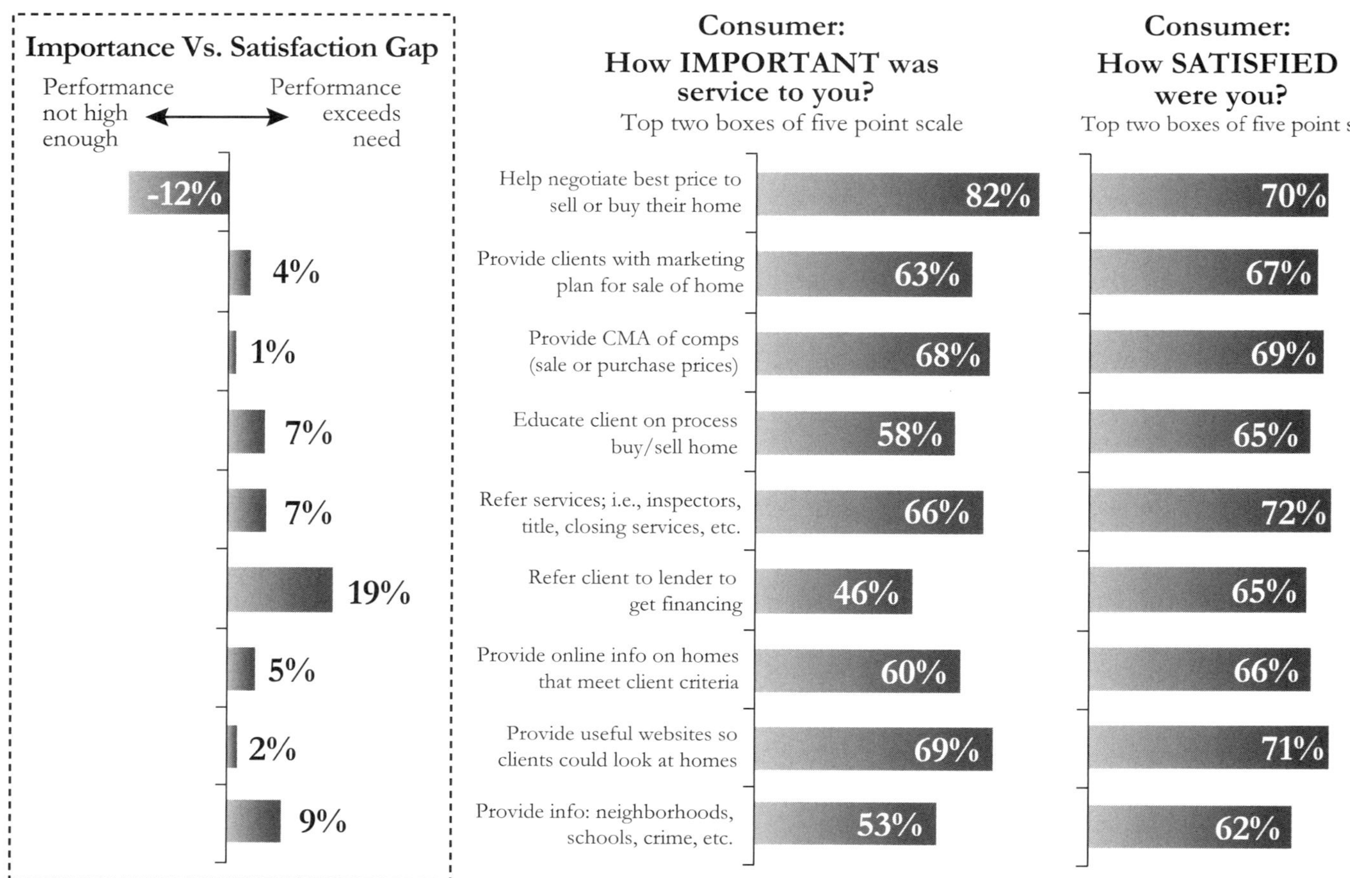

Source: Harris Interactive: Jan. 2014 survey of 1,004 consum Does not include 178 (18%) that didn't use an agent or consumers that selected "Not applicable" for a given question (e.g., first-time buyers and "marketing plan for my home")

The graph on the right shows how satisfied the consumers were with the service provided by the agent. Finally, the graph on the left shows the performance gap between the consumer's perception of the importance of the service, and how well the agent did. One topic, "help negotiate the price," had a negative score. Here, consumers felt this was the most important service, but that agents generally did not perform as well as the consumers wanted. This is a training opportunity for agents and brokerages to improve service levels. Unlike many important activities performed by agents, negotiation is highly visible to the consumer and easy to explain and demonstrate.

The next exhibit, 9-3, displays consumer ratings of service importance, but this time segmented by client generations. You can see how Millennials, Gen X and Boomers, and Traditional clients rated these real estate services. During the survey, we asked consumers which two services were most important to them.

The graph on the left side of the chart shows the gap in importance ratings between the youngest and oldest consumer groups.

Exhibit 9-3: Consumers by Generation: Value of Services provided by Agents. Gen X and Boomers were almost the same.

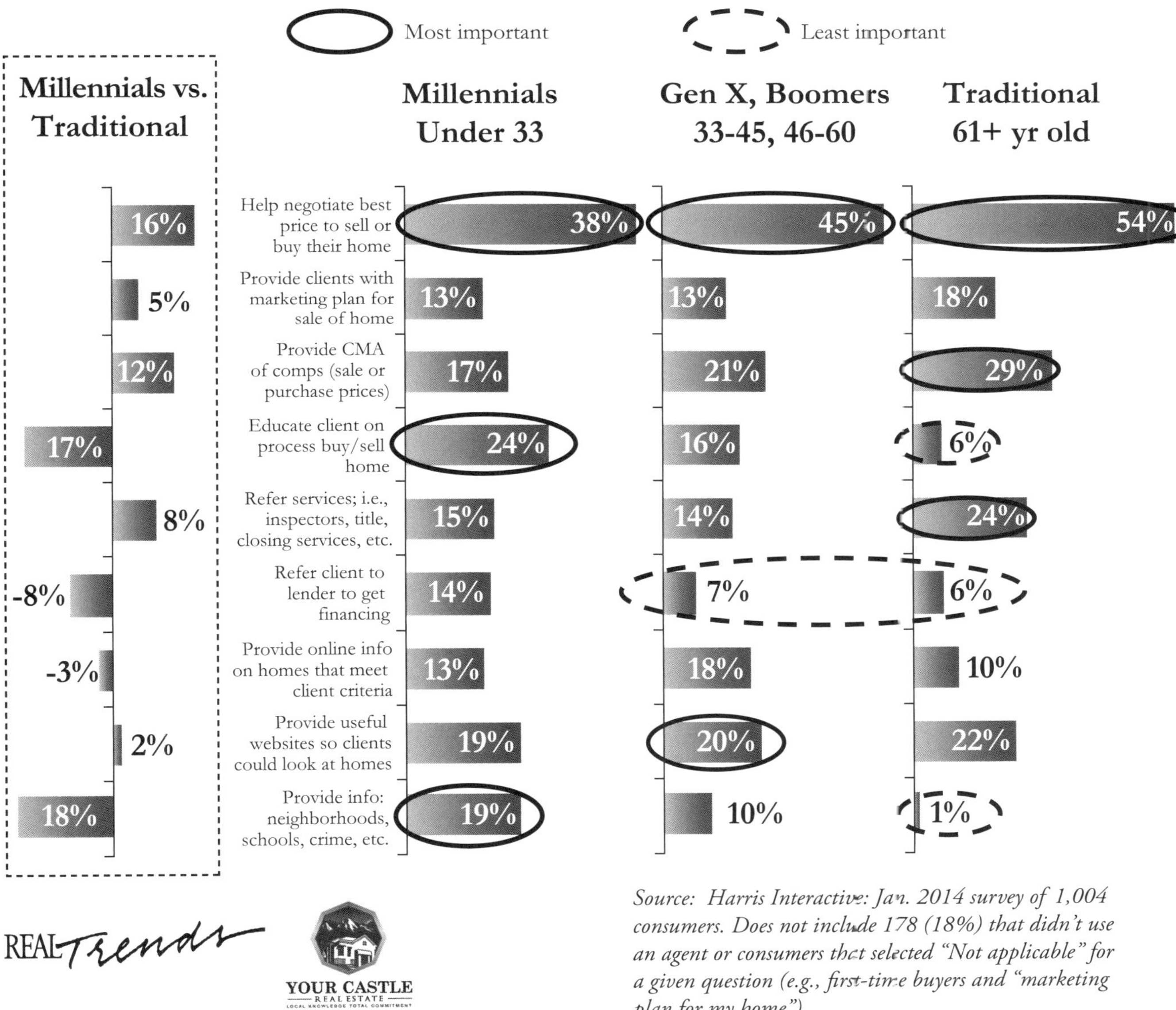

Source: Harris Interactive: Jan. 2014 survey of 1,004 consumers. Does not include 178 (18%) that didn't use an agent or consumers that selected "Not applicable" for a given question (e.g., first-time buyers and "marketing plan for my home")

Here are some of the most useful findings:

- Help with negotiation is the most important agent skill from the consumer's point of view. Older clients (54 percent) were much more likely than younger clients (38 percent) to feel this way.
- From our interviews, we got the sense that many agents think consumers are doing their own CMA with online services like Zillow and Trulia. That is increasingly the case, but the agent's CMA is still very important, too. Older clients (29 percent) were more likely to think so than younger clients (17 percent).
- Not surprisingly, "Educate me on the process of buying or selling a home" was much more useful to younger clients (24 percent) than older clients (6 percent).
- None of the groups were overly likely to find lender referrals useful. Younger buyers (mostly first-time buyers) were more likely (14 percent) than older buyers to find these referrals helpful.

One of the biggest gaps between generations was with "provide neighborhood information." There are many resources (often conflicting) on the Internet for this information. While we would commonly consider younger people as more adept with the Internet, they had a much higher opinion of the agent's value-added (19 percent) than older consumers (1 percent). Our hypothesis is that older consumers already know what they want in housing and where to find it. The agent does not bring much to their decision process.

The younger consumers told us they did extensive research online, but they still want the advice and opinions of the agent to help them synthesize and prioritize their findings, resolve conflicting information, and guide them to a great decision. Since they often have limited funds for their first home, they usually cannot get everything they want. This results in many tradeoffs in the purchase decision process. Agents who can explain how they can help with this decision process will likely have a competitive advantage with a sizable number of younger clients.

Linking these insights to agent reviews

As reviews are becoming increasingly important to consumers, agents could ask their clients to showcase their skills in negotiation and decision-making support in their write-ups. This will likely resonate with prospective clients who read their reviews. The more specific the examples, the more persuasive they will be.

For agents:

- If you work with many first-time buyers, or first-time move-up clients, have your reviews document your time, care, and attention in explaining the process.
- While it might be just considered a "given," if you focus on older clients, have at least a few reviews comment on your extensive network of trusted suppliers (e.g., stagers, handymen, inspectors) and how they made the transaction easier. Also with older clients, the detail and accuracy of your CMA and the care with which you explained it would be persuasive.

For all reviews, agents should coach their clients to be truthful, specific, and positive in their write-ups.

Linking these insights to the first client meeting or interview

Winning with younger clients, then, is not all about being perceived as tech savvy. That is simply the price of entry for the agent to be seen as a possible service provider. The real differentiators are:

- Providing (and confirming) the younger clients' online research about neighborhoods, and helping them make good decisions about their housing trade-offs.
- For the minority of younger buyers without a lender relationship, providing that referral.
- Providing great negotiation support.
- And of course, taking the time to hold clients' hands and really explain how the process works. Most agents who regularly work with first-time buyers and first-time move-up buyers excel at this. The previous three points offer much more opportunity.

Winning with older clients requires a slightly different mix of skill mastery:

- Negotiation is the biggest opportunity area.
- Most of these consumers experience agents as very good at developing a market analysis. They very much value your expertise here! Keep doing what you are doing.

- While younger consumers are more likely to want to find their own service providers (e.g., home inspectors, stagers), older consumers are more likely to rely on the agent's network of trusted sources. Most experienced agents have no problem in this area. Be sure to talk about this during your listing appointments. It's easy to gloss over as you might not think it's important. But for many older clients, it is important and is an easy win for you.
- Certainly ask if the client wants help with lending, neighborhood information, and how the process works. But most of these older clients will not feel that they need help here.

Winning with Gen X and Baby Boomer clients:

- Negotiation is the biggest opportunity.
- Interestingly, these age cohorts were most likely to want to rely on the agent for "online info about homes that met criteria." The industry has come to assume that consumers will use their own online sources for this. For many clients that is true—but not for all of them. There could be several explanations. People in these age groups tend to be very busy with careers and family. They are generally move-up buyers, often with children. While they have the technical sophistication to find homes online, some would rather pay you to think through it.

You should consider developing some questions in the initial interview to determine this. Consumers who want a concierge-type approach are really telling you they want a "counselor" and not a "facilitator." The services you offer, and the commission fees you charge, could be based on your interview findings.

- Middle-aged consumers' reliance on agents to provide (or more likely confirm) their online research about neighborhoods (e.g., schools, crime) falls between that of Millennials and Traditional groups. This makes sense.
- You should consider adding an interview question to probe how much interest a particular client has in your support in this area. Many will feel they can handle it on their own—which is probably what you suspected anyway. A minority will really appreciate your input.

Room for improvement

We surveyed very-high-production real estate agents and teams. We conducted extensive personal interviews with about 25 people. Exhibit 9-4 explores the gap between consumer and agent assessments of the value of different services.

- The graph in the middle shows how agents rated the importance of these real estate services.

Exhibit 9-4: Consumers vs. Agent: Opinions of service importance.

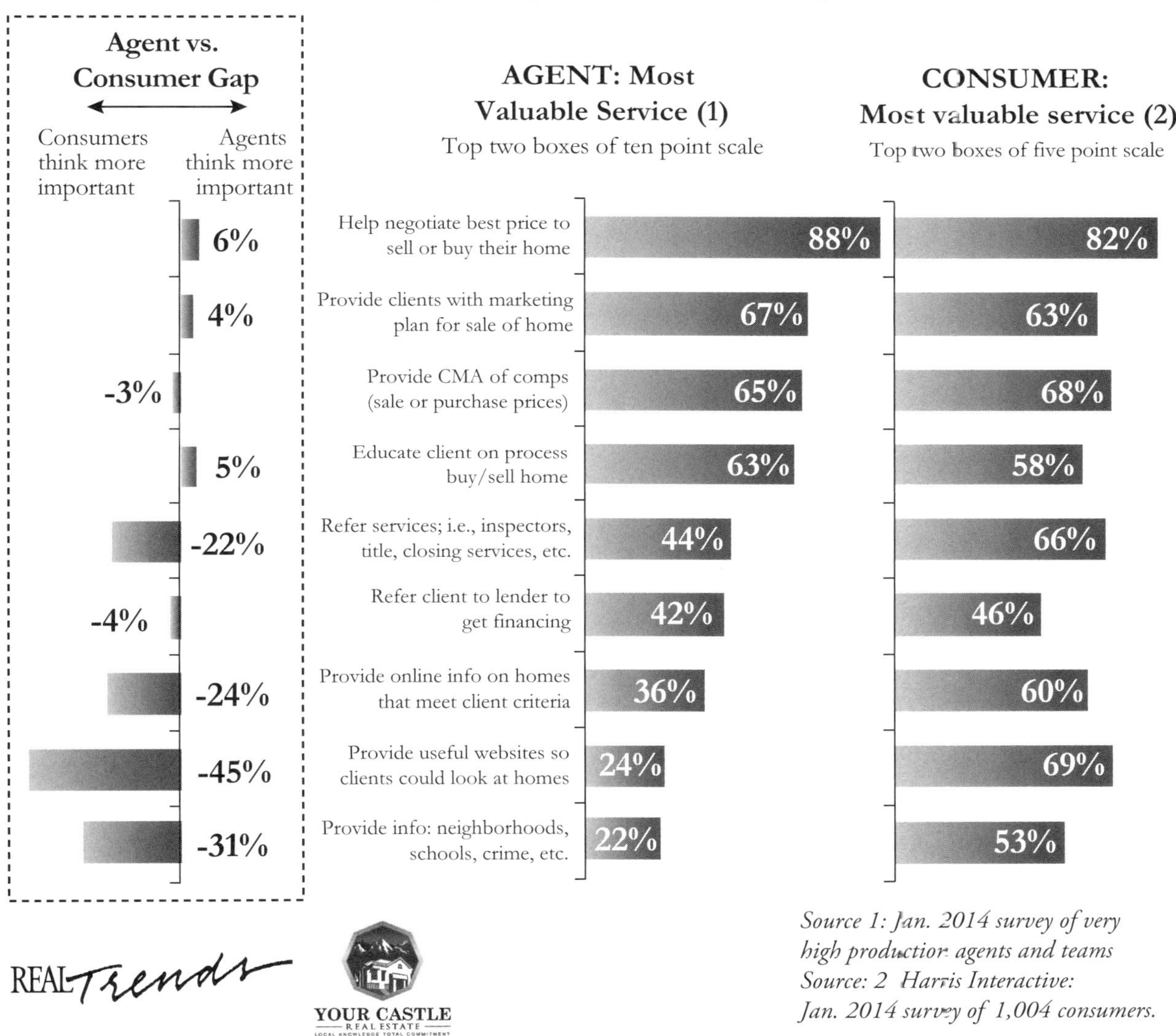

Source 1: Jan. 2014 survey of very high production agents and teams
Source: 2 Harris Interactive: Jan. 2014 survey of 1,004 consumers.

- The graph on the right also appeared in Exhibit 9-1; it is the consumer's importance rating.
- The graph on the left is the gap between the consumer and agent assessments.

The agents graded themselves more negatively than the consumers did. The main exceptions were their negotiation support, and their help in educating the client about the buy/sell process. Here the agents thought these services were a little more important than the consumers did. There is room for agents to improve in both areas.

The bigger surprise was in those services consumers found useful that agents did not think were particularly valuable. The biggest gaps were:

- "Provide websites so clients can look at homes." Consumers find real estate agents' websites much more valuable than the agents think. As discussed before, this could be driven by the delays in real-time data updates for many online sites (e.g., the home shows as active when it is actually under contract or sold). Or it could be driven by the concern shared by many buyers that they will miss the "perfect" home, and they want as many sites to search as possible. You should discuss this with your client, so you can customize how you can address this information gap.
- "Provide info on neighborhoods, schools, etc." This is also discussed above.
- "Provide online info on homes that meet criteria." We hypothesize that most clients, particularly Millennials, have strong Internet search skills. However, they do not purchase or sell a home often. This lack of experience, and the large financial impact of their choice, drives them to seek the advice of an expert to double check or corroborate their findings. This is a critical element of real estate agent value to the consumer that is unlikely to go away, even as Internet tools become more powerful. You should take the time to discuss this with your clients.
- "Refer service providers." The same logic from the prior point applies here.

Agents vs. broker/owners: Assessments of the value of specific services

We surveyed the owners of the largest firms in the U.S. Exhibit 9-6 is similar to Exhibit 9-4. The only difference is that we are exploring the difference between agent and brokerage owner assessments of service importance. How do agents' views of which services are important compare to the degree of support and training provided by realty owners? Is there a misallocation of resources?

- The graph in the middle displays agents' assessments of service importance. You have seen this in previous charts.
- The graph on the right shows broker/owners' assessments. These are generally a lot higher than agents' views.
- The graph on the left is the perception gap between agents and owners.

Exhibit 9-5: Agents and Owners: Gap analysis: value of consumer support services.

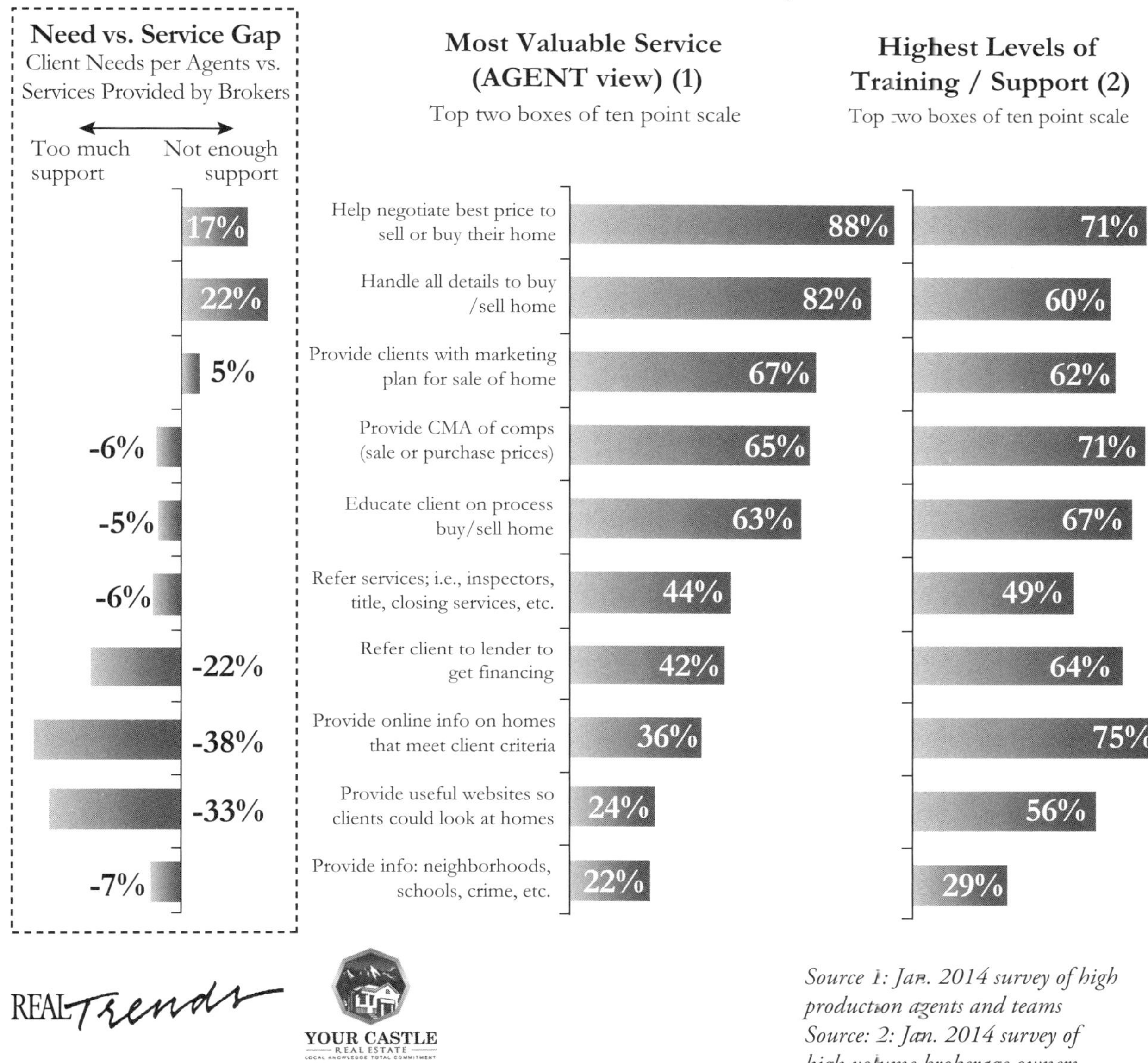

Where brokerages can do more

These are the biggest areas where agents felt they needed more support from their brokerage:

- Negotiation training and support
- "Handle all the details to buy and sell my home." For agents—and brokerages—that want to follow a facilitator path, this is less important. For those that wish to

position themselves as "counselors," this might be the biggest area where you can make a difference.

- Odds are you already do many things to make a stressful move easier for your clients. It could potentially benefit all parties were you to take the time to integrate processes to make them work together more smoothly.
- You should document the breadth of concierge services you provide in marketing materials that would be appropriate at listing presentations and/or buyer consultations (if first-time buyers—and especially for busy professionals).

You might want to consider developing some case studies—what did the client need, and how did the brokerage and agent develop and deliver a comprehensive set of services to solve the challenge? These case studies would vary according to the agent's specialization, and specific services would probably remain the agent's responsibility in developing, managing, and communicating them. However, some of the counselor concierge services would no doubt be held in common for most clients, and could be developed at a brokerage level. This could provide an enduring strategic advantage to the brokerage in recruiting and retaining high-performance agents. Since this is a difficult-to-find, difficult-to-copy service with high value to agents and clients, it would enable the brokerage to maintain (or even grow) margins, too.

Below are a few case study examples for your consideration:

- Investor buyer who wants to build a portfolio of rental properties. What to buy? How many? Where to buy? What lenders are the right match? Property managers? CPA for support? Legal and insurance?
- Older empty nester needs to transition to assisted living. He or she will be moving from a 4,000-square-foot home lived in for 40 years to a 1,000-square-foot "apartment." There is a lot of deferred maintenance; many different contractors are needed. Pre-packing and staging would be a big issue for many. Advice on home furnishings: what to keep, what to sell, what to give away. Emotional support that transcends a normal transaction: Not everyone selling their last home is happy about this transition. Managing multiple decision makers, as the kids might be prompting the change. Homes that have 30-year-old kitchens and baths might benefit from a referral to a general contractor that can do these updates before selling, so the family can get top dollar. Which GC? Which updates to do?

- Landlord-by-accident has moved to another city due to a job transfer. Either could not sell prior home (perhaps it had negative equity, or did not want to sell at the bottom of the market) or did not want to. Now, either due to market appreciation, frustration with tenants, or vacancy, owner wants to sell. This client may need concierge support for home "detailing" and maintenance, support services while the home is available for showing (e.g., shoveling snow and yard maintenance for absentee owner), staging, and perhaps CPA/legal support on how to optimize the transaction.
- Very busy two-income professional couple wants to trade up. They want a real estate agent concierge to project-manage every element of the move. Beyond traditional real estate, staging, and home detailing, what else might that include? We would bet several of your high-production agents have stories for this.

Where brokerages might be able to work differently

Here's what we recommend, based on the survey's findings:

- "Provide online info on homes that meet criteria." Brokerage owners felt they were providing a lot of value here. The agents did not generally agree. However, the consumers generally found this to be a very valuable service. These gaps likely indicate an opportunity for agents and owners. Perhaps some of your agents' best clients could come in for a focus group after closing to provide feedback to agents and owners. How many of them used the brokerage's website? What were the best and worst features? Is it cost effective to make improvements? Share the results with your agents.
  - If you can demonstrate that your company website does, in fact, greatly meet consumer needs, you need to make your agents aware of this. This will drive retention and help with erosion of company dollar.
  - If your company website is not impressive or useful to end consumers, your brokerage is at a competitive disadvantage. Your retention of top agents could suffer as a result. You need to know the facts.
- "Refer client to lender." Other than Millennials, most clients did not find this to be very helpful. Agents considered it more useful than consumers did. We would hypothesize that consumers do not have much experience in evaluating the quality of the lender. Most every agent has lost a deal due to a low-quality mortgage

broker. Brokerage owners feel even more strongly about the importance of their lending referrals. Often they have a large financial interest in referring traffic, in a RESPA-compliant way, to preferred lenders. There is clearly a ommunication gap. Developing better consumer marketing materials to explain why all lenders are "not the same" and why preferred lenders can bring advantages to the consumer could narrow some of the gaps.

- "Provide info on neighborhoods, schools, etc." Both owners and agents gave low ratings to this service. Yet many segments of consumers rated it quite a lot higher. Brokerages could take advantage of economies of scale to develop materials for their agents that would address this type of information. This is another way that owners with a "counselor" strategy can add value in supporting their agents' sales efforts.

Chapter Ten

Challenges for brokerage owners today—and tomorrow

We surveyed 1,350 brokerage owners in January 2014. We asked them to assess their biggest challenges—today and in the future—regarding a number of topics. This chapter presents their concerns; they also offer some ideas about how to address these challenges. If you think the market will be more challenging in the future, you are not alone!

For more than a decade, REAL *Trends* has compiled an annual list of the 500 largest firms. REAL *Trends* also assembles a list of "up and comers," which are the firms that are not quite large enough (as measured by closed sides) to make the REAL *Trends* 500 list. In 2013 (the rankings we used for this survey), a firm needed to close 1,282 sides to make the REAL *Trends* 500. Up and comers' sides ranged from 500 to 1,458.

Exhibit 10-1: Owners: Demographics of survey respondents vs. brokerage owner population.

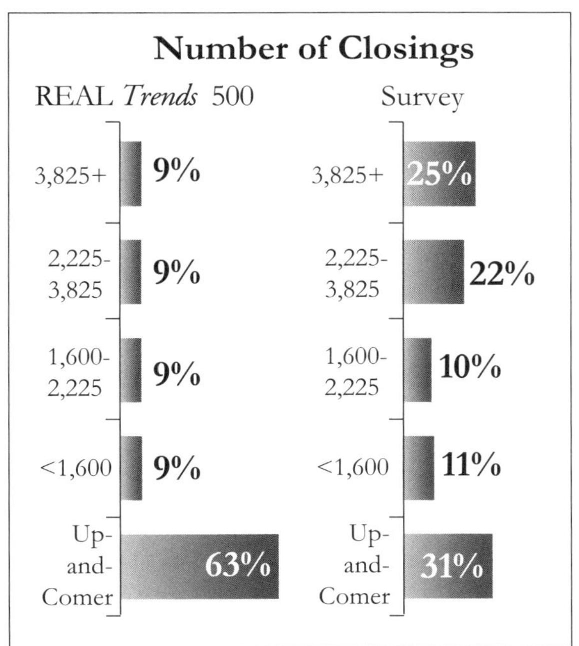

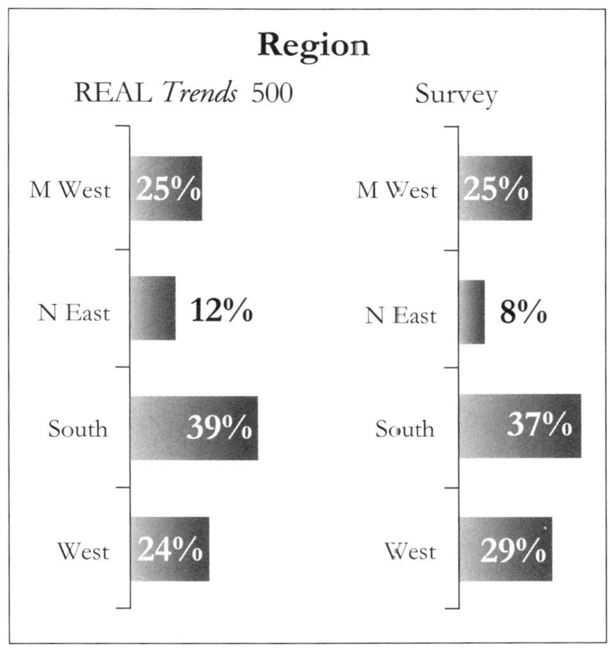

Source: Jan. 2014 survey of 1,350 brokerage owners

REAL Trends

Exhibit 10-1 displays the demographics of our survey respondents by both number of closings and region; Exhibit 10-2 displays demographics by the owner's age and years at the helm.

The owners who responded to the survey were skewed to the largest firms, as measured by closed transaction sides. Their geographic reach closely mirrored the overall U.S. average for large brokerages. Here is a summary of the firms that responded to the survey:

- Average volume: $845,000,000
- Average number of units sold: 3,450
- Average number of agents: 380
- Average units sold per agent: 9.1

Exhibit 10-2: Owners: Demographics of survey respondents.

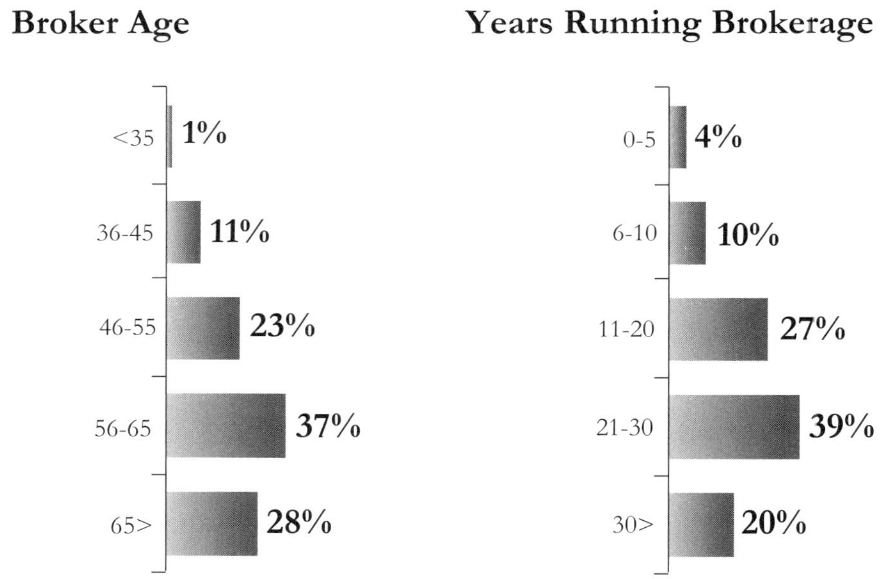

Broker Age

Age	Share
<35	1%
36-45	11%
46-55	23%
56-65	37%
65>	28%

Years Running Brokerage

Years	Share
0-5	4%
6-10	10%
11-20	27%
21-30	39%
30>	20%

REAL Trends

YOUR CASTLE REAL ESTATE LOCAL KNOWLEDGE TOTAL COMMITMENT

Source: Jan. 2014 survey of 1,350 brokerage owners

Today's challenges: What do brokerage owners consider their biggest vs. smallest?

When we asked owners to share their perspectives on today's challenges, here is what we found:

- Owners consider today's biggest challenges to be recruiting and retaining agents with the right pay plan (commission splits).
- Interestingly, a large number of respondents found "finding new managers" and "aging agents" to be among the biggest challenges, while not an insignificant number (16 and 10 percent respectively) found these to be among the smallest challenges.
- Most owners have completed their office right-sizing efforts. This is not a high concern any more.
- While off-market listings generated a lot of discussion, few owners see them as a big challenge.
- E+O (errors and omissions insurance) is not seen as a problem.

Exhibit 10-3: Owners: Biggest vs. smallest challenges today.

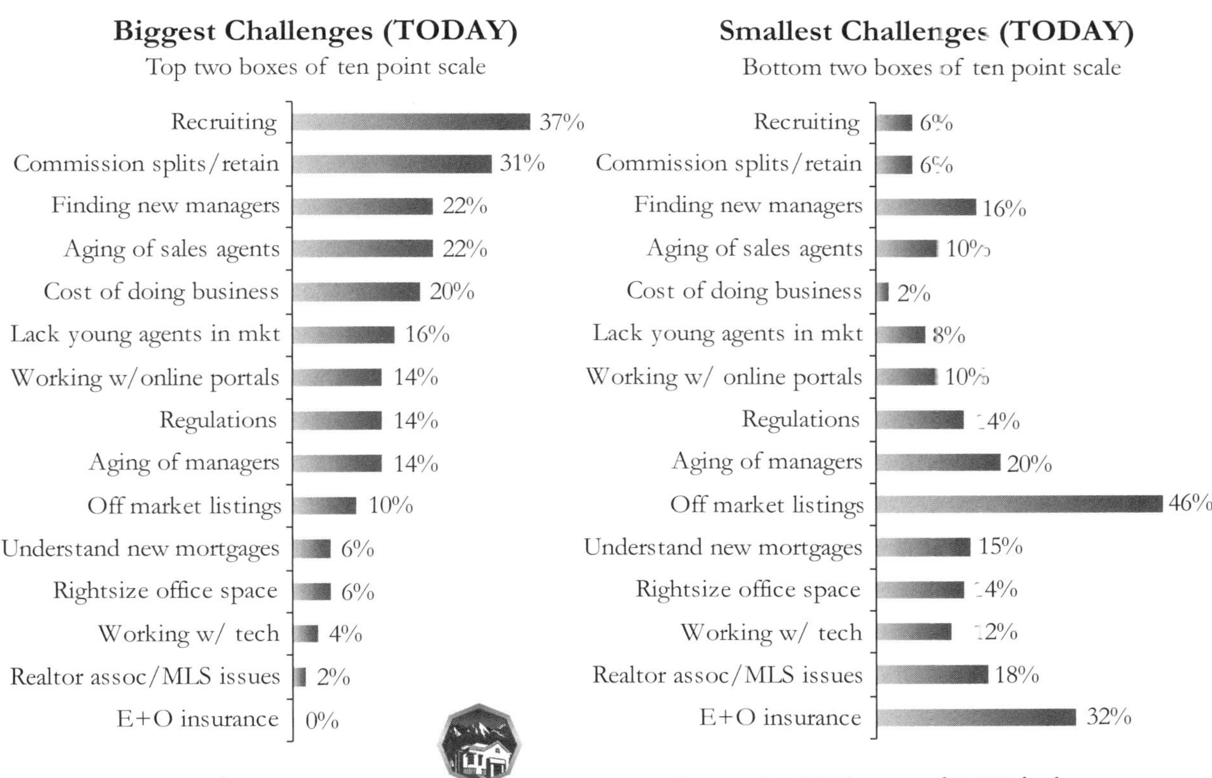

Source: Jan 2014 survey of 1,350 brokerage owners

We will discuss recruiting in more depth later in the chapter.

Here are some comments about the aging of real estate agents gleaned from detailed interviews with industry leaders:

President of a large independent firm with 1,900 agents:

> *Gen Y agents are behaviorally different. Many are less formal in their business dress. They rely more on electronic versus face-to-face communication. They do not come into the office as much and when they do it's for shorter periods of time. When recruiting, our focus is always on our culture; therein lies the challenge. We need to adapt our ideas as far as office attendance being a big part of our culture, and slightly relax our policy on dress. For instance, a suit without a tie, or a jacket and slacks, may be appropriate.*
>
> – Merle Whitehead, President, Realty USA

President of a large independent firm with 1,400 agents:

> *The real estate industry is dealing with a work force that works longer just like many other industries do. The challenge becomes attracting and retaining four different age demographics to your platform. They want different types of physical space, different types of communication, different types of technology, and different types of training/education. It also appears that the consumers prefer to deal with their same age demographic and that makes it tricky when you are either trying to build a business or wind down a business. As an agent you end up without a balance of buyers and sellers. One thing that is consistent among all age groups. They do gravitate toward and appreciate strong leadership. Continuing to attract and grow your leadership team will be paramount.*
>
> – Phyllis Brookshire, President, Allen Tate Realtors

Owner of a large independent firm with 250 agents:

Changes in the economy along with a lack of jobs have led more of the Gen Y group to want to be in charge of their own future. Real estate is becoming an option for them. These new, younger, tech savvy agents should do well. They understand how to network face to face and how to use social media.

– Nancy Fennell, President, Dickson Realty

President of a large franchise brokerage with 4,000+ agents:

During the recession, we had few new agents entering the real estate business. If they did come into the business, most were not as successful as the seasoned veterans. The experienced agents continued to do most of the business and reap the benefits of their longevity. In the last two years, there has been an influx of new agents who are experiencing improved market conditions. The gap that was created during the recession, however, is still apparent. Our industry needs to do a better job of attracting young new talent in order to thrive in the future.

– Joan Docktor, President, Berkshire Hathaway HomeServices Fox & Roach, Realtors/The Trident Group, Philadelphia, PA

Today's biggest challenges: larger firms vs. smaller firms

Exhibit 10-4: Owners: Biggest challenges today (large firms vs. smaller firms).

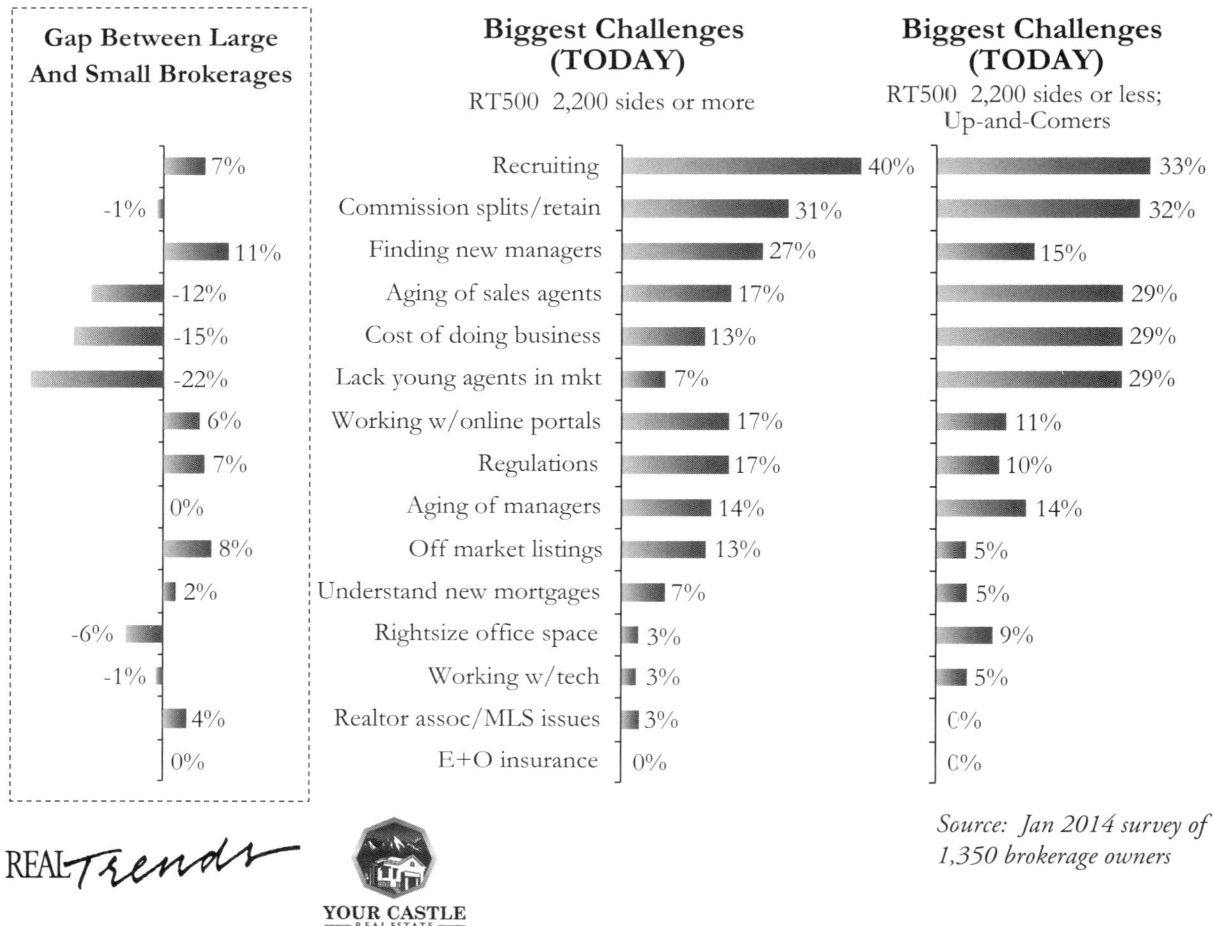

How do the larger firms differ from smaller firms in their views on today's biggest challenges? Our findings:

- Both large- and smaller-firm owners said that their biggest current concerns were recruiting and commission plans.
- Smaller firms are more concerned about finding new managers. This might be because larger firms have more experience in locating great managers. The process of bringing in new management talent might be a rare experience for a smaller firm (especially if it has only been managed by the owner for its entire history).

- Larger firms are more concerned than smaller firms about the aging of sales agents, cost of doing business, and the lack of young sales agents in the market.
- Virtually no one is worried about:
    - Changes with mortgage regulations
    - Off-market listings
    - Technology
    - MLS/associations, and E+O

Today's biggest challenges: younger vs. older owners

Younger brokerage owners and older brokerage owners were frequently divided in what they chose as their biggest challenges. Here's what we learned:

- Younger owners were more concerned about (younger vs. older owners):
    - Changes in regulations (20 percent vs. 10 percent)
    - Working with technology (10 percent vs. 0 percent)
- Older owners were more concerned about (older vs. younger owners):
    - Recruiting (48 percent vs. 20 percent)
    - Cost of doing business today (26 percent vs. 10 percent)
    - Finding new managers (27 percent vs. 15 percent)
- Concerns shared by owners of all ages (older vs. younger owners):
    - Splits (29 percent vs. 35 percent)
    - Aging of sales agents (19 percent vs. 25 percent)
    - Lack of younger agents entering the market (13 percent vs. 20 percent)

Exhibit 10-5: Owners: Biggest challenges today (younger vs. older owners).

Gap Between Young And Old Owners	Biggest Challenges (TODAY)	Owner Under 55	Owner Over 55
-28%	Recruiting	20%	48%
6%	Commission splits/retain	35%	29%
-12%	Finding new managers	15%	27%
6%	Aging of sales agents	25%	19%
-16%	Cost of doing business	10%	26%
7%	Lack young agents in mkt	20%	13%
-7%	Working w/online portals	10%	17%
10%	Regulations	20%	10%
2%	Aging of managers	15%	13%
0%	Off market listings	10%	10%
-2%	Understand new mortgages	5%	7%
-10%	Rightsize office space	0%	10%
10%	Working w/tech	10%	0%
-3%	Realtor assoc/MLS issues	0%	3%
0%	E+O insurance	0%	0%

Source: Jan 2014 survey of 1,350 brokerage owners

REAL Trends

YOUR CASTLE REAL ESTATE

Future biggest vs. smallest challenges

What are brokerage owners most concerned about in terms of what their firms may face down the road? Here's what we found:

- Today's biggest challenges were recruiting and retaining agents with the right split. These were important future issues as well. Owners expect recruiting to get harder and managing splits to get easier.
- Finding new managers, the aging of agents, and the cost of doing business were all perceived as a bigger challenge in the future than today.
- The aging of managers is not a concern today (14 percent)—but it's a significant future concern (31 percent).

- The topics whose challenge level increased the most between today and the future were: the aging of managers (+17 percent), the aging of agents (+10 percent), and the cost of doing business (+8 percent).
- Working with tech, off-market listings and E+O were at the bottom of the worry list in the future, just as they are in the present.

Exhibit 10-6: Owners: Biggest vs. smallest challenges in future

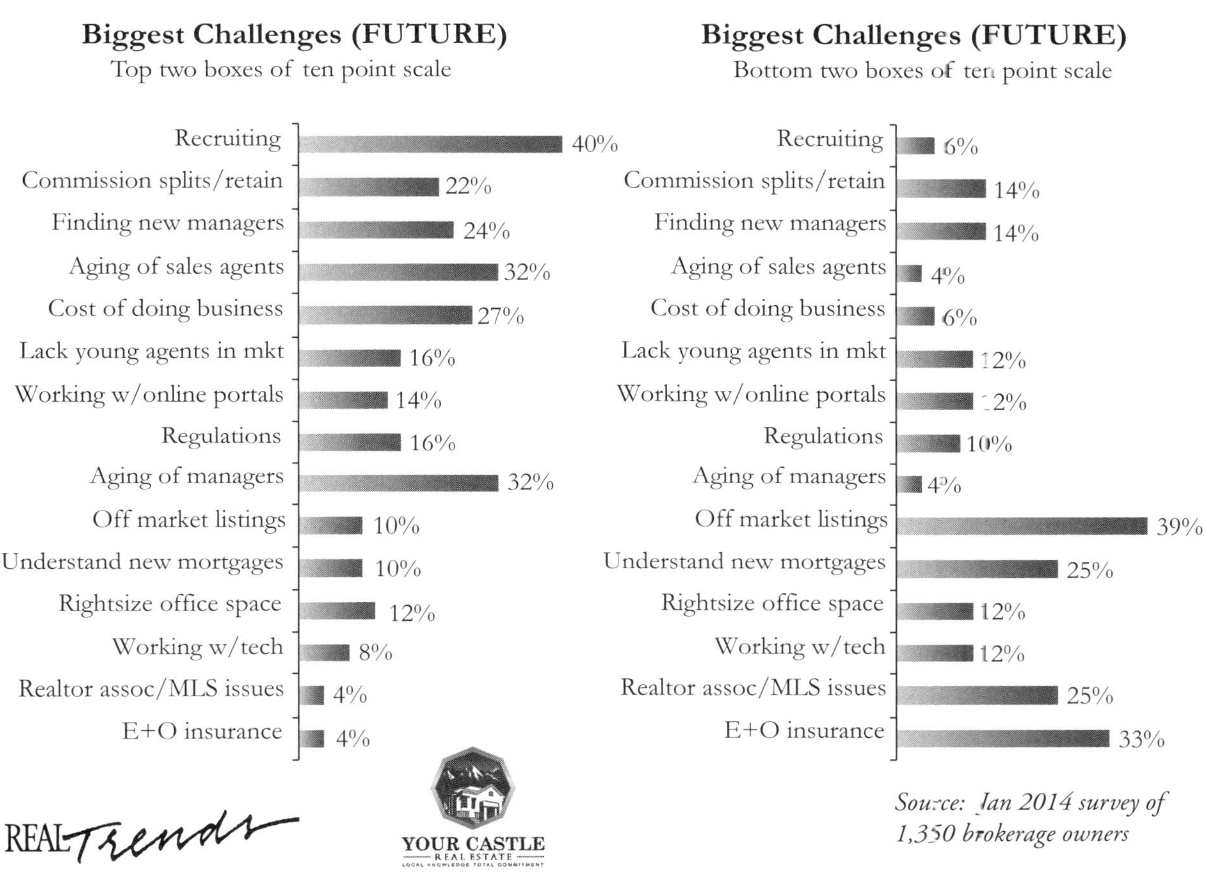

One interesting finding from our survey (which is not illustrated here): In considering their present situation, smaller firms were twice as likely to rate a challenge as small. But when asked about the future, both small and large firms, on average, ranked their challenges about the same. Does this imply that smaller firms think their advantage over large firms might narrow over time?

Future big challenges: younger vs. older owners

Younger and older owners diverged on many assessments of what they considered to be the largest future challenges. Younger owners were more concerned about:

- The lack of new agents entering the market (30 percent of younger owners were concerned vs. 6 percent of older owners)
- Finding new managers (30 percent vs. 19 percent)

Older owners were more concerned about:

- The cost of doing business in the future (42 percent of older owners vs. 5 percent of younger owners)
- Working with online portals (19 percent vs. 5 percent)
- Recruiting (45 percent vs. 35 percent)

Exhibit 10-7: Owners: Biggest future challenges (younger vs. older owners).

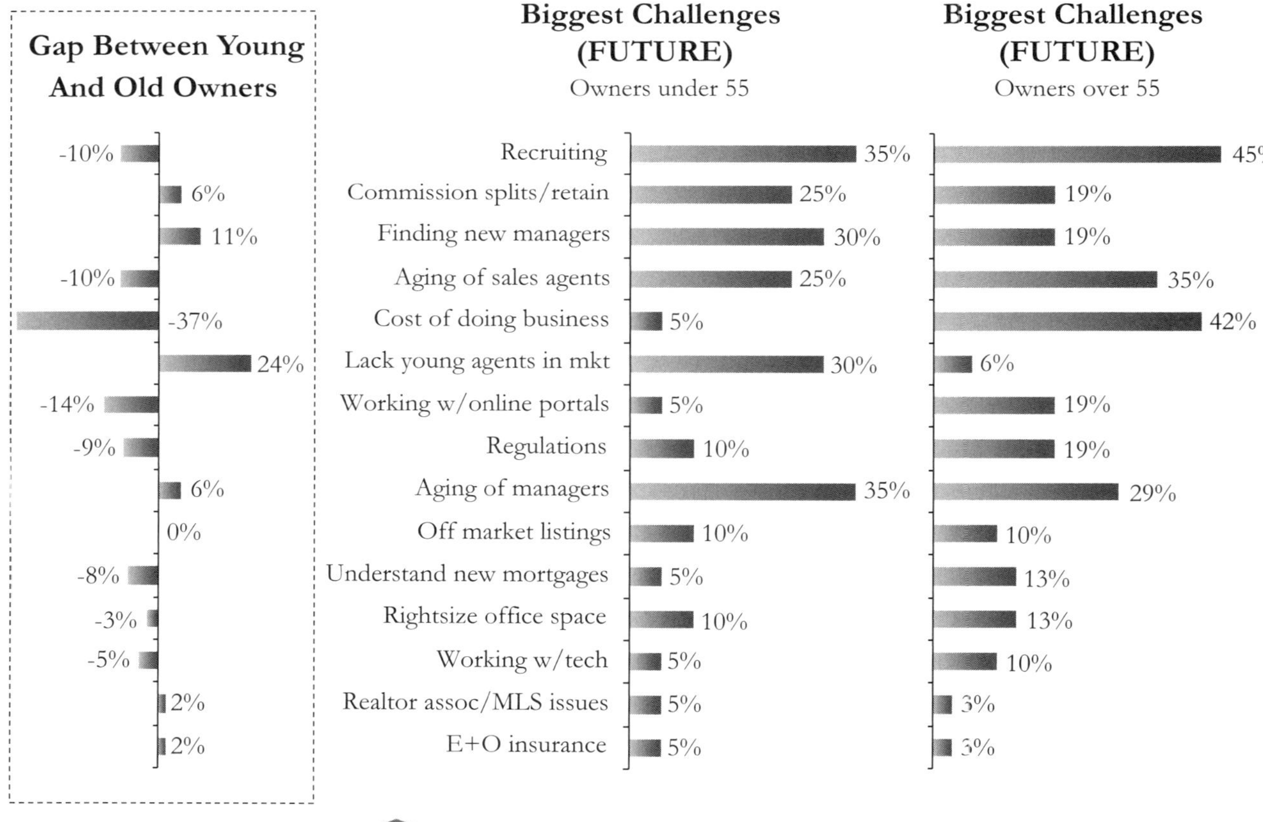

Source: Jan 2014 survey of 1,350 brokerage owners

All respondents were fairly equally concerned (in terms of concern level) about issues such as managing splits, the aging of managers, off-market listings, technology, MLS and Realtor associations, and E+O insurance.

Recruiting

To get at information on recruiting, we segmented brokerage owners into four groups, based on their changes in closed sides between 2008 and 2012. We chose this metric instead of sales volume to eliminate bias, as many markets appreciate at different rates. The four groups were segmented in this fashion:

- Flat or declining growth (REAL *Trends* 500)
- 10-50 percent growth (REAL *Trends* 500)
- 51 percent or higher growth (REAL *Trends* 500)
- All owners on the up-and-comer list

We knew that recruiting would come up as a challenge. On our survey, we asked brokerage owners how they currently find the people who join their firms. Options included:

- New hire was referred to me by my agent
- My sales manager found them
- Through a co-op deal with my agent
- Independent real estate school
- My recruiter found them
- Found via online ad
- My (company-owned) real estate school
- Other

Exhibit 10-8: Owners: How do Brokerages attract agents to their firm?

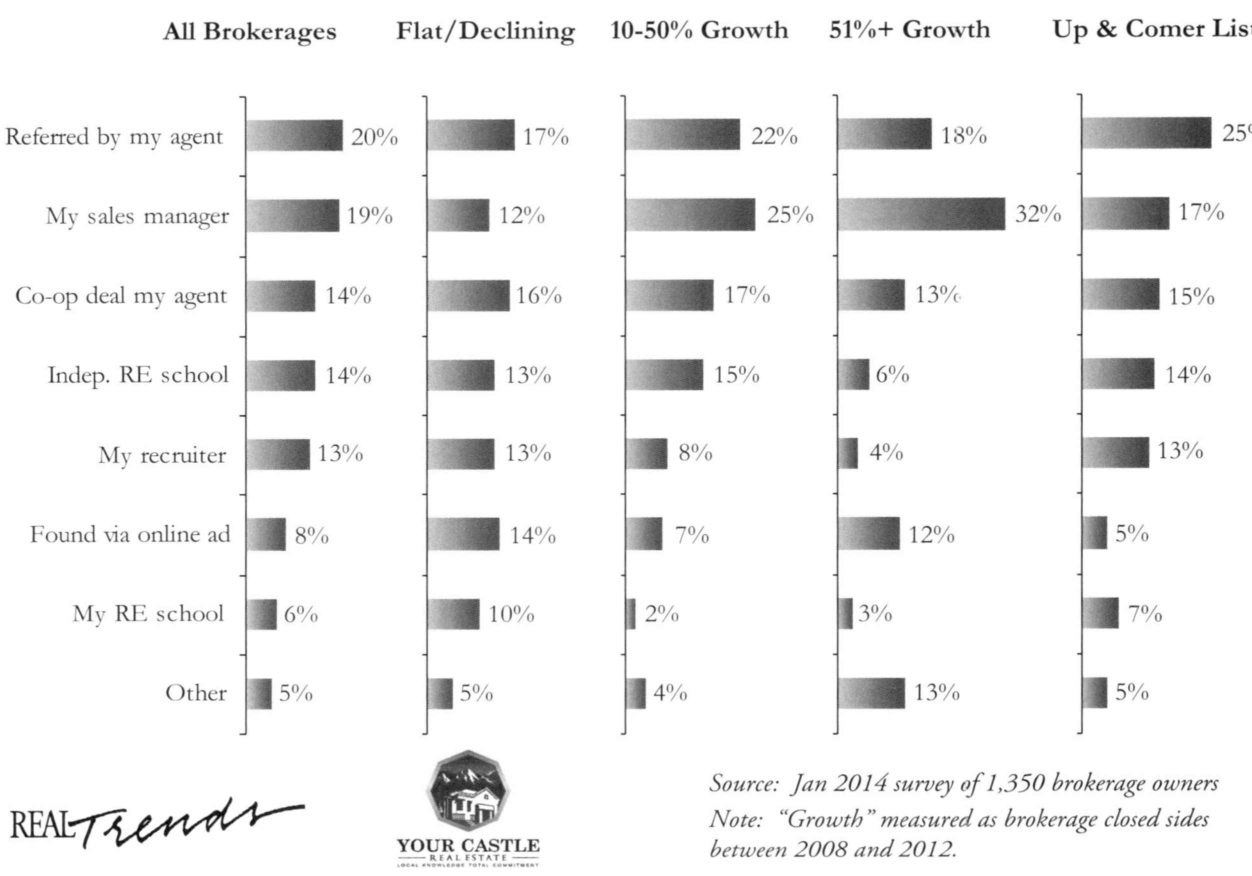

Source: Jan 2014 survey of 1,350 brokerage owners
Note: "Growth" measured as brokerage closed sides between 2008 and 2012.

We found some differences in the patterns of recruiting, depending on firms' revenue trends:

- Most firms rely on referrals from their agents and sales managers for most of their hires.
- Firms with flat or declining revenue used every source with about the same level of success. No one source led the pack.
- Large firms with moderate growth over the four years (10-50 percent) relied most on their sales managers to drive recruiting growth. Agent referrals were almost as important.
- Larger firms with the fastest growth (over 51 percent) relied the most on their sales managers for recruiting, and did not use a recruiter at all. Real estate schools were not very important to this high-growth group, either.

- Smaller firms (up-and-comer list) tended to use agent referrals to drive recruitment growth. The next four sources were almost a tie:
  - Sales managers: 17 percent
  - Coop deals with my agents: 15 percent
  - Independent real estate school: 14 percent
  - Recruiter: 14 percent

In talking with industry leaders, these are some of the key comments they made about the importance of culture, recruiting, and retention of agents:

President of a large independent firm with 1,400 agents:

> *We believe that culture is critical to the differentiation of our firm and is a major reason we have been successful. Attracting new talent is obviously a priority. I think it is harder for the younger agents to get started in real estate than it was when many of us started right out of college. They are carrying more debt and there is a lot of competition, and in many ways, the playing field is very leveled. Keeping a balance of experienced, older agents and younger agents who have great new ideas and approaches becomes an opportunity to grow our companies. If we can figure out how to attract a wider diversity of agents, both in ethnicity and age, we will be able to give the consumer what they want and need.*
>
> – Phyllis Brookshire, President, Allen Tate Realtors

President of a large independent firm with 1,900 agents:

> *Although we keep the core of our culture in place, we exhibit flexibility in our programs. For instance we did away with the "Sales Associate of the Month" award because the top agent or team would always win. We switched to a monthly "Personal Best" award, so that more people get to participate in recognition.*
>
> – Merle Whitehead, President, Realty USA

Owner of a large independent firm with 190 agents:

> *If you had to start over, what would you do? Centralized recruiting could be a better process than what we do now. I would specialize more among the staff. Managing brokers for deal doctor vs. being a manager vs. being a coach: different roles; different people.*
>
> – David Stark, President, Stark Company Realtors

President of a large franchise brokerage with 4,000+ agents:

> *It is important to have a culture where you can provide agents with a path to achieve success to meet their goals and dreams. Some things that agents value include training and coaching opportunities, state-of-the-art technology, recognition and rewards, a collaborative environment, networking opportunities, marketing support for personal branding, and management that not only listens, but hears. With the size and resources of our company, we can provide agents with all the tools that they need to create a growing business.*
>
> – Joan Docktor, President, Berkshire Hathaway HomeServices Fox & Roach, Realtors/The Trident Group, Philadelphia, PA

Senior manager at a national franchise:

> *The aging of our industry and the inability to consistently attract the next generation of talent is a major concern. In some respects the topic has been concealed in recent years with industry consolidation and lower business levels, though with the recovery will come a greater sense of urgency about succession planning. Greater opportunities within the industry as a result of rising business levels will enhance the attraction, though are there more structural elements to the business that must change to effect the generational transfer? The need for focused succession planning is at every level from the organizational leader, branch managers, through the sales professional. This is not a new discussion, but each year we see the need growing and unless we demonstrate real progress in the next five years it is going to be a train wreck.*
>
> – Budge Huskey, President, Coldwell Banker Real Estate LLC, Madison, NJ

* * * * * * *

The survey results suggest that there is no one way to succeed at recruiting. The best firms might leverage agent referrals, sales managers, trips to real estate schools, AND an in-house recruiting team to maximize results.

Conclusion

Many business books about the future attempt to scare the reader into believing that the future is dim, that forces of change will soon make all existing participants obsolete. This is not one of those books.

Our goal was to examine some of the great fears about the future that exist in the residential realty business and through surveys, interviews and research determine whether the foundation for these fears was warranted. We outlined the forces that favor the change, those that oppose it, the implications should a change happen and lastly some solutions. We know that the fears we have outlined are not a complete list of everyone's concerns nor do we think that we have covered every possible outcome within the fears that we outline in the book.

We think that while no one issue that we cover in *Game Changers* is likely to cause catastrophic disruption in the industry, each has the ability to force change at the margin – to push agents, brokerage firms and housing consumers into change that is not comfortable to contemplate, much less easy to accommodate. We think that there will be change in each of these areas and mostly in the direction cited in the book. Further we believe that some industry participants will not adjust their businesses to these changes and will have diminished prospects as a result.

Change in the residential realty industry has historically been evolutionary, not revolutionary. Many who thought they could dramatically change this industry from the outside found that they had to make peace with the industry and become partners, not antagonists. We think much will be the same going forward. Put another way we think that if you found a way to adapt and survive the last ten years, you will likely be able to adapt and survive over the next ten years.

Executive Summary for Real Estate Agents

If you do not have time to read the entire book, this will give you the key points for real estate agents. Four of the Game Changers really apply to you:

1. Agent segmentation: Facilitators and Counselors
3. Ratings and reviews begin to matter
6. Commission rates continue to sink
8. The listing portals lock up the consumer relationship

Relevant, but as not critical, are one Game Changer and two appendices:

5. Homeownership rate declines
A. What realty services do consumers really value?
C. How very high production agents find their clients

Five Key Points for Real Estate Agents

- You will not wake up one morning and discover Google or Zillow invented a death ray to put you out of business.
- Anyone who survived the last ten years will survive the next ten years.
- As with all industries, competition intensifies over time.
    - o Margins are compressed unless you innovate.
    - o Real estate is no exception.
- "The fundamentals of the real estate deal remain the same—tech helps, but is both a distraction and an enabler." – David Stark
- The changes in this book will be gradual.

<u>Agent segmentation: Facilitators and Counselors</u>

The opportunities and challenges are the same. Maybe 60% of real estate sales people are Facilitators; they do not have the skill set, because they have not done enough transactions. They have not moved their game up to a high-enough level to be a Counselor in the future. They just present offers and show properties. Ten years ago—that was all you needed.

Now the clients have all the information and you need to be an interpreter, not a provider. All that shifts to the counseling side of things. The concern: How much will the industry shift to facilitating needs for the clients versus counseling needs for clients?

In the future, we will have two groups:

1. *High-level advisory and counseling because of experience, knowledge and skills. You're able to really add value to your client's decision making on buying a home or investment property.*
2. *Somebody who says, "You want to go to those four homes, I will take you there. I will help you fill out that documentation, do the paperwork and get the deal closed."*

Facilitators and Counselors get the same commission today, but not in the future.

– Dan Elsea, President, Real Estate One, Detroit, MI
($4+ billion in sales)

Technology is attempting to devalue the role of the Realtor. The average buyer or seller has gone online and done their homework on pricing. It is critical to develop the relationship with the clients by providing value added services such as expertise in the local market and transaction management. Prepare buyers and sellers with the mechanics of the transaction and highlight the pain points. This includes the hurdles of the mortgage process. These items are much more valuable than taking the clients in a car and driving them around, although that is a good opportunity to develop the relationship.

– Ayoub Rabah, Great Street Properties, Chicago, IL (600+ sides)

We did a survey of consumers. We asked, "Are real estate agent services less valuable now that so much information is available on the Internet?"

- Millennials, those under 33 years old, agreed 49% of the time.
- Traditional consumers, those over 61 years old, agreed 30%.

According to the most recent NAR consumer survey, 23% of Millennial sellers preferred a limited-service brokerage rather than a full-service brokerage, compared to 8% for all sellers. Additionally, only 42% of Millennial sellers were very satisfied with the selling process, according to NAR.

Market trend:

- High production agents and teams have a large share of the market, and they will continue to capture more market share in the next decade.
    - o They close more deals, generate more revenue, invest more in business… creates a positive feedback loop.
    - o Many on-line ad systems require scale to be efficient. This is a barrier to entry for lower production agents.

Foundation ideas:

- Portals (Zillow, Trulia) provide market trends and valuation tools.
- Online MLS resources are plentiful and easy for consumers to use.
- Consumers will be able to do more of the research and planning on their own.
    - o Consumer reliance on agents to provide market and MLS data will continue to decline.
    - o Consumer reliance on agents to interpret their research – often with conflicting sources – will increase.
- The real estate transaction is complex. We believe regulations will make it more complex in the future.
- The fundamentals of the real estate deal remain the same—tech helps, but is both a distraction and an enabler. Homes are a perfectly non-commoditized asset. That does not lend itself to "Amazon marketplace." (David Stark)

Results:

- The high value of the transaction, the inability to return the product if you are not happy, and lack of experience (most consumers buy every 7-10 years) ensures agents will always have a role.
- FSBO (For Sale By Owner) will not grow much in market share in the next decade.
- However, many Millennials may shoulder more of the workload of the home buy/sell and assign less responsibility (and commission) to real estate agents.
- The Facilitator is the middle path between high value, high cost, high service traditional Counselor and the low cost, little service FSBO. We expect this segment to grow at the expense of the traditional real estate "generalist" agent.

- The change will be gradual over time, as Millennials become a larger share of the market.
- We believe that large teams succeed, in part, because they are process driven. They will be best positioned to capture the growing market share from the Facilitator transactions.

Your strategic choices:

- If you have less than ten years to retirement:
  - You can coast.
  - These trends will not happen fast enough to threaten your core repeat and referral business.
- If you have more than ten years in your career:
  - You need to make this trend work for you.
  - Defend your core (repeat and referral business) with the outstanding service and relationship skills you already have.
  - Exploit this Counselor / Facilitator trend to capture additional market share.
- Pick a model.
  - Both Nordstrom and Walmart are profitable.
  - Both are highly defendable market niches.
  - Real estate will not polarize as much as the retail industry in the next decade, but the trend is already in place.
  - Being an undifferentiated generalist killed Montgomery Ward, K-Mart and Sears.

Your next steps:

- Facilitator Track
  - You need more deals. You should have less work per deal, at a lower commission. Your dollar per hour should increase.
  - You will need very efficient transaction management processes.
  - Develop marketing that attracts and incubates the price sensitive clients Counselors cannot or don't want to handle.

- o This is an economy of scale game. If you are a big producer now, this trend is likely very right for you.
- Counselor Track
  - o Not as many deals, more work per deal, higher commissions per deal. Your dollar per hour should increase.
  - o Develop market knowledge and "concierge" service.
  - o Develop marketing that attracts clients that want high service and are willing to pay a premium to get it.
- Enablers for either Track
  - o Highly efficient CRM and core support processes
  - o Strong "Core" transaction management
  - o Pay attention to time management and productivity; defend prospecting time as you scale up.

<u>Ratings and reviews begin to matter</u>

Consumers research virtually everything based on ratings—cameras, hotels, restaurants, etc. HAR surveyed 7,000 real estate consumers last year, and 90 percent found agent ratings to be helpful in their decision of which real estate professional to hire. Yelp, Redfin, ZipRealty, Coldwell Banker brokers, Better Homes & Gardens brokers, Trulia and Zillow (400,000+ agent ratings) all offer consumers some form of agent ratings. HAR offers agent ratings on a voluntary basis and currently 4,200 agents are being rated with 83,000 clients surveyed responding favorably about their experience with their agent.

– Bob Hale, CEO, Houston Association of REALTORS, Houston MLS

....

The consumer is going to love it [ratings], and Realtor.com will not be able to do it because 70% of the agents do not want ratings because it favors the top producers. Therefore, they [NAR, associations, MLSs] will not be able to get it done and somebody from the outside will.

Most people know 10 realtors—which one to pick? Look online for ratings—who sells the most homes in my neighborhood. Even if you are referred to three Realtors, what is the tiebreaker? Ratings.

– Neal Hanks, President, Beverly Hanks Brokerage (250+ Realtors)

....

We did a survey of consumers. We asked, "Will you look at agent performance website for next deal?"

- Consumers in all generations value relationships. Regardless, adoption of ratings is poised to take off rapidly.
    - o Traditional, over 61 years old: 15%
    - o Millennial, under 33: 45%
- This will shift market share, probably to agents who are more productive or have more experience in a particular segment of the market.

We asked, "For your next real estate transaction, how many ratings websites will you consult?"

- Oldest consumers: **None**, or about the same number as last time.
    - o They have a trusted advisor and they plan to be loyal to them.
- Millennials generally have limited agent relationships (relative to older consumers).
    - o Much more expected reliance on future ratings sites.
    - o Millennials are already doing more web research currently.
    - o That gap should grow dramatically in the near term.

"Would you prefer the agent you knew well or an agent with specific skills?"

- For all generations, "the agent I know" won the majority of the time.
- However, a sizable minority of young consumers (33%!) were either much more likely or somewhat more likely to choose a "specialized agent found by a website."

"If there were a website that offered ratings of real estate agents and consumer reviews, how likely would you be to use such a website?"

- Millennials had significantly more reliance on websites.
- Older consumers did not.

"How helpful do you think it would be to know how many real estate deals an agent was involved in, in the neighborhood you are interested in?"

- EVERY generation tended to find this information to be helpful.
- Even older consumers, with agent strong relationships, want this.

"How likely are you to use your last transaction's agent again for a future transaction?"

- A large number of people of all ages were happy with their agent. Most plan to use this person again.
- However, cracks are forming in the wall with younger consumers.
    - o They were less likely than older consumers to select "definitely will use again." NAR research has had the same findings.
    - o Merely "likely" was selected much more often.
    - o For this group, the strength of intent for repeat business is not as powerful as it is for older consumers.

Implications

- Repeat and referral is a powerful channel for agent selection today and will continue to be in the future.
    - o This is especially true for older consumers who tend to be loyal and tend to have very established relationships with agents.
    - o Millennials generally do not have these established connections and a meaningful share of their transactions will probably NOT be referral based.
- We expect the percentage of agents selected by repeat and referral to erode gradually over time.

Your next steps:

- If you do not have an area of specialization, consider developing one.
    - o Works well with the Counselor vs. Facilitator trend.
    - o Also lends itself to rating / review marketing channel.
- Learn how to guide your clients through giving you reviews.
    - o Make it a regular part of your post-close process.
- Set up profiles on all of the sites.
- Make maintaining and updating your profiles a regularly occurring (perhaps quarterly) process.
- For review sites that also have Q+A with consumers (e.g., Trulia), consider investing some time into building a "reputation" there, too.

- Do not overlook the obvious tools like LinkedIn.
- Set up a Google alert for your name, so you know when new material is posted about you.
- While you are at it, set up Google alerts for your key neighborhoods and/or areas of interest, to maintain your leading edge expertise.

"While downward pressure on commissions may continue into the next decade, hopefully with continued increase in home values, the impact on Realtors may not be that significant. There will always be a place for flat fee and discounters, but the savvy consumer will still adhere to the adage of getting what you pay for. There will be Realtors that have the knowledge, technology and tools to justify their fees and those that won't be able to invest in their business that will be forced to discount their services."

– Chad Ochsner, Owner, RE/MAX Alliance Colorado (800 agents)

Discussion points:

- The book has an outline for the arguments for continued average commission erosion over time. We will not cover them in this summary.
- Just because the *average* commission declines does not mean that your commissions will decline.
- Implement the Facilitator / Counselor ideas, and you will thrive.

Your next steps:

- If you choose Facilitator, become the low cost provider.
  - o Rapidly scale up your operations.
  - o Biggest, lowest cost provider in market wins: Think Walmart.
  - o While you might not want to adopt all of the counselor ideas, you might selectively implement a few. That alone might help add enough additional value to retain your commission rates while others in your market have to discount more.

- Avoid expensive technology "shiny objects." Just get efficient.
- Do not fall into trap of thinking Nordstrom "Counselor" approach is best since it is more prestigious.
- Walmart makes a lot of money and they have a VERY strong competitive position.

The listing portals lock up the consumer relationship

- An industry **leader**, "In the past, the firm with the most listings drove the most leads. With the strength of the portals, that is becoming less and less the case."
- Another **leader** said, "They have 60 million consumers a month visiting their site and 400,000 agent ratings and growing. They have over 20 individual mobile web apps. No broker has that or is ever going to have that. We have heard that they intend to start charging referral fees as well."
- One **top agent**: "I spend tens of thousands of dollars a month on the portals and make a large profit doing so. I plan to increase that spending because it makes sense for my business."
- Another **top agent**: "I have found it is the most effective manner of reaching new, younger customers whom I don't know personally yet. It's the future of my business."
- **MLS CEO**: "Portals can't eliminate Realtors, but they could replace the MLS."

As business markets move from information asymmetry to information parity, there will be pressure on the suppliers of service in that market to add new value (D. Pink). So it is in residential brokerage – we have moved from where the agent had all the information (information asymmetry) to where the customer has access to the same information (information parity) as the agent. Nothing about the market will ever be the same again.

> *I think they're accelerating. Zillow and Trulia get a lot of press in our industry, so we get drawn into thinking how big they are. You talk to an average consumer and they are only casually engaged with them. So it really hasn't taken hold yet but it will, in terms of lead generation for our industry.*

The next generation (the Millennials) will certainly be more used to going online to gather all their information, as well as their friends, clients, and social conversation. So I think the reason it took so long for web leads to grow is because we had control of the information. The consumers had to come to us for information and that also made us a little bit lazy as an industry. Our service was providing information, which meant you didn't have to have a skill set as high as you might if the client came to you with the information. Going forward we will have to be the interpreter and the manager of information.

It happened to stockbrokers the same way. Stock data became available online so consumers could get that information quickly. I think technology has facilitated that change, but it's access to information that is the real driver. Access to information greatly changed the relationship between agents and brokers back in the 70s as well with the creation of the MLS. So this is just the next phase, shifting the information access from the agent to the consumer.

– Dan Elsea, President, Real Estate One, Detroit, MI ($2.5B+ sales in 2012)

Key findings from our custom research:

- Consumers are almost as familiar with large online real estate portals (e.g., Zillow, Trulia) as they are with traditional "brick-and-mortar" real estate brokerages (e.g., RE/MAX, Coldwell Banker, Keller Williams).
- **The level of trust consumers feel towards portals and major brokerage brands are almost the same.**
- While portals are newer to the industry, they have already had an impact on consumers, and have changed the way they shop for homes.

Implications:

- We think the portals pose the biggest threat to the MLS.
- We think the portals pose the smallest threat to the agents.
- Most consumers that have relied on repeat and referral in the past will continue to do so.
- The small, but growing consumer base (particularly Millennials) that do not use repeat and referral will segment between those that want Facilitators and those that prefer Counselors.

- The ratings and review websites will serve a role in playing matchmaker between consumers and agents. So will the portals. The portals (which will almost certainly increase their ratings and reviews over time) will become increasingly efficient at reselling those leads.

Your next steps:

- If you are a high production agent or team, this Game Changer plays to all of your strengths. You will take share from the agents that do not adapt. You will continue the trend of consolidation among agents.
- If you pick Facilitator, you will likely see the most share gain from your portal leads.
- If you choose to be a Counselor agent, you probably will not see as much incremental lead flow. However, these consumers will likely be **highly** attracted to your unique skills. They should be very high margin for you.
- If you elect to stick with your current repeat and referral business, you will never even notice the change. Odds are your business will not decline due to this Game Changer, it will simply stay relatively flat or not grow as much as the overall market.

Homeownership rate declines

Owner of a large RE/MAX with $3.6+ billion in closed sales volume in 2013:

> *If homeownership rates declined to 55% by 2025, the biggest challenge may be our message. How can our industry continue to sell the dream of homeownership and wealth creation to a generation that may not care?*
>
> *Fortunately, studies have shown that Millennials do want to own their home, but clearly face headwinds preventing them from buying and selling as soon and as often as generations before them (i.e., student loan debt). The sheer size of Generation Y will hopefully prevent this percentage decline from actually occurring. Fewer Millennials may be able to purchase a home, but because their numbers are so great, the impact may not be all that threatening.*
>
> – Chad Ochsner, President, RE/MAX Alliance, Denver, CO ($3.6+ Billion)

Every home has an owner. A decline in the homeownership rate just means more investor owners. Investors sell homes more often than owner occupants. Change means the buyers of homes change (owner occupants vs. investors) so agents need different skill sets. It's mainly a training issue.

– David Stark, President, Stark Company Realtors (200 Realtors)

Foundation ideas:

- Historically, about 65% of Americans have owned their home.
- The desire to do so is an ingrained habit with young and old alike.
- Government regulation, tax policy and financial markets have created highly favorable conditions for homeownership.
- The drive to enable more families to become homeowners was the biggest contributor to the housing downturn of 2005-2011. Too many were chasing home ownership without the financial means.

Results:

- Since 2004, the home ownership rate has declined 5%.
- Six million incremental families that rent versus own.
- First time homebuyers historically are about 35% of the market. They are notably absent from the current housing recovery.
- Although their desire to become owners remains strong, substantial student loan debt and a weak job market inhibit them.
- Stricter mortgage underwriting standards have had a chilling effect.
- Each factor may drive homeownership to permanently, lower levels.

The average small investor…

- Owns four properties.
- On average, buys and sells every five years. Owner occupants are closer to ten years on average.
- According to a large brokerage that did a detailed study, the average investor commission rate is identical to the average owner occupant commission rate.

- As a result, a decline in the home ownership rate will likely increase the number of transactions. The deal flow will be concentrated in the hands of a smaller number of property owners that select the real estate agents.

Your choices:

- Do nothing. Focus on the repeat and referral, mostly owner occupant business you have now. As with some other Game Changers, you will notice little change in your business, other than a slower rate of growth.
- Embrace the Facilitator track for investors.
  - o If you have a large Facilitator owner occupant practice, this is an obvious add-on to your business to drive enormous growth.
  - o Since Facilitators are not expected to bring much detailed expertise – just efficient transaction management – you already have most of what is needed.
  - o Our hypothesis is that investors, particularly on the listing side, will seek efficient Facilitators.
- Embrace the Counselor track for investors.
  - o Our hypothesis is that investors, particularly newer investors on the buy side, will be very attracted to the expertise of the Counselor.
  - o If you can develop the right skills and offering, you can build a lucrative practice. The book has extensive idea checklists.

What realty services do consumers really value?

We did customized survey of consumers that recently bought or sold a home. Most important real estate services, from consumer's point of view:

- Help negotiate best price to sell or buy their home, 82%.
- Provide useful web sites so clients could look at homes, 69%.
- Provide CMA of comps (sale or purchase process), 68%.

Thoughts:

- The big surprise is "provide web sites".
- Clients certainly have plenty of choices for MLS-type access online.

- They can use the portals (e.g., Zillow, Trulia), agent specific sites, or number of other options.
- We would guess that when clients get deep into the search process, real time data is very useful.
- Agents may feel they have nothing to offer clients for web listing access, but clients do not share that opinion.
- It is an opportunity for agents and firms.

We compared how important consumers found services vs. how well their agent actually performed.

- One topic, "help negotiate the price," had a negative score.
- Here, consumers felt this was the most important service, but that the agents generally did not perform as well as the consumers wanted.
- This is a training opportunity for agents to improve service levels. Unlike many important activities performed by agents, negotiation is highly visible to the consumer, easy to explain and demonstrate.

We checked to see if different consumer generations had different opinions:

- Help with negotiation is the most important agent skill from the consumer's point of view.
  - o Older clients (54%) were much more likely than younger clients (38%) to feel this way.
- From our interviews, we got the sense that many agents think consumers are doing their own CMA with online services like Zillow and Trulia.
  - o That is increasingly the case, but the agent's CMA is still very important, too.
  - o Older clients (29%) were more likely to think so than younger clients (17%)
- Not surprisingly, "Educate me on the process of buying or selling a home" was more useful to younger clients (24%) than older clients (6%).
- One of the biggest gaps was with "provide neighborhood information."
  - o There are many sources on the Internet for this information.
  - o While we would commonly consider younger people as more adept with the internet, they had a much higher opinion of the agent's value added (19%) than older consumers (1%).

- Our hypothesis is that older consumers already know what they want in housing and where to find it. The agent does not bring much to their decision process.
- The younger consumers told us they did extensive research on line, but they still want the advice and opinions of the agent to synthesize and prioritize their findings.

Your next steps: Reviews

- As reviews become more important, have your clients highlight your skills in negotiation and decision making support in their write-ups.
    - This will resonate with prospective clients reading your reviews.
    - The more specific the examples, the more persuasive they will be.
- If you work with a lot of first time buyers, or first time move-up clients, have your reviews document your time, care and attention in explaining the process.
- While it might be just considered a "given," if you focus on older clients, have at least a few interview comments on your extensive network of trusted suppliers (e.g., stagers, repair people, inspectors).
    - Show how they really made the transaction easier.
    - Also with older clients, the detail and accuracy of your CMA and the care in which you explained it would be persuasive.
- For all reviews, you want to coach your clients to be truthful, specific, and positive in their write up. Only dogs thrive on non-specific feedback.

FIRST CLIENT MEETING – MILLENNIALS

- Winning with younger clients is not just about being perceived as tech savvy. That is just the price of entry for agent to be considered as a possible service provider. The real differentiators are:
    - Providing (and confirming) the younger clients' on-line research about neighborhoods and helping them make good decisions about their housing trade-offs.
    - For the minority of younger buyers without a lender relationship, providing that referral.

- o Providing great negotiation support.
- o Taking the time to hold their hand and really explain how the process works.
  - Most agents that regularly work with first time buyers and first time move-up buyers excel at this.
  - The other three points offer much more opportunity.

FIRST CLIENT MEETING – TRADITIONAL (61+ years old)

- Negotiation is the biggest opportunity area.
- Most experienced agents are very good at developing a market analysis. These consumers very much value your expertise here! Keep doing what you are doing.
- While younger consumers are more likely to want to find their own service providers (e.g., home inspectors, stagers), older consumers are more likely to rely on the agent's network of trusted sources. Most experienced agents have no problem in this area. Be sure to talk about this during your listing appointments. It is easy to gloss over it, as you might not think it is important. For many older clients, it is important and it is an easy win for you.
- Certainly ask if the client wants help with lending, neighborhood information, and how the process works. However, most of these older clients will not feel that they need help here.

FIRST CLIENT MEETING – Gen X, Baby Boomers

- Negotiation is the biggest opportunity.
- Interestingly, these age cohorts were most likely to want to rely on the agent for "online info about homes that met criteria." The industry has come to assume the consumers will use their own online sources for this. For many clients that is true – but not for all of them.
  - o There could be several explanations.
  - o People in these age groups tend to be busy with career and family.
  - o They are generally move-up buyers, often with children.
  - o While they have the technical sophistication to find homes online, some

would rather pay you to think through it.

  - o Consider developing some questions in the initial interview to discover this.
  - o Consumers that want a "concierge" type approach are really telling you they want a "counselor" and not a "facilitator".

- Middle age consumer reliance on the agent to provide (or more likely confirm) their online research about neighborhoods (e.g., schools, crime) falls between Millennials and Traditional groups. That makes sense.
  - o Consider adding an interview question to probe how much interest any particular client has in your support in this area.
  - o Many will feel they can handle it on their own – which is probably what you suspected anyway.
  - o A minority will really appreciate your input. Be sure to provide that support when needed.

<u>How very high production agents find their clients</u>

Individual agents

- 67% of their closed business was from repeat business from past clients and referrals from people in their network.
  - o As you might expect, the amount of repeat and referral business declines as their overall production goes up.
  - o Thus, the absolute number of repeat and referral deals hits a ceiling.
  - o Further growth beyond that ceiling requires different prospecting methods.
- Third party referrals (generally relocation work) comprise about 9% of closed volume.
  - o This grows slightly as overall volume grows.
  - o However, it only accounts for a small fraction of that growth.
- 15% of closed volume, on average is from web leads, 9% is from sign calls and cold calls.
  - o For both lead sources, the reliance on these lead sources grows a lot after the agent "maxes out" their repeat and referral database.

Teams

- They follow the same general patterns as the individual producers.
- While reliance on web leads for individuals grows about 50% (from the lowest to highest production quartile), the teams use of web leads grows almost 300%.
- Similarly, for sign calls and cold calls, individuals see about 50% growth and teams see 200% growth.

Your next steps:

Mid-level producers (and teams) wishing to join the ranks of the largest producers will need to:

- Grow their repeat and referral process as far as they practically can. There seems to be a ceiling for most agents on how far this will scale.
- Add relocation business if practical to do so. While it is only 8-10% for most of the people we surveyed, that is still a sizable amount of volume.
- Develop systems and infrastructure (CRM, drip systems, call coordinators, tailored marketing materials) to capture growth from web leads and calls.

Web lead traffic could be from review and rating sites if the mid-level producer is able to develop an attractive profile. Alternatively, it could be from more "traditional" methods such as SEO optimization, outstanding content in a blog, or other approach.

* * * * * *

Many business books about the future attempt to scare the reader into believing that the future is dim, that forces of change will soon make all existing participants obsolete. This is not one of those books. We think there is incredible opportunity for real estate agents to grow in the next decade. We wish you the best of success.

Executive Summary for Brokers, Owners and Managers

If you do not have time to read the entire book, this will give you the key points for brokers, owners and managers. Three of the Game Changers really apply to you:

1. Agent segmentation: Facilitators and Counselors

6. Commission rates and gross margins continue to sink

8. The listing portals lock up the consumer relationship

Relevant, but as not critical, are two Game Changers and two appendices:

3. Ratings and reviews begin to matter

5. Homeownership rate declines

A. What realty services do consumers really value?

B. How very high production agents find their clients

<u>Five Key Points for Brokers, Owners and Managers</u>

- You will not wake up one morning and discover Google or Zillow invented a death ray to put you out of business.
- Anyone who survived the last ten years will survive the next ten years.
- As with all industries, competition intensifies over time.
  - Margins are compressed unless you innovate.
  - Real estate is no exception.
- "The fundamentals of real estate deal remain the same—tech helps, but is both a distraction and an enabler." – David Stark
- The changes outlined here will be gradual.

<u>Agent segmentation: Facilitators and Counselors</u>

The opportunities and challenges are the same. Maybe 60% of real estate sales people are Facilitators; they do not have the skill set, because they have not done enough transactions. They have not moved their game up to a high-enough level to be a Counselor in the future. They just present offers and show properties. Ten years ago—that was all you needed. Now the clients have all the information and you need to be an interpreter, not a provider. All that shifts to the counseling side of things. The concern: How much will the industry shift to facilitating needs for the clients versus counseling needs for clients?

In the future, we will have two groups:

1. *High-level advisory and counseling because of experience, knowledge and skills. You're able to really add value to your client's decision making on buying a home or investment property.*
2. *Somebody who says, "You want to go to those four homes, I will take you there. I will help you fill out that documentation, do the paperwork and get the deal closed."*

Facilitators and Counselors get the same commission today, but not in the future.

– Dan Elsea, President, Real Estate One (Detroit MI) 2013: $4.2 Billion

Technology is attempting to devalue the role of the Realtor. The average buyer or seller has gone online and done their homework on pricing. It is critical to develop the relationship with the clients by providing value added services such as expertise in the local market and transaction management. Prepare buyers and sellers with the mechanics of the transaction and highlight the pain points. This includes the hurdles of the mortgage process. These items are much more valuable than taking the clients in a car and driving them around, although that is a good opportunity to develop the relationship.

– Ayoub Rabah, Great Street Properties, Chicago, IL (600+ sides)

We did a survey of consumers. We asked, "Are real estate agent services less valuable now that so much information is available on the Internet?"

- Millennials, those under 33 years old, agreed 49% of the time.
- Traditional consumers, those over 61 years old, agreed 30%.

According to the most recent NAR consumer survey, 23% of Millennial sellers preferred a limited-service brokerage rather than a full-service brokerage, compared to 8% for all sellers. Additionally, only 42% of Millennial sellers were very satisfied with the selling process, according to NAR.

Market trend:

- High production agents and teams have a large share of the market, and they will continue to capture more market share in the next decade.
  - o They close more deals, generate more revenue, invest more in business… creates a positive feedback loop.
  - o Many on-line ad systems require scale to be efficient. This is a barrier to entry for lower production agents.

Foundation ideas:

- Portals (Zillow, Trulia) provide market trends and valuation tools.
- Online MLS resources are plentiful and easy for consumers to use.
- Consumers will be able to do more of the research and planning on their own.
  - o Consumer reliance on agents to provide market and MLS data will continue to decline.
  - o Consumer reliance on agents to interpret their research – often with conflicting sources – will increase.
- The real estate transaction is complex. We believe regulations will make it more complex in the future.
- The fundamentals of real estate deal remain the same—tech helps, but is both a distraction and an enabler. Homes are a perfectly non-commoditized asset. That does not lend itself to "Amazon marketplace." (David Stark).

Results:

- The high value of the transaction, the inability to return the product if you are not happy, and lack of experience (most consumers buy every 7-10 years) ensures agents will always have a role.
- FSBO (For Sale By Owner) will not grow much in market share in the next decade.
- However, many Millennials may shoulder more of the workload of the home buy/sell, and assign less responsibility (and commission) to real estate agents.
- The Facilitator is the middle path between high value, high cost, high service traditional Counselor and FSBO. We expect this segment to grow at the expense of the traditional real estate "generalist" agent.
- The change will be gradual over time, as Millennials become a larger share of the market.

- We believe that large teams succeed, in part, because they are process driven. They will be best positioned to capture the growing market share of the Facilitator transactions.

Lessons from other industries:

- Between the 1950's and today, broadcast media went from three major networks to hundreds of cable channels.
- The hyper-focused niche channels pulled the highest household income viewers from the major networks – and the advertising revenue that went with them.
- The majors, left with a lower income demographic, can't command the advertising rates they could in the past.
- In real estate, specialist Counselors will capture an increasing share of the highest value clients. Facilitator focused agents and brokerages CAN make it up on volume, but you'll need to chase scale economies to do it.

Agent Segmentation

We can learn from what happened to broadcast media. Specialist networks have siphoned high income households (high ad revenue per person) from major networks. Mainstream media is stuck with "common denominator" shows with lower income viewership and ad rates. ***Margin has transferred to the specialists.***

1920's Radio

1950's TV — 3 Dominant Stations

TV in 2014
Hundreds of Channels

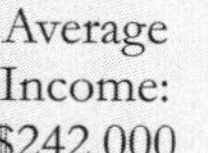

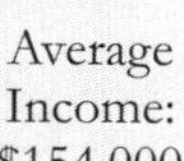

Average Income: $242,000	Average Income: $154,000	Average Income: $148,000	Average Income: $145,000	Average Income: $144,000	On FOX Avg. Income: $144,000	On FOX Avg. Income: "lowest on TV"

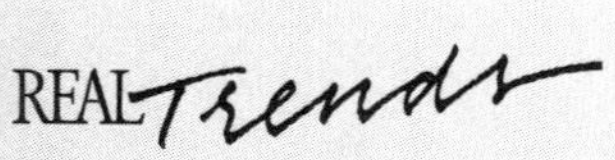

Source: http://www.tennischannel.com/mediakit2012.pdf the networks, YCRE research

Your strategic choices:

- If you have less than five years to retirement:
    - o You can coast.
    - o These trends will not happen fast enough to threaten the core repeat and referral business of most of your agents.
- If you have more than five years in your career:
    - o You need to make this trend work for you.
    - o Help your agents defend their core repeat and referral business with their outstanding service and relationship skills.
    - o Exploit this Counselor / Facilitator trend to capture additional market share.
- Pick a model.
    - o Both Nordstrom and Walmart are profitable.
    - o Both are highly defendable market niches.
    - o Real estate will not polarize as much as the retail or broadcast industries in the next decade, but the trend is well underway.
    - o Being an undifferentiated generalist killed Montgomery Ward, K-Mart and Sears.

Your next steps:

- Pick a strategy and think through the implications:
    - o Top-producing sales agents and teams compress brokerage margins (they hit their cap, then don't pay much more after that).
        - Counselors likely need less in the way of management—yet more in the way of training and accountability.
        - How will firms fund the more skilled managerial talent to support the more-sophisticated Counselor agents?
    - o Lower producers require much more of both (management and support), yet do not provide the splits to fund their support.
    - o Firms that try to train new agents, support cost-driven facilitators AND give expensive, high-value training to counselors could find themselves short of resources. They could disappoint all three groups. Higher turnover could result, placing the firm in a death spiral.
    - o You might need to have minimum production standards.

- Facilitator Track
  - Benefits: lower overhead, lower complexity.
  - Your agents will be under commission pressure – so you will be, too.
  - Learn to express your value as a firm clearly. Help your agents do the same.
  - Find value-added services to boost margins (websites, CRM, marketing packs)
  - Get very efficient; reduce costs best in class levels.
- Counselor Track
  - Benefit: higher margin, excellent for recruiting and retention.
  - Market intelligence. Neighborhood level, packaged for agents, easy to explain.
  - Advanced training, coaching and recurring accountability.
  - Partner with vendors to get access to transaction management; integrate as seamlessly into your ops as you can.
  - Consider having production minimum standards. Many training and support costs are per agent, you will need a certain amount of margin per agent to make this work.
- Enablers for either Track
  - Highly efficient CRM and core support processes
  - Strong "core" transaction management
  - Pay attention to time management and productivity; defend prospecting time as you scale up.

Ratings and reviews begin to matter

Consumers research virtually everything based on ratings—cameras, hotels, restaurants, etc. HAR surveyed 7,000 real estate consumers last year, and 90 percent found agent ratings to be helpful in their decision of which real estate professional to hire. Yelp, Redfin, ZipRealty, Coldwell Banker brokers, Better Homes & Gardens brokers, Trulia and Zillow (400,000+ agent ratings) all offer consumers some form of agent ratings. HAR offers agent ratings on a voluntary basis and currently 4,200 agents are being rated with 83,000 clients surveyed responding favorably about their experience with their agent.

– Bob Hale, CEO, Houston Association of REALTORS, Houston MLS

The consumer is going to love it [ratings], and Realtor.com will not be able to do it because 70% of the agents do not want ratings because it favors the top producers. Therefore, they [NAR, associations, MLSs] will not be able to get it done and somebody from the outside will.

Most people know 10 realtors—which one to pick? Look online for ratings—who sells the most homes in my neighborhood. Even if you are referred to three Realtors, what is the tiebreaker? Ratings.

– Neal Hanks, President, Beverly Hanks Brokerage (250+ Realtors)

....

We worked with Harris Interactive, a noted global research firm, to do a survey of consumers. We asked, "Will I look at agent performance website for next deal?"

- Consumers in all generations value relationships. Regardless, adoption of ratings is poised to take off rapidly.
  - o Traditional, over 61 years old: 15%
  - o Millennial, under 33: 45%
- This will shift market share, probably to agents who are more productive or have more experience in a particular segment of the market.

We asked, "For your next real estate transaction, how many ratings websites will you consult?"

- Oldest consumers: **None**, or about the same number as last time.
  - o They have a trusted advisor and they plan to be loyal to them.
- Millennials generally have limited agent relationships (relative to older consumers).
  - o Much more expected reliance on future ratings sites.
  - o Millennials are already doing more web research currently.
  - o That gap should grow dramatically in the near term.

"Would you prefer the agent you knew well or an agent with specific skills?"

- For all generations, "the agent I know" won the majority of the time.
- However, a sizable minority of young consumers (33%!) were either much more likely or somewhat more likely to choose a "specialized agent found by a website."

"If there were a website that offered ratings of real estate agents and consumer reviews, how likely would you be to use such a website?"

- Millennials had significantly more reliance on websites.
- Older consumers did not.

"How helpful do you think it would be to know how many real estate deals an agent was involved in, in the neighborhood you are interested in?"

- EVERY generation tended to find this information to be helpful.
- Even older consumers, with strong agent relationships, want this.

"How likely are you to use your last transaction's agent again for a future transaction?"

- A large number of people of all ages were happy with their agent. Most plan to use this person again.
- However, cracks are forming in the wall with younger consumers.
  - o They were less likely than older consumers to select "definitely will use again." NAR research has had the same findings.
  - o Merely "likely" was selected much more often.
  - o For this group, the strength of intent for repeat business is not as powerful as it is for older consumers.

Implications

- Repeat and referral is a powerful channel for agent selection today and will continue to be in the future.
  - o This is especially true for older consumers who tend to be loyal and tend to have very established relationships with agents.
  - o Millennials generally do not have these established connections, and a meaningful share of their transactions will probably NOT be referral based.
- We expect the percentage of agents selected by repeat and referral to erode gradually over time.

Next steps for managers and owners:

- Develop in-house training programs for all of the "Agent" topics.
- Have an in-house expert who can be a single point of contact for helping all of your agents with implementing the ideas.
  - o You may have to do most of the work for them.
  - o College interns are a great (and affordable) way to do this.
- Collect success stories of agents (especially tech challenged people) getting closed referrals from these new marketing channels.
  - o Package up the stories into case studies.
  - o Give them to your recruiters, so they can share this with prospects as yet another thing that makes your brokerage special.
- Proactively (intern job?) do a social media "audit" of all of your producers
- Show them where they are relatively strong and where they can improve.
- Have the intern sit with them 1:1 to implement the improvement ideas.
- Implementing some of the "Counselor" ideas from Chapter 1 around market knowledge will make it easier for your agents to become specialists.
- Set up Google alerts for the firm's name and areas of specialization. Have someone monitor it.

Commission rates continue to sink

> *"While downward pressure on commissions may continue into the next decade, hopefully with continued increase in home values, the impact on Realtors may not be that significant. There will always be a place for flat fee and discounters, but the savvy consumer will still adhere to the adage of getting what you pay for. There will be Realtors that have the knowledge, technology and tools to justify their fees and those that won't be able to invest in their business that will be forced to discount their services."*
>
> – Chad Ochsner, Owner, RE/MAX Alliance Colorado (800 agents)

Discussion points:

- The book has an outline for the arguments for continued average commission erosion over time. We will not cover them in this summary.
- Just because the average commission declines does not mean that your commissions will decline.
- Implement the Facilitator / Counselor ideas, and you will thrive.

Company gross margin declines

The brokerage is being disintermediated over time, but at a slow pace so it is hard to notice. Drivers include:

- *MLS, trade associations. They provide a lot more training and other traditional "brokerage services" than they did in the past.*
- *Portals (e.g., Zillow) sell leads direct to agent. The brokerage used to provide the majority of the leads to agents (e.g., relocation).*
- *Tools directly sold to agent – CRM, marketing tools, electronic contracts by MLS and others.*
- *Technology. Equipment and services that used to be prohibitively expensive for the individual – e.g., fax machines, color printers, fast internet connections – are now cheap and common place.*

As a result, a Realtor's competitive differentiators that used to be only available from a sophisticated brokerage office are now easily available to solo agents. Collectively, it erodes the value of the brokerage, and you see that in the declines in the company dollar retained over time. The brokerage owner has to provide great service, great marketing, and great support. This will slow GM erosion, but it doesn't stop it. It only slows it down.

In Canada, RE/MAX and Royal LePage have 50% share – so economies of scale really come to play. They use the franchise training, web sites, support, etc. much more in Canada than they do in U.S. Collectively, this shifts costs from the brokerage to the franchise. This enables Canadian brokers to make money on lower margins. As you might predict, there are only a few large independents in Canada – generally one per large market. This might be where the U.S. market is going.

– Senior executive of a very large independent brokerage.

Huge brokerage consolidation opportunities—you have to be good and really know your model. Be market centric—different models in different cities. You now have to be a solid business person too.

Each market will have a critical mass required for the dynamics of that unique city—but you will have to hit that threshold to truly be successful and profitable on any reasonable level. Have a unique model approach to business—do NOT follow the pack.

– Mark Stark, CEO, Prudential Americana Group and Prudential Arizona Properties (1,400 agents)

....

Broker / owner next steps:

- Increase company leads, perhaps through online marketing efforts that require the economy of scale only a larger brokerage can manage.
- Focus on developing new agents as the primary emphasis of the firm.
- Firms can change course away from pursuit of market share at all costs and focus on the development of agents and teams who embrace the tools, resources and culture of the firm and gracefully allow those who value higher splits to depart.
- Implement Chapter 1 ideas (Counselor vs. Facilitator).
- Consider if your market requires you to attain a critical mass or scale for future success. Can you formulate a plan to get there?

<u>The listing portals lock up the consumer relationship</u>

- An industry **leader**, "In the past, the firm with the most listings drove the most leads. With the strength of the portals, that is becoming less and less the case."
- Another **leader** said, "They have 60 million consumers a month visiting their site and 400,000 agent ratings and growing. They have over 20 individual mobile web apps. No broker has that or is ever going to have that. We have heard that they intend to start charging referral fees as well."
- One **top agent**: "I spend tens of thousands of dollars a month on the portals and make a large profit doing so. I plan to increase that spending because it makes sense for my business."

- Another **top agent**: "I have found it is the most effective manner of reaching new, younger customers whom I don't know personally yet. It's the future of my business."
- **MLS CEO:** "Portals can't eliminate Realtors, but they could replace the MLS."

I think they're accelerating. Zillow and Trulia get a lot of press in our industry, so we get drawn into thinking how big they are. You talk to an average consumer and they are only casually engaged with them. So it really hasn't taken hold yet but it will, in terms of lead generation for our industry.

The next generation (the Millennials) will certainly be more used to going online to gather all their information, as well as their friends, clients, and social conversation. So I think the reason it took so long for web leads to grow is because we had control of the information. The consumers had to come to us for information and that also made us a little bit lazy as an industry. Our service was providing information, which meant you didn't have to have a skill set as high as you might if the client came to you with the information. Going forward we will have to be the interpreter and the manager of information.

It happened to stockbrokers the same way. Stock data became available online so consumers could get that information quickly. I think technology has facilitated that change, but it's access to information that is the real driver. Access to information greatly changed the relationship between agents and brokers back in the 70s as well with the creation of the MLS. So this is just the next phase, shifting the information access from the agent to the consumer.

– Dan Elsea, President, Real Estate One (Detroit MI). $2.5B+ sales in 2012.

Key findings from our custom research:

- Consumers are almost as familiar with large online real estate portals (e.g., Zillow, Trulia) as they are with traditional "brick-and-mortar" real estate brokerages (e.g., RE/MAX, Coldwell Banker, Keller Williams).
- **The level of trust consumers feel towards portals and major brokerage brands are almost the same.**
- While portals are newer to the industry, they have already had an impact on consumers, and have changed the way they shop for homes.

Implications:

- We think the portals pose …
    - o The biggest threat to the MLS.
    - o The smallest threat to the real estate agents.
    - o Brokerages that generate leads via the internet might see some pressure on that revenue source.
- Most consumers that have relied on repeat and referral in the past will continue to do so.
- The small, but growing consumer base (particularly Millennials) that do not use repeat and referral will segment between those that want Facilitators and those that prefer Counselors.
- The ratings and review websites will serve a role in playing matchmaker between consumers and agents. So will the portals. The portals (which will almost certainly increase their ratings and reviews over time) will become increasingly efficient at reselling those leads.

Broker owner and manager next steps:

- Based on the dominant strategy of your sales agents, develop support programs to help them with this opportunity.

Homeownership rate declines

If homeownership rates declined to 55% by 2025, the biggest challenge may be our message. How can our industry continue to sell the dream of homeownership and wealth creation to a generation that may not care?

Fortunately, studies have shown that Millennials do want to own their home, but clearly face headwinds preventing them from buying and selling as soon and as often as generations before them (i.e., student loan debt). The sheer size of Generation Y will hopefully prevent this percentage decline from actually occurring. Fewer Millennials may be able to purchase a home, but because their numbers are so great, the impact may not be all that threatening.

– Chad Ochsner, President, RE/MAX Alliance, Denver, CO ($3.6+ Billion)

Every home has an owner. A decline in the homeownership rate just means more investor owners. Investors sell homes more often than owner occupants. Change means the buyers of homes change (owner occupants vs. investors) so agents need different skill sets. It's mainly a training issue.

– David Stark, President, Stark Company Realtors (200 Realtors)

Foundation ideas:

- Historically, about 65% of Americans have owned their home.
- The desire to do so is an ingrained habit with young and old alike.
- Government regulation, tax policy and financial markets have created highly favorable conditions for homeownership.
- The drive to enable more families to become homeowners was the biggest contributor to the housing downturn of 2005-2011. Too many were chasing home ownership without the financial means.

Results:

- Since 2004, the home ownership rate has declined 5%.
- Six million incremental families that rent versus own.
- First time homebuyers historically are about 35% of the market. They are notably absent from the current housing recovery.
- Although their desire to become owners remains strong, substantial student loan debt and a weak job market inhibit them.
- Stricter mortgage underwriting standards have had a chilling effect.
- Each factor may drive homeownership to permanently, lower levels.

The average small investor…

- Owns four properties.
- On average, buys and sells about every five years. Owner occupants are closer to ten years on average.
- According to a large brokerage that did a detailed study, the average commission rate for investors and owner occupants is identical.

- As a result, a decline in the home ownership rate will likely increase the number of transactions. The deal flow will be concentrated in the hands of a smaller number of property owners that select the real estate agents.

Broker / owner choices:

- Provide the training and support for your agents for the agent "what to do now" steps.
- Evaluate if property management is a good fit for your brokerage.
- When you get everything running, use this as a recruiting tool to get established investor-oriented agents from other brokerages that do not offer the levels of support and knowledge that you do.
- Consider sponsoring investor groups in your community to generate leads for your agents.

What realty services do consumers really value?

We did a customized survey of consumers that recently bought or sold a home. Most important real estate services, from consumer's point of view:

- Help negotiate best price to sell or buy their home, 82%.
- Provide useful web sites so clients could look at homes, 69%.
- Provide CMA of comps (sale or purchase process), 68%.

Thoughts:

- The big surprise is "provide websites".
- Clients certainly have plenty of choices for MLS-type access online.
- They can use the portals (e.g., Zillow, Trulia), agent specific sites, or number of other options.
- We would guess that when clients get deep into the search process, real time data is very useful.
- Agents may feel they have nothing to offer clients for web listing access, but clients do not share that opinion.
- It is an opportunity for agents and firms.

We compared how important consumers found services vs. how well their agent actually performed.

- One topic, "help negotiate the price," had a negative score.
- Here, consumers felt this was the most important service, but that the agents generally did not perform as well as the consumers wanted.
- This is a training opportunity for agents to improve service levels. Unlike many important activities performed by agents, negotiation is highly visible to the consumer, easy to explain and demonstrate.

We checked to see if different consumer generations had different opinions:

- Help with negotiation is the most important agent skill from the consumer's point of view.
    - o Older clients (54%) were much more likely than younger clients (38%) to feel this way.
- From our interviews, we got the sense that many agents think consumers are doing their own CMA with online services like Zillow and Trulia.
    - o That is increasingly the case, but the agent's CMA is still very important, too.
    - o Older clients (29%) were more likely to think so than younger clients (17%).
- Not surprisingly, "Educate me on the process of buying or selling a home" was more useful to younger clients (24%) than older clients (6%).
- One of the biggest gaps was with "provide neighborhood information."
    - o There are many sources on the Internet for this information.
    - o While we would commonly consider younger people as more adept with the internet, they had a much higher opinion of the agent's value added (19%) than older consumers (1%).
    - o Our hypothesis is that older consumers already know what they want in housing and where to find it. The agent does not bring much to their decision process.
    - o The younger consumers told us they did extensive research online, but they still want the advice and opinions of the agent to synthesize and prioritize their findings.

Next steps for managers and owners:

- The book has many detailed recommendations for agents, not reprinted here.
- The biggest gaps where agents felt they needed more support from their brokerage:
    - o Negotiation training and support.
    - o "Handle all the details to buy and sell my home." For agents – and brokerages – that want to follow a facilitator path, this is less important. For those that wish to position themselves as "counselors", this might be the biggest area where you can make a difference.
- Odds are you already do many things to make a stressful move easier for your clients. Take the time to integrate the processes to make them work together more smoothly
- Document the breadth of "concierge" services you provide in marketing materials that would be appropriate at listing presentations and/or buyer consultations (if first time buyers… especially for busy professionals).
- Consider developing some case studies – what did the client need, and how did the brokerage and agent develop and deliver a comprehensive set of services to solve the housing problem?
- The case studies would look different depending on the agent's specialization. Those specific services would likely remain the responsibility of the agent to develop, manage, and communicate. However, some of the counselor "concierge" services would likely be in common for most clients, and could be developed at a brokerage level. This could provide an enduring strategic advantage to the brokerage for recruiting and retaining high performance agents.

The biggest concerns of brokerage owners

Key findings

- Owners consider today's biggest challenges to be recruiting and retaining agents with the right pay plan.
- Many, not all, expressed concern about the rising average age of agents and managers.
- Most owners have completed their office rightsizing efforts. This is not a high concern anymore.
- While off market listings generated a lot of discussion, few owners see them as a big challenge.

Recruiting - There are some differences in the patterns of recruiting, depending on firm's revenue trend:

- Most firms rely on referrals from their agents and sales managers for most of their hires.
- Firms with flat or declining revenue used every source with about the same level of success. No one source led the pack.
- Large firms with moderate growth over the four years (10 – 50%) relied most on their sales managers to drive growth. Agent referrals were almost as important.
- Larger firms with the fastest growth (over 51%) relied the most on their sales managers, and did not use a recruiter at all. Real estate schools were not very important to this high growth group, either.
- Smaller firms (up & comer list) tended to use agent referrals to drive growth. The next four sources were almost a tie:
    - o Sales managers, 17%
    - o Co-op deals with my agents, 15%
    - o Independent real estate school, 14%
    - o Recruiter, 14%

* * * * * *

Exhibit 10-8: Owners: How do Brokerages attract agents to their firm?

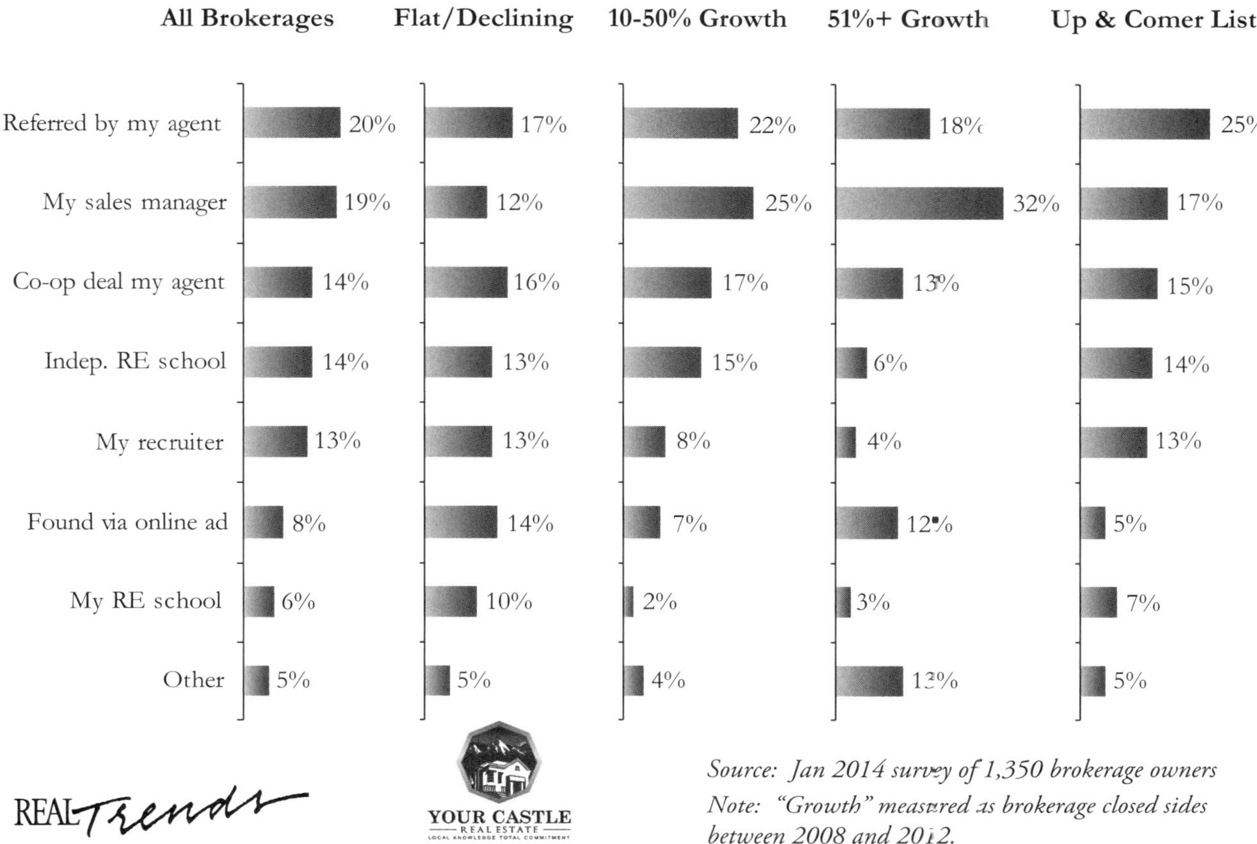

Many business books about the future attempt to scare the reader into believing that the future is dim, that forces of change will soon make all existing participants obsolete. This is not one of those books. We think there is incredible opportunity for real estate brokers, owners and managers to grow in the next decade. We wish you the best of success.

Appendix 1: Detailed Results from Consumer Survey

The following information provides key insights into how those who purchased and/or sold a home in 2013 feel about real estate agents, current trends and other key information regarding real estate transactions. You will find some overall thoughts followed by the key findings per question afterwards. Please note that in the key findings, sub group analysis is provided for those distinctions that are significant.

High-level Thoughts

Before going into any detail on the key findings and then the detailed findings, some of the overall takeaways from this study are:

- Personal connections matter! Whether it's an agent they used before or one that was referred to them, 2013 home buyers/sellers care about having some sort of connection with the real estate agent they are using. In addition, once they have that connection, they keep it, which is why such a high number either definitely will use their real estate agent again or are very likely to do so.
- Age, however, may take a little away from the personal connection. Younger 2013 home buyers/sellers are still getting their real estate legs, so to speak. This is why the education they get on the process is so important to them. They are the ones most likely to look for new and/or different ways to find agents. This is the generation that grew up knowing nothing but the Internet and they rely on it for everything… Buying and selling a home falls into that category as well. Age was also the one demographic that really showed significant differences throughout the survey. It is hard to know how this younger generation is going to mature… will they always rely on the Internet or will they fall into line with the older generations.
- Urbanicity also matters. It rather is intuitive that someone buying or selling a home in the big city has a different perspective than someone doing the same in a more rural setting. However, the differences are seen throughout that it is worth pointing out and remembering.

- Buying a home and selling a home are two different things… and there are two different mindsets for it. Those buying seem to need their agents a bit more than those selling. It is not in every question, but it occurs enough that there seems to be a trend there.

Key Findings

Buying and/or selling a home can be a major life changer. In addition, not surprisingly three-quarters of those who bought and/or sold a home in 2013 agree that buying a home is a stressful process (74%) and just slightly less agree that selling a home is a stressful process (72%). However, while it may be stressful, these 2013 home buyers/sellers have mixed feelings about the process. Half (51%) say the process of buying a home is easy to understand while three in ten disagree with this. On the other side, just under half (47%) agree that the process of selling a home is easy to understand with 27% disagreeing with this.

> 74% of buyers say buying is stressful and 72% of sellers say the same thing. Only about half of all buyers and sellers say that the process is easy to understand.

There has been a lot of talk about those taking the process of buying and/or selling a home on their own, but among those who bought and/or sold a home in 2013, four in five (81%) did it with a real estate agent and just one in five (19%) did not. Why? Well, seven in ten (70%) agree they prefer to use a real estate agent because they are professionals. Moreover, a similar number (71%) agree they think of their real estate agent as a trusted partner. These agents also worked for their money as seven in ten 2013 home buyers/sellers (69%) agree that their real estate agent received fair compensation for the work he/she did during the transaction.

> 69% of buyers and sellers say that their agent received fair compensation for the work they did during the transaction

One reason for the talk of not using an agent is that all the information is available online now. But 2013 home buyers/sellers aren't sure of that; under half (45%) agree that the services provided by real estate agents are less valuable now that the Internet has all the information on homes for sale, but 19% neither agree nor disagree and one-third (34%) disagree with this statement.

> 45% of sellers and buyers think that the services provided by real estate agents are less valuable now due to the internet having all the information on homes. However, 34% disagree with this position.

In addition, it is not an easy process to find the right agent. First, there is research to be done. On average, those who used an agent for a home sale or purchase in 2013 checked 3.6 websites before hiring their agent. In the future more websites may be available, the next time they may need to hire a real estate agent two in five (40%) say they will check even more websites while 38% will check about the same number.

More than one-third of those who used an agent said referrals from people they trust were extremely important to them in making their final decision (37%) while one-quarter said having a personal relationship (27%) and finding agents who had similar listings to what they were looking for (23%) was extremely important. One in five said having the agent as a member of a realtor organization (22%), having used the agent previously (22%) and looking at websites with ratings of agents (18%) was extremely important. But, among all six of these, when asked what was most important to them in making their decision about which agent to work with, there are two that stand out as one-quarter each say it is referrals from people they trust (25%) and having a personal relationship with the agent (24%).

> 37% of all who used an agent said that referrals from trusted source were extremely important in choosing an agent while 27% said that having a personal relationship was extremely important.

While working with their agent there are services that these agents provided throughout the real estate buying and/or selling process. Some of these services are more important to buyers and sellers than others. Half (52%) say that having their agent assist them in negotiating the best price to buy and/or sell was extremely important to them while two in five say being provided a list of homes to look at (40%) and a market analysis of comparable properties (38%) were extremely important. Not surprisingly, when asked which service was most important to them, these three also rose to the top as 44% said negotiating the best price was most important and one in five each say providing the market analysis of comparable properties (21%) and providing a list of homes to look at (20%) were most important.

There is how important something is to a buyer and/or seller, then there is how satisfied they were with the services the real estate agents actually provided. Overall, 2013 buyers/sellers were satisfied with the list of nine services. At least half said they were extremely/very satisfied with eight of the nine and for the ninth, being referred to a lender for mortgage financing, it was not that they were not satisfied, it was that one-third (32%) said this was not applicable to them.

Looking ahead to the next time a home buyer/seller may have need of a real estate agent, seven in ten (70%) say they are more likely to choose an agent they know while just one-quarter (24%) are more likely to choose a specialized agent they found online. But, there is a likelihood that the next time they need an agent, they may check a ratings website as two in five say they would be extremely/very likely to do so (41%) and 22% would be likely to do so. In addition, in that website, they may want to include how many real estate transactions in the neighborhood of interest an agent was involved in as almost half (47%) say that would be extremely/very helpful to know while 37% say it would be helpful. However, when it comes to the next time, the home buyer/seller may not have to look very far as one-third (33%) say they will definitely use their previous agent again and three in ten (31%) are very likely to use that agent again.

> 70% of consumers said they are more likely to use an agent they know while just 24% said they would choose a specialized agent they found online.

Detailed Findings:

1. *Did you use a real estate agent to assist you with any of your real estate transactions? (n=1,004)*
    - Four in five Americans who conducted a real estate transaction in 2013 (81%) used an agent to assist them with a transaction while one in five (19%) did not.
    - Income and education definitely show a difference in using an agent. Over one-quarter of those with a high school education or less did not use a real estate agent compared to one in ten of those with at least a college degree (27% vs. 12%). Having a lower household income also seems to lead someone to go it alone as about one-quarter of those with a household income of less than $50,000 (27%) and between $50,000 and $74,999 (23%) did not use an agent compared to 12% of those with a household income of $100,000 or more.

> The higher the educational level of the housing consumer the more likely they are to use an agent to buy or sell a home. The same is true for income levels where those with lower household incomes are less likely to use an agent than those with higher income.

2. *When you were looking for your real estate agent, how important were each of the following to you in making your final decision? (n=826)*

	Extremely /Very important (NET)	Extremely important	Very important	Important	Not important (NET)	Not that important	Not at all important
Referrals from people I trust	63%	37%	26%	23%	14%	9%	5%
Having a personal relationship with the agent	57%	27%	29%	23%	21%	14%	7%
Finding agents that had listings similar to what I was looking for	53%	23%	30%	23%	24%	15%	10%
Being a member of a realtor organization	47%	22%	26%	29%	23%	13%	11%
Having used the agent in a previous transaction	44%	22%	22%	19%	38%	19%	19%
Looking at websites with ratings of agents' performance	40%	18%	22%	25%	35%	21%	14%

As the table shows, when it comes to the importance of these criteria when choosing an agent…

- More than three in five (63%) say that referrals from people they trust are extremely/very important.
- Over half say having a personal relationship with the agent (57%).
- Finding agents that had listings similar to what they were looking for (53%) are very important.
- Just under half (47%) said being a member of a realtor organization was extremely/very important to them when they were choosing a real estate agent.
- 44% said having used the agent in a previous transaction was extremely/very important.
- Two in five (40%) said looking at websites with ratings of agents' performance was very important.

Almost half of those living in urban areas (48%) say referrals from people they trust are very important compared to one third of those living in suburban (33%) and rural (32%) areas. Younger adults are also more likely to say this as over two in five of those 18-34 (44%) and 35-44 (43%) say referrals are extremely important compared to 21% of those 45-54 and 31% of those 55 and older.

Two-thirds of those living in urban areas (68%) say having a personal relationship with the agent was extremely/very important to them in making their final decision compared to 53% of suburbanites and 46% of those living in rural areas.

Over three in five (62%) of those 18-34 say finding agents that had similar listings to ones they were looking for is extremely/very important in making their final decision compared to 47% of those 45-54 and 41% of those 55 and older. One-third of those living in rural areas (34%) say this is not important compared to 22% of both urbanites and suburbanites.

Over half of those in rural areas (53%) say having used the agent before is not important to them compared to 38% in suburban areas and 28% in urban areas. Age also shows differences here as over half of those 55 and older (53%) and almost half of those 45-54 (48%) say this is not important while only about three in ten of those 35-44 (32%) and 18-34 (27%) feel the same. Men are more likely than women to say having used the agent before is extremely/very important (49% vs. 37%) while women are more likely than men to say it is not important (43% vs. 33%).

Over half of those 18-34 (55%) and almost half of those 35-44 (48%) say looking at websites with ratings of agents' performances was extremely/very important in making their final decision compared to just 23% of those 45-54 and 16% of those 55 and older. Over half of those in urban areas (54%) also said this was extremely/very important compared to 37% of those in the suburbs and 23% of those in rural areas.

3. *While all of these may have been important, which one would you say was most important to you in making your decision about which real estate agent to work with? (n=826)*

Looking at all six of the items, two rise to the top:

- One-quarter of those who used an agent in a real estate transaction in 2013 say referrals from people they trust (25%) and having a personal relationship with the agent (24%) are the most important items in making their decision.
- Fewer numbers said finding agents that had similar listings to what they were looking for (17%).
- Having used the agent in a previous transaction (13%).
- Looking at websites with ratings of agents' performances (8%).
- Being a member of a realtor organization (7%) was most important.
- 5% said something else was most important.

For those 45-54 and 55 and older having a personal relationship rises to the top as most important (29% and 30% respectively).

4. *Before you met with a real estate agent, what research, if any, did you do before you hired that agent to help you with your real estate transaction? Please select all that apply. (n=826)*

Over two in five who used an agent for a real estate transaction in 2013 (44%) talked with people who referred the agent to them before hiring them while two in five (39%) checked real estate sites. Over one-third (36%) checked the agent's personal web site while one-third (33%) checked the agent's brokerage web site.

Around one-quarter checked ratings sites (27%) and did a generic online search using sites like Google or Yahoo to check their reputation (23%) while lesser numbers checked professional networking sites (19%) and social media sites (15%). Almost one in five (17%) did not do any research before hiring their real estate agent, while 8% did something else.

More than nine in ten 18-34 year olds (93%) and 85% of 35-44 year olds did any research compared to 74% of those 45-54 and 71% of those 55 and older. These younger home buyers/sellers are more likely to have done all the various research options presented than their older counterparts are.

5. *How important were each of the following services your real estate agent may have provided you? (n=826)*

	Extremely /Very important (NET)	Extremely important	Very important	Important	Not important (NET)	Not that important	Not at all important	N/A
Assisted in negotiating the best price to buy and/or sell	76%	52%	24%	13%	5%	3%	2%	5%
Provided a market analysis of comparable properties	65%	38%	27%	21%	8%	4%	3%	6%
Provided a list of homes to look at	62%	40%	22%	18%	8%	3%	5%	12%
Referred me to service providers such as inspectors, title insurance, etc.	60%	34%	26%	21%	11%	7%	4%	7%
Provided an online service that sent me info about homes that matched criteria	57%	31%	26%	17%	14%	6%	9%	11%
Education on the process of buying and/or selling a home	56%	33%	23%	21%	15%	10%	5%	8%
Provided a marketing plan for selling my home	52%	29%	23%	15%	12%	6%	7%	20%
Provided info about neighborhoods, schools and crime rates	51%	28%	23%	18%	17%	10%	7%	14%
Referred me to a lender for mortgage	38%	19%	20%	18%	26%	12%	13%	18%

Women are more likely than men to say that having the agent assist in negotiating the best prices to buy and/or sell is very/extremely important (82% vs. 73%). Those who both bought and sold a home in 2013 are more likely than those who only bought a home to say this is extremely important (61% vs. 48%).

Urbanites and Suburbanites are more likely than rural residents to say having the agent provide a market analysis of comparable properties was extremely important (39% and 42% vs. 26%). Those who are married are more likely than those who are not to say this was extremely/very important (71% vs. 56%).

Providing an online service to send information about homes that match their criteria is more important to younger home buyers/sellers than older ones. Three in five of those 18-34 (60%) and 70% of those 35-44 say this is extremely or very important compared to 46% of those 55 and older. The more educated one is and the higher one's income is, the more likely you are to say this is important. Two-thirds of those with at least a college degree (66%) say this is extremely/very important compared to 53% of those with some college and 49% of those with a high school degree or less. Two-thirds of those with a household income of $100,000 or more (68%) also say this is extremely/very important compared to 46% of those with a household income of less than $50,000 and half (50%) of those with a household income between $75,000 and $99,999.

Those 18-34 and 35-44 are more likely than those 45-54 and 55 and older to say education on the process is an extremely/very important thing that their agent provided them (67% and 58% vs. 43% and 45% respectively).

Interestingly, one-third of those 45-54 (33%) said the agent providing a marketing plan was not applicable to them. Those in an urban or suburban area, however, are more likely than those in a rural one to say that having the agent provide a marketing plan for selling their home is extremely/very important (56% and 54% vs. 42%).

When it comes to providing information on neighborhoods, schools and crime rates, those 18-34, 35-44, and 45-54 are all more likely than those 55 and older to say this was an extremely important service provided by their real estate agent (30%, 34%, and 31% vs. 16%). Those with a child under 18 are also more likely than those without to say this was an extremely important service (34% vs. 22%).

Those 18-34 are more likely than those 45-54 and 55 and older to say that the referral to a lender for mortgage financing was an extremely/ very important service (52% vs. 27% and 20%).

6. *While all of these may have been important services that your real estate agent provided, which two would you say were the most important services they provided? (n=826)*

- Over two in five buyers/sellers in 2013 who used an agent (44%) say the most important service they provided was they assisted in negotiating the best price to buy and/or sell.
- One in five each says that the most important service was providing a market analysis of comparable properties (21%) and providing a list of homes to look at (20%).
- Less than one in five (16%) say the most important service an agent provided was they referred them to other service providers.
- 15% say it was that they provided an education on the process for buying and/ or selling a home.
- 14% each say it was that they provided a marketing plan for selling their home and they provided an online service that sent information about homes that matched their criteria.
- Around one in ten said the most important service the agent provided was information about neighborhoods, schools and crime rates (12%).

Those 55 and older are more likely than those 18-34, 35-44, and 45-54 to say the most important service their agent provided was assistance in negotiating the best price to buy and/or sell (60% vs. 32%, 47%, and 41% respectively). As might be imagined, those 18-34 are more likely than those in the other three age groups to say the most important thing was an education on the process of buying and/or selling a home (23% vs. 12%, 11%, and 8% respectively).

7. Thinking of these same services, how satisfied were you with the services your real estate agent may have provided you? (n=826)

	Extremely /Very satisfied (NET)	Extremely satisfied	Very satisfied	Satisfied	Not satisfied (NET)	Not that satisfied	Not at all satisfied	N/A
Assisted in negotiating the best price to buy and/or sell	68%	38%	30%	22%	6%	4%	2%	5%
Provided a market analysis of comparable properties	65%	32%	33%	21%	5%	4%	1%	9%
Referred me to other service providers such as inspectors, title insurance, etc.	64%	33%	31%	20%	4%	3%	1%	11%
Provided a list of homes to look at	60%	31%	29%	20%	5%	4%	1%	15%
Education on the process of buying and/or selling a home	56%	29%	27%	25%	5%	3%	2%	14%
Provided an online service that sent me info about homes that matched my criteria	56%	26%	29%	21%	6%	4%	2%	17%
Provided information about neighborhoods, schools and crime rates	54%	26%	28%	19%	7%	5%	2%	20%
Provided a marketing plan for selling my home	53%	27%	26%	18%	4%	3%	1%	25%
Referred me to a lender for mortgage	43%	20%	23%	17%	8%	5%	3%	32%

Across all of the various activities a real estate agent can do, satisfaction is high across the board. The only time it hovers around the 50% mark for those who were extremely/very satisfied is because there are large numbers who say this is not applicable to them. Satisfaction is also consistent across groups and these services. There are, however, a few exceptions.

Three-quarters of those 35-44 (77%) were extremely/very satisfied with the market analysis of comparable properties their agent provided compared to 61% of those 18-34, 57% of those 45-54 and 64% of those 55 and older.

Three in five of those 18-34 (61%) and 35-44 (63%) were extremely/very satisfied with the education on the process of buying/selling a home compared to 41% of those 45-54 and 50% of those 55 and older. Again, these older groups were not dissatisfied; they just were more likely to say this was not applicable to them.

8. *Before you hired your real estate agent, how many websites, if any, did you check before hiring your agent? (n=826)*

On average, those who used an agent for a home sale or purchase in 2013, checked 3.6 websites before hiring their agent. Almost three in ten (28%) did not check any while 27% checked between 1 and 2, 23% checked between 3 and 4 and 22% checking 5 or more.

Over half of those 55 and older (52%) did not check any websites, and, on average, checked only 2.1 sites. Those 18-34 checked, on average, 4.6 websites and those 35-44 checked, on average, 4.2 websites.

9. *How strongly do you agree or disagree with each of the following statements. (n=1,004)*

I prefer to use a real estate agent for real estate transactions because they are professionals.

- Seven in ten of those who bought/sold a home in 2013 (70%) agree that they prefer to use a real estate agent because they are professionals.
- 43% strongly agreeing and 28% somewhat agreeing.
- One in ten (11%) disagree with 6% somewhat disagreeing.
- 4% strongly disagreeing; 17% neither agree nor disagree.
- 2% are not at all sure.
- Three-quarters of those 55 and older (77%) agree with this compared to two-thirds of those 18-34 (65%) and 45-54 (66%).
- Those who both bought and sold a home in 2013 are more likely to agree with this than those who just bought or just sold a home (81% vs. 67% and 68%).

Services provided by agents are less valuable now that the Internet has all of the information on homes for sale.

- Over two in five of those who bought/sold a home in 2013 (45%) agree.
- 19% strongly agreeing and 26% somewhat agreeing.
- One-third (34%) disagree with 20% somewhat disagreeing and 14% strongly disagreeing.

- 19% neither agree nor disagree and 2% are not at all sure.
- Half of those 55 and older (49%) disagree with this compared to 24% of those 18-34 and 35% of those 35-44. On the other side, over half of those 18-34 (55%) agree with this.
- Males are more likely to agree with this than females (49% vs. 39%) while females are more likely to disagree (42% vs. 28%).

Buying a home is a stressful process.

- Three-quarters of those who bought/sold a home in 2013 (74%) agree.
- 45% strongly agreeing and 29% somewhat agreeing.
- One in ten (11%) disagree with 7% somewhat disagreeing.
- 4% strongly disagreeing; 12% neither agree nor disagree and 3% are not at all sure.

Selling a home is a stressful process.

- Seven in ten of those who bought/sold a home in 2013 (72%) agree.
- 41% strongly agreeing and 31% somewhat agreeing.
- One in ten (9%) disagree with 5% somewhat disagreeing and 4% strongly disagreeing.
- 9% neither agree nor disagree and 11% are not at all sure.

I think of my real estate agent as a trusted advisor.

- Seven in ten of those who bought/sold a home in 2013 (71%) agree.
- 43% strongly agreeing and 28% somewhat agreeing.
- One in ten (11%) disagree with 6% somewhat disagreeing.
- 6% strongly disagreeing; 15% neither agree nor disagree.
- 2% are not at all sure.
- Those in the Northeast are more likely to agree with this than those in the Midwest and South (81% vs. 69% each).

- Those who both bought and sold a home in 2013 are more likely to agree with this than those who just bought or just sold a home (82% vs. 69% and 67%).

My real estate agent received fair compensation for the work he/she did during the transaction.

- Seven in ten of those who bought/sold a home in 2013 (69%) agree.
- 42% strongly agreeing and 27% somewhat agreeing.
- One in ten (9%) disagree with 6% somewhat disagreeing and 3% strongly disagreeing.
- 17% neither agree nor disagree and 5% are not at all sure.
- Those who both bought and sold a home in 2013 are more likely to agree with this than those who just bought or just sold a home (84% vs. 65% and 62%).

The process of buying a home is easy to understand.

- Half of those who bought/sold a home in 2013 (51%) agree.
- 20% strongly agreeing and 30% somewhat agreeing.
- Three in ten (30%) disagree with 23% somewhat disagreeing.
- 8% strongly disagreeing; 17% neither agree nor disagree.
- 3% are not at all sure.
- Men are more likely than women to agree with this (55% vs. 45%).

The process of selling a home is easy to understand.

- Almost half of those who bought/sold a home in 2013 (47%) agree.
- 17% strongly agreeing and 30% somewhat agreeing.
- Over one-quarter (27%) disagree with 19% somewhat disagreeing.
- 9% strongly disagreeing; 18% neither agree nor disagree.
- 8% are not at all sure.
- Those in the Midwest are more likely to agree with this than those in the West (52% vs. 39%).

10. *In the future, there will probably be more websites for information regarding real estate agents. Thinking of the next time you may need to hire a real estate agent, how many more websites do you think you will check before hiring a real estate agent? (n=826)*

Two in five of those who purchased or sold a home in 2013 and used a real estate agent (40%) say, the next time they have a need for an agent again, they will check more websites with 16% checking many more websites than the last time and 25% checking a few more websites than last time. Two in five will check about the same number of websites (38%) and just 5% will check many less (2%) or a few less websites (4%); 16% will not check any websites.

Almost three in five of those 18-34 (58%) will check more websites next time they are in the need for an agent compared to 24% of those 45-54 and 22% of those 55 and older who say the same thing.

Men are more likely than women to say they will check more websites the next time they are in the need of a real estate agent (46% vs. 33%).

11. *Assume you had two choices for finding a real estate agent.*

- *First, you could use one that you personally knew, maybe one you had worked with previously.*
- *Second, you could search online to find a real estate agent that had a specific skill or expertise that you were looking for, maybe an expert in a certain neighborhood or type of property.*
- *Which type of agent would you more likely choose for your next real estate transaction? (n=826)*

Seven in ten 2013 home buyers/sellers who used an agent (70%) are more likely to choose an agent they know, with over two in five (43%) much more likely to do so and 27% somewhat more likely. Just one-quarter (24%) are more likely to choose a specialized agent they found online with 7% much more likely to choose the specialized agent and 16% somewhat more likely to do so; 7% are not at all sure which they would choose.

Younger 2013 home buyer/sellers are more likely than their older counterparts to choose the specialist they found online. One-third (35%) of 18-34 year olds are choosing the specialist compared to 17% of those 35-44, 20% of those 45-54, and 13% of those 55 and older.

Those in urban areas and the suburbs are more likely than those in rural areas to choose a specialized agent they found online (30% and 24% vs. 13%).

Marital status and having a child in the household affect which type of agent they would choose. Those with a child in the household (28%) and those who are not married (29%) are more likely than those without a child (20%) are and those who are married (20%) to choose the specialized agent from the website.

12. *Thinking about the next time you might need a real estate agent, if there was a website that had ratings of real estate agents and featured consumer reviews of these agents, how likely would you be to use such a website before hiring your next agent? (n=826)*

Two in five 2013 home buyers/sellers who used a real estate agent (41%) say they would be extremely/very likely to use a ratings website the next time they might need a real estate agent with 22% saying extremely likely and 19% saying very likely. One-third (34%) are likely to use such a website and one in five (18%) are not likely.

Those 18-34 and 35-44 are more likely to say they would be extremely/very likely to use the ratings website than those 55 and older (46% and 47% vs. 32%).

Men are more likely than women to say they would be extremely/very likely to use the ratings website the next time they needed a real estate agent (46% vs. 34%).

Urbanites are more likely than those living in rural areas to say they would be extremely/very likely to use the specialized website next time they needed a real estate agent (45% vs. 31%).

Those with a child under 18 in the household are more likely than those without one to say they would be extremely/very likely to use the specialized website the next time they needed an agent (49% vs. 35%).

13. Again, thinking about the next time you might need a real estate agent, how helpful do you think it would be to know how many real estate transactions in the neighborhood you are interested in that agent was involved in? (n=826)

Almost half of 2013 home buyers/sellers who used an agent (47%) said it would be extremely/very helpful to know how many real estate transactions in the neighborhood they are interested in that agent was involved in with 19% saying extremely helpful and 28% saying very helpful. More than one-third (37%) say it would be helpful while 8% say it would be not that helpful and 2% say not at all helpful; 7% are not at all sure.

Over half of those 18-34 (53%) say this would be extremely/very helpful compared to just over one-third (36%) of those 55 and older.

Over half of those in urban areas (52%) and almost half of those in the suburbs (48%) say it would be extremely/very helpful to know the number of real estate transactions in the neighborhood they are interested in that the agent was involved in compared to one-third of rural residents (33%).

Over half of those with children under 18 in the household (54%) say this would be extremely/very helpful compared to 41% of those without children under 18 in the household.

14. Thinking of the real estate agent you used on the last transaction, how likely are you to use that agent again for a future transaction? (n=826)

One-third of 2013 home buyers/sellers who used an agent (33%) say that they definitely will use that agent again for a future transaction. Three in ten (31%) say they very likely will use that agent again while 19% are likely to use that agent again for a future transaction. Slightly over one in ten (13%) say they are not likely to use that agent again with 7% not that likely and 6% not at all likely; 4% are not at all sure.

Those who bought a home in 2013 are more likely than those who sold a home in 2013 to say they definitely will use that agent again the next time they have a real estate transaction (36% vs. 22%) while those who sold a home are more likely than those who bought a home to say they are not likely to use that agent again (23% vs. 9%).

15. *Thinking of the last real estate transaction you made, how much did you buy/sell the property for? If you are not sure, please provide your best estimate.(n=1,004)*

- On average, the last real estate transaction made was for $216,022.
- For one-third (36%) the transaction was under $100,000.
- While for 16% the transaction was between $100,000 and $149,999.
- For 16% it was between $150,000 and $224,999.
- Looking at the higher end transactions, for about one in ten (9%) it was between $225,000 and $299,999, for 7% it was between $300,000 and $399,999 and for 14% it was over $400,000.

16. *Over the course of your lifetime, how many real estate transactions have you closed? If you are not sure, please provide your best estimate. (n=1,004)*

On average, they have completed 6.8 transactions.

- One-quarter (25%) have made 1 transaction.
- 22% have made 2.
- 16% have made 3 transactions.
- Just under one in five (17%) have made between 4 and 5.
- 8% have made between 6 and 9.
- 13% have made 10 or more transactions

Full Methodology

This survey was conducted online within the United States between January 14 and 22, 2014 among 1,004 adults aged 18 and older, who bought a home in 2013, sold a home in 2013 or did both of whom 826 used a real estate agent by Harris Poll on behalf of REAL *Trends*. Figures for age, sex, race/ethnicity, education, region and household income were weighted where necessary to bring them into line with their actual proportions in the population. Propensity score weighting was used to adjust for respondents' propensity to be online.

All sample surveys and polls, whether or not they use probability sampling, are subject to multiple sources of error which are most often not possible to quantify or estimate, including sampling error, coverage error, error associated with nonresponse, error associated with question wording and response options, and post-survey weighting and adjustments. Therefore, the words "margin of error" are avoided as they are misleading. All that can be calculated are different possible sampling errors with different probabilities for pure, unweighted, random samples with 100% response rates. These are only theoretical because no published polls come close to this ideal.

Respondents for this survey were selected from among those who have agreed to participate in surveys. The data have been weighted to reflect the composition of the adult population. Because the sample is based on those who agreed to participate in the panel, no estimates of theoretical sampling error can be calculated.

Appendix 2: High Production Agent and Team Survey

The authors developed a number of ideas to test for this book. We did a pre-survey test among agents just in the Denver market in December 2013. Based on those results, we tuned the questions, deleted several, and added a few. We did the national survey of high production agents at the end of December 2013.

REAL *Trends* and *The Wall Street Journal* compile a list of the top individual and team real estate agents in the U.S. Many more people and teams apply than there are positions on the list. Based on several years of applications, we emailed surveys to the top 2,000 teams and 4,000 individual producers.

We compared the demographics of the responses to the overall lists. Here is what we found:

Appendix 2-1: Agents and Teams: Demographics of survey respondents.

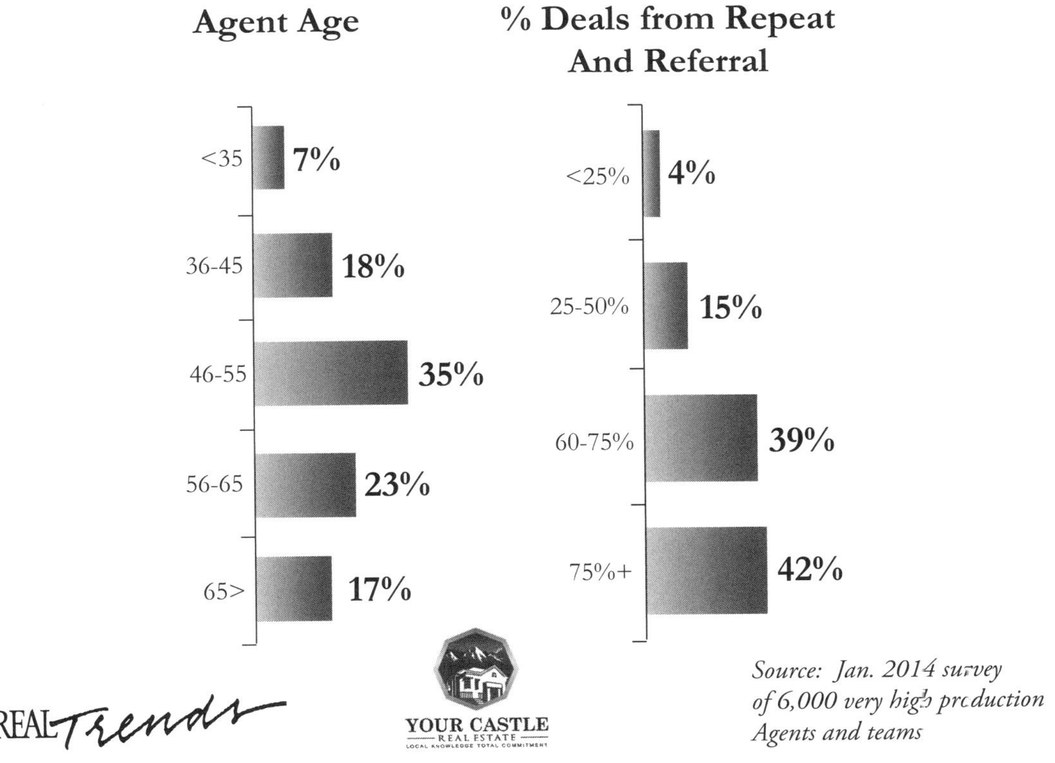

Source: Jan. 2014 survey of 6,000 very high production Agents and teams

See Chart "A2-1." Most agents are between 46 and 55 years old. They generally match the NAR (National Association of Realtors) average age of 57.

Most of the agents and teams get the majority of their business from repeat and referral

Please see "Chart A2-2." The median number of sides closed in the prior year for individual agents was 65. Thus we had a tendency to get responses from higher production agents.

Appendix 2-2: Agents and Teams: Demographics of survey respondents.

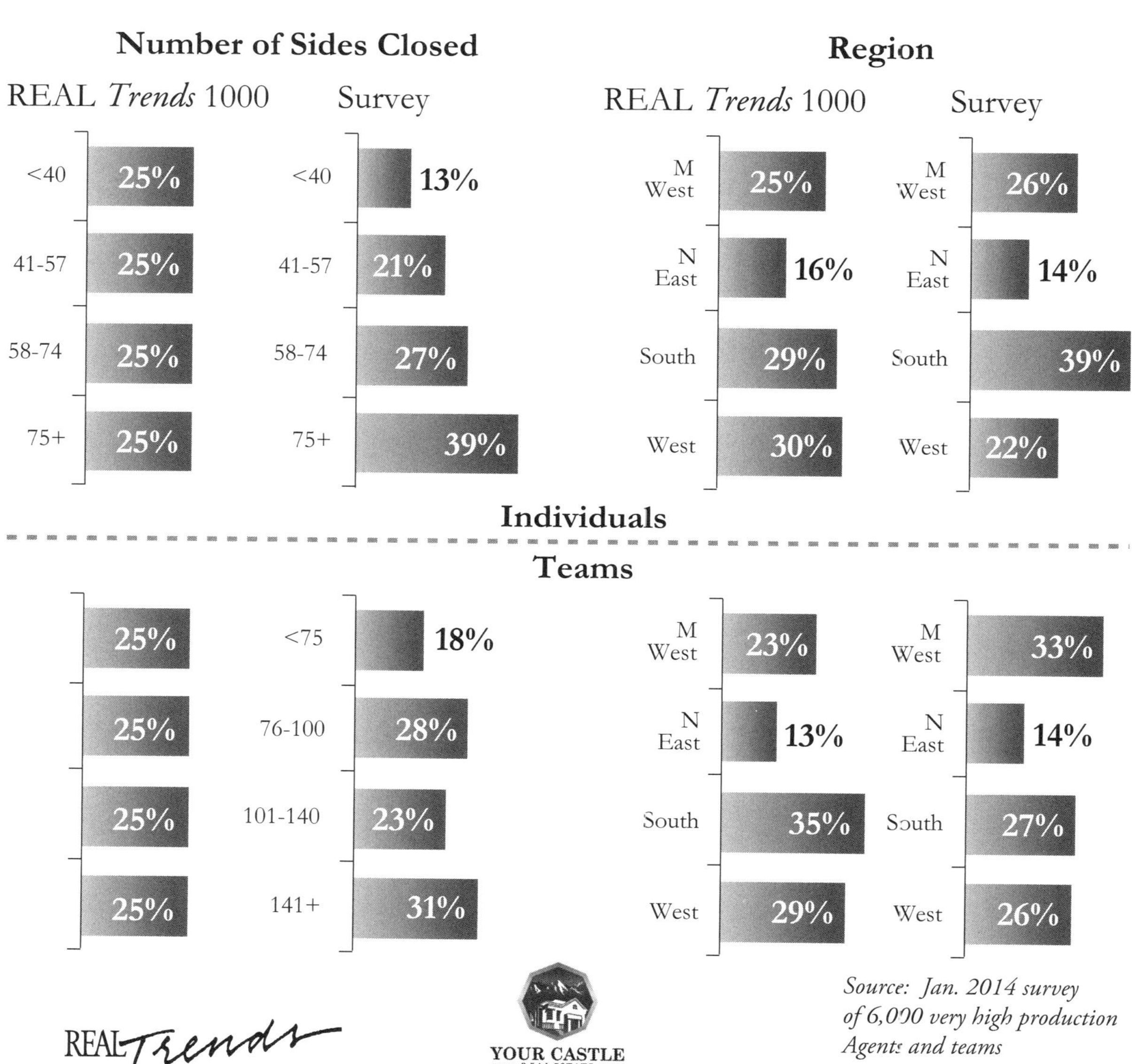

Source: Jan. 2014 survey of 6,000 very high production Agents and teams

Similarly, for teams, the median sides closed was 105.

The regions represented in the survey results were very close for both teams and individuals.

For the text comments throughout the book, we interviewed about 25 high production agents and team leaders. Our goal was to bring the numbers "to life" and add additional context and insight to the results. We also wanted to validate our interpretations. We hope you enjoy their quotes as much as we did. Conducting the interviews with this amazingly talented group was a highlight of writing this book.

Appendix 3: How High Producers Get Leads

As with making a movie, writing a book requires endless editing. As a result, a lot of great material ends up on the "cutting room floor." This final analysis is from our survey of high production teams and individual real estate agents. The insight is interesting, but it did not fit in any of our chapters. We included it here, for those that are interested.

Appendix 3-1: Agents and Teams: Where they get their leads.

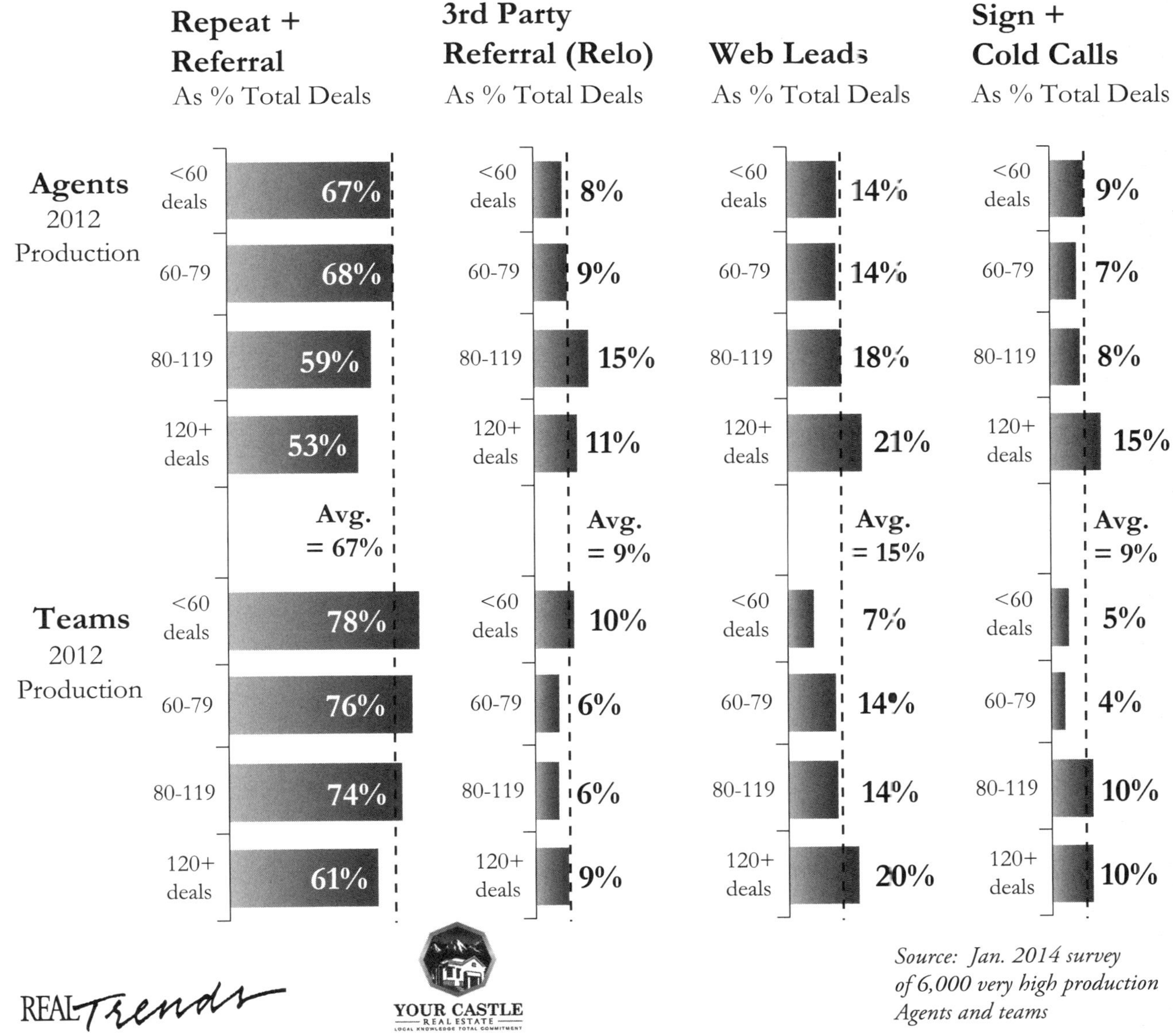

Source: Jan. 2014 survey of 6,000 very high production Agents and teams

In chart A3-1, we examine how high producers get leads. The top of the chart has individual agents. 67% of their closed business was from repeat business from past clients and referrals from people in their network. As you might expect, the amount of repeat and referral business declines as their overall production goes up. In other words, the absolute number of repeat and referral deals hits a ceiling. Further growth beyond that ceiling requires different prospecting methods.

You can see that third party referrals (generally relocation work) comprises about 9% of closed volume. This grows slightly as overall volume grows. However, it only accounts for a small fraction of that growth.

15% of closed volume, on average is from web leads, 9% is from sign calls and cold calls. For both lead sources, the reliance on these leads grows significantly after the agent "maxes out" their repeat and referral database.

On the lower half of the chart, you can see the same analysis for high production teams. They follow the same general patterns as the individual producers. While reliance on web leads for individuals grows about 50% (from the lowest to highest production quartile), the teams use of web leads grows almost 300%. Similarly, for sign calls and cold calls, individuals see about 50% growth and teams see 200% growth.

Earlier chapters in the book discussed several themes:

- The highest producers are taking more market share from the lower producers.
- Portals are likely to continue to grow and generate more lead volume.
- Consumers eagerly seek review and ratings sites. Most consumers will continue to rely on repeat and referral, but the rating sites will gradually erode that market share, too.

The result of the three macro-drivers is that high producers will continue to gather an increasingly larger share of the transactions. Of these large teams and high producers here, we would expect the "largest of the large" to capture most of this upside.

Mid-level producers (and teams) wishing to join the ranks of the largest will need to:

- Grow their repeat and referral process as far as they practically can. There seems to be a ceiling for most agents on how far this will scale
- Add relocation business if practical to do so. While it is only 8-10% for most of the people we surveyed, that is still a sizable amount of volume.
- Develop systems and infrastructure (CRM, drip systems, call coordinators, tailored marketing materials) to capture growth from web leads and calls.

Web lead traffic could be from review and rating sites if the mid-level producer is able to develop an attractive profile. Alternatively, it could be from more "traditional" methods such as SEO optimization, outstanding content in a blog, or other approach.

Regardless, there will be plenty of amazing growth opportunities for real estate agents and teams in the future.

Also by the Authors

- *Game Plan*
  by Steve Murray with Ian Morris
- *Valuing a Residential Real Estate Firm*
  by Steve Murray
- *People Still Matter*
  by Steve Murray
- *Against All Odds*
  by Steve Murray

Current Editions

- *The 2013 Guide to Colorado Real Estate Investing*
  by Lon Welsh, Charles Roberts, Tony Girard
- *How to Thrive with Social Media and Blogging*
  by Lon Welsh, Greg Parham
- *Unlocked: Revealing the Eight Secrets of Highly Efficient Sales Professionals*
  by Darice Johnston, Lon Welsh, Bruce Gardner
- *Thrive: How Realtors Can Succeed in a Down Market*
  by Lon Welsh, Bruce Gardner, Mike Welk, Drew Shope
- *The Real Estate IRA Retirement Planning Guide*
  by Jeff Sibel, with Lon Welsh and Charles Roberts

In Development

- *The 2015 Guide to Colorado Real Estate Investing*
  by Lon Welsh, Charles Roberts, Tony Girard, Greg Parham

Older Editions

- *The 2011 Guide to Colorado Real Estate Investing*
  by Lon Welsh, Charles Roberts, Tony Girard
- *The 2009 Guide to Denver Real Estate Investing*
  by Lon Welsh, Charles Roberts